Date Due

GLOBAL COMPETITION
IN CAPITAL GOODS

GLOBAL COMPETITION IN CAPITAL GOODS

An American Perspective

ROBERT S. ECKLEY

QUORUM BOOKS

New York • Westport, Connecticut • London

Library of Congress Cataloging-in-Publication Data

Eckley, Robert S.
    Global competition in capital goods : an American perspective /
Robert S. Eckley.
        p. cm.
    Includes bibliographical references and index.
    ISBN 0–89930–559–8 (alk. paper)
    1. Industrial equipment industry—United States—Case studies.
    2. Competition, International.   I. Title.
    HD9680.U52E25   1991
    338.4′76218′0973—dc20   90–26489

British Library Cataloguing in Publication Data is available.

Library of Congress Catalog Card Number: 90–26489
ISBN: 0–89930–559–8

First published in 1991

Quorum Books, 88 Post Road West, Westport, CT 06881
An imprint of Greenwood Publishing Group, Inc.

Printed in the United States of America

The paper used in this book complies with the
Permanent Paper Standard issued by the National
Information Standards Organization (Z39.48–1984).

10 9 8 7 6 5 4 3 2 1

Copyright Acknowledgment

The author and publisher gratefully acknowledge permission to use the following material:

Robert S. Eckley, "Caterpillar's Ordeal: Foreign Competition in Capital Goods." Reprinted
from *Business Horizons* 32, no. 2 (1989):80–86. Copyright 1989 by the Foundation for the
School of Business at Indiana University. Used with permission.

For Nell

CONTENTS

TABLES AND FIGURES

FIGURES

PREFACE

The purpose of this study is to investigate and compare the performance of seven leading capital goods companies—goods used to produce other goods and services—relative to their domestic and foreign competitors over the last twenty years. Much of the international competition is occurring between these companies, and the experiences of the seven leaders are indicative of how U.S. firms are doing in this engagement.

These companies and their principal competitors, fifty in number—half American and half foreign—were observed in considerable detail. Another fifty firms were followed closely enough to observe when they were influencing the industry's behavior. Information came from books, articles, published company reports, case studies, the business and trade press, investment analysts' reports, videotapes, and interviews. A plethora of data exists on the computer industry; others are observed by enough interested parties to provide at least a handful of different views of each company. The MIT Commission on Industrial Productivity provided a 1989 review of computers, aircraft, and machine tools, enabling me to build on their work and that of others. Generally, ample information was available to answer most questions, despite occasional frustrations. The companies are a diverse lot, although common themes can be found in the volatility of demand for most capital goods, the role of technology and the generally informed buyer, the importance of economic growth in creating demand, exposure to foreign exchange risk, and other similar influences.

The author has been involved in the management of a large capital goods company, as a teacher of international business, and in management questions, including service on several corporate boards. The approach used in this study is primarily empirical, viewing the companies as a business manager would, enlightened by a background in economics. The companies are viewed as national entities, despite their multinational roles—American, Japanese, or European firms headquartered in one nation and engaged in worldwide business. The world may be evolving toward "the borderless world" of Kenichi Ohmae, but it is not there yet, and it would be foolhardy to act as if it is. Having said that, it is important to concede and acknowledge that the multinational or transnational character of international business is becoming more significant as the interdependence of the world's economies increases.

I am heavily indebted to my two sons, Robert George and Paul N. Eckley, for information, ideas, and helpful discussions. One was employed in marketing at IBM for ten years, ending in 1989, and is now a commercial photographer. The other is an investment analyst, who has studied several of the companies considered. My daughter, Jane E. Lennon, an attorney, has helped by giving me an outside observer's perspective on several of the chapters. Another daughter, Rebecca E. Melchert, has provided an example of successful entrepreneurship under adverse circumstances, a reminder of the possibilities available to those willing to try.

I owe a unique debt to an uncle, Wayne F. Eckley, recently deceased, for indirect assistance on several chapters. He taught nuclear engineering for more than thirty years at the U.S. Naval Academy and was always in a teaching mode, in or out of the classroom. Whether his efforts succeeded in my case is problematical, but they made me more confident in tackling several technical subjects.

Edward M. Bernstein, guest scholar at the Brookings Institution and first research director at the International Monetary Fund and also former central bank adviser, has assisted in a number of ways by providing information, guidance, and reviewing several chapters. In particular, he was useful in discussing the effects of exchange rate fluctuations on international business and in alerting me to pitfalls in analyzing international economics.

The accounting practice of translating sales or revenue at year-end exchange rates is suspect when rates have changed significantly during the year. Consequently, I have used average rates for translating sales figures, and if wide fluctuations have occurred, alternatives were tested to avoid spurious conclusions.

Colleagues at Illinois Wesleyan University contributed in a number of important instances. Adlai Rust Professor Mona J. Gardner, director of Business and Economics, provided encouragement and assistance from that division, including a student assistant, Brian Harper, who was extremely reliable and helpful. Robert M. Leekley kindly assisted in the preparation of illustrations. The Sheean Library staff were tolerant of my many requests and working style.

In addition to the people mentioned above, the following have helped by reviewing individual chapters and giving me many useful comments: Rex James Bates, Jim T. Gordon, E. Hugh Henning, L. W. Lees, Jim McStay, Robert R. Pratt, and Clarence B. Teagle.

My greatest debt is to my wife, to whom this book is dedicated, for constant support, encouragement, and inspiration when each was needed. Without her, there would not have been a book.

GLOBAL COMPETITION
IN CAPITAL GOODS

1

CAPITAL GOODS: AMERICA'S LEADING SECTOR

In 1971 the United States ran its first foreign trade deficit in almost a hundred years. Not since 1888, when the nation was primarily dependent on agricultural exports, had America imported more than it exported. In 1981, ten years later, it had its last surplus in foreign trade, which was followed by massive deficits. While these deficits have declined in recent years, there is little prospect that they will soon disappear.

Capital goods, those used in the production of other goods and services, have been in the forefront for many decades in the competition for world markets. U.S. leadership was clearly evident in the manufacture of machinery and equipment of various kinds as global trade in these goods rapidly grew in the fifties and sixties. That leadership has been eroded significantly in the last twenty years, but not lost. The task undertaken in this book is the examination of several leading U.S. capital goods companies and the industries in which they compete, in order to learn the reasons behind recent developments as well as the direction of future prospects.

THE IMPORTANCE OF CAPITAL GOODS

According to the definition followed by the Department of Commerce, capital goods include nonelectrical machinery, electrical and electronic equipment, transport equipment except automobiles, and instruments and related equipment, all excluding military equipment.[1] As defined, these industries constitute roughly a quarter of the total U.S. manufacturing activity as measured by the value of shipments or employment. They are even more important relative to world trade, constituting a third of total U.S. exports.

Within the capital goods sector, the leading industry by far is now the manufacture of computers and semiconductor chips, sometimes referred to as two industries, although in fact they are clearly only one. With the advent of deregulation, the telecommunications equipment industry has become increasingly global in nature and is beginning to commingle with the computer industry as the technologies join in information transmittal. The manufacture of electronic components and accessories, an amorphous mixture of capital and consumer goods, has long been well established across national boundaries. The aerospace industries, including aircraft, aircraft engines and parts, and spacecraft, have been more internationally oriented than almost any other throughout the last forty-five years. Instruments, including scientific, engineering, and photographic, and medical equipment and supplies constitute many small and often highly specialized manufacturing activities, some of which are growing rapidly, occasionally explosively, on a global basis. All of the above industries are generally considered to be "high technology" in everyday parlance, although some "high tech" classifications, based on research and development spending as a percentage of sales, also include several noncapital goods industries as well. These are inorganic chemicals, plastic and other synthetic materials, and pharmaceuticals.[2]

Heavy machinery and equipment is seldom recognized as a high technology field, but it is nevertheless an important component of U.S. capital goods and involves a large engineering input. The industries included in this category are extensively exposed to foreign competition, and most have experienced little growth in demand during the past decade. They include the manufacture of electrical generating and transmission equipment, construction and mining machinery, machine tools, and specialized industrial machinery. Another relatively mature U.S. industry is the production of trucks, buses, and engines and turbines, also undergoing readjustment and competitive realignment.

Capital goods exports from the United States have more than quadrupled during the last fifteen years, largely reflecting price inflation. In the same period, however, imports have grown much faster and in 1989 were eleven times their earlier level. Both now exceed $100 billion a year, as shown in Figure 1.1. The excess of exports over imports narrowed to only 3 percent in 1987, although it recovered to 22 percent in 1989. The leading categories of capital goods exports are computers and semiconductors and aircraft and aircraft engines, which constitute about half of the total. Consistently, capital goods exports have accounted for more than one-third of total U.S. exports, including agricultural products and minerals. More than half of the fifty leading industrial exporters from the United States are capital goods

Figure 1.1
U.S. Exports and Imports of Capital Goods, 1965–90

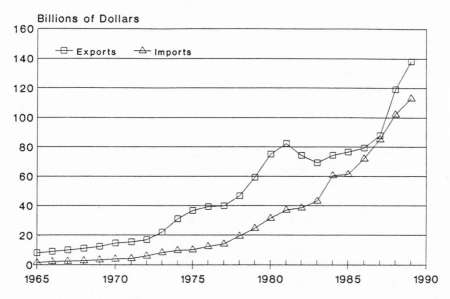

Billions of Dollars

Source: U.S. Department of Commerce.

companies. The implication is clear: capital goods lie at the heart of America's ability to compete in world markets.

The ability of U.S. multinational companies to compete in global markets has become increasingly dependent on their ability to supply markets abroad from foreign sources. Recent studies by the National Bureau of Economic Research argue that the declining share of U.S. exports of manufactured goods does not reflect a decline in the share of world exports supplied by U.S. multinational companies. They indicate that U.S. multinationals supply almost half of their world exports from majority-owned affiliates abroad and argue that "it is not declines in the competitiveness of American firms' managements and technology that were responsible for the deterioration of the U.S. trade position."[3]

THE CHALLENGE FROM ABROAD

Capital goods exports from the United States in 1970 were four times imports. But the situation soon changed drastically. By then the economies of Europe and East Asia had enjoyed more than a decade of prosperity following recovery in the earlier post–World War II years. The Kennedy Round of tariff reductions was completed in 1967, opening the markets of the industrial nations to increased competition, especially in capital goods. Shortly thereafter, from 1971 to 1973, the flexible exchange rate system emerged, adding another element of uncertainty to international prices on the eve of the first energy crisis. Businesses attempted to take advantage of widening markets. The intensity of this competition became more evident as the dollar appreciated from 1980 to 1985. Public policy measures and business repositioning to improve access to markets are evident in Japan and East Asia, in Europe, and elsewhere.

The Japanese challenge has raised the greatest apprehension. Its bilateral trade surplus with the United States averaged $53 billion from 1986 to 1989, and its surplus with the rest of the world averaged $38 billion, raising concern also in Europe and other regions. In 1989, capital goods accounted for more than half of Japanese exports to the United States. The Japanese Ministry of International Trade and Industry (MITI) sponsored a number of projects, such as the Very Large Scale Integrated Circuit Program in semiconductor chips and another in machine tools, which helped it gain world leadership in these two fields. Other projects have been less successful, such as the Fifth Generation computer project and participation in a multi-nation jet engine project, in which it has made large expenditures and has yet to achieve commensurate results. The success in machine tools and semiconductors, and even more dramatic success in automobiles and consumer electronic equipment, has sounded alarms in other industrial countries. In the United States, the Congress in 1989 criticized the transfer of technology from General Dynamics to Mitsubishi Heavy Industries in the FSX military aircraft project.

Actually, many of the global market penetrations have been by private firms without overt government sponsorship, although the Japanese government has maintained economic, political, and social conditions very favorable to exporting. Fuji Photo Film has been able to achieve an important position in world markets for photographic supplies, as have Ricoh, Canon, and others in copiers. Similarly, Komatsu's dogged pursuit of Caterpillar brought some success in the early 1980s.

Elsewhere in Asia, South Korea has developed several companies that are participating in the semiconductor and heavy equipment industries. Taiwan, Hong Kong, and Singapore have penetrated primarily the consumer electronic industries, and they may have the capability of moving into some capital goods fields soon.

The European trade surplus with the United States has not been large or persistent, but Europe, too, has had its successes, the most spectacular by Airbus Industrie in commercial aircraft. Heavily subsidized by the French, German, and British governments, it made its first sales in the United States in 1977 and seems assured of achieving profitability by the mid–1990s. Another joint European Community, governmental, and business project, the $5 billion Joint European Submicron Silicon program, aims to develop new generations of semiconductors involving Philips, Siemens, and SGS-

Thomson, a French-Italian joint venture. A second Community project, Esprit, is more diffused in assisting many cooperative projects directed toward the improvement of microelectric technology. The private sector also is readjusting to the prospects for 1992 when many remaining barriers to a free flow of transactions among the economies of the twelve Common Market Countries will be removed.

Siemens, one of Germany's two largest industrial companies, heretofore heavily dependent on sales in Germany, is moving to better position itself in United States and other European markets. In 1988 it acquired Bendix Electronics (automotive) in the United States and announced the acquisition of Rolm PBX communications business in forming a joint marketing venture with the International Business Machines Corporation (IBM). Siemens and British General Electric (GEC, not affiliated with General Electric (GE) in the United States) acquired the British defense electronics company, Plessey. The other large German company, Daimler-Benz, recently took over Messerschmitt-Bölkow-Blohm, the German portion of Airbus Industrie, in addition to several others. France's Compagnie Générale d'Électricité (CGE) was active also in taking over minority positions in Alsthom (power engineering) and Alcatel (telecommunications) and formed a joint venture with GEC to become the largest power equipment manufacturer within the European Community.

Outside the Community, other European firms were taking steps in anticipation of increased competition. Volvo joined General Motors (GM) in the U.S. truck market, and in perhaps the boldest move of all, Asea of Sweden merged with Switzerland's Brown Boveri to form the world's largest electrical and power-generating equipment company. The acquisition of Combustion Engineering gives Asea Brown Boveri an enhanced presence in the U.S. market.

In the Western Hemisphere, international competitors are also emerging. Canada's Northern Telecom has established itself in the telecommunications field with original technological contributions. The Brazilian government is attempting to foster an independent capability in microcomputers, and Mexico could develop as a low-cost supplier in the same manner that several East Asian countries have, given a continuation of appropriate public policies and business determination.

These illustrations of developments and possibilities are suggestive of the kinds of evolution and repositioning occurring within world markets. Although the illustrations are inadequate to fully describe global competition, they are indicative of the type of activity that must be constantly monitored and evaluated by U.S. multinationals in charting their own future activities.

METHODOLOGY: CHOICE OF INDUSTRIES AND COMPANIES

The approach employed in this study is essentially an empirical one of attempting to investigate how well seven leading U.S. capital goods companies have responded to the market forces confronting them during the last two decades. It asks how they have reacted to external forces and competitive moves in shaping their internal management decisions. Attention is focused on their positioning for market growth, product development technology and strategy, the management of manufacturing costs, and their deployment of resources on a global basis. In six of the seven companies, a large majority of sales revenues is represented in the activities investigated. Only in the case of GE is the analysis limited to electrical generating and distribution equipment, which now accounts for only one-tenth of total revenues.

More than fifty multinational firms are scrutinized within the seven industries examined—twenty-four U.S. based and the others about evenly divided between Europe and Japan. Another fifty require some awareness of their presence and potential activity. The emphasis on large companies risks the accusation of focusing on bigness, were it not for the fact that the computer and chip industry has been a playground for start-up firms in the 1970s and 1980s. Some of the other six industries also have responded to entrepreneurial effort, but the barriers to entry are substantial and difficult to overcome without large investments or governmental assistance in such areas as commercial aircraft, heavy electrical equipment, or engines.

It is easy to overemphasize the diversity of conditions facing capital goods companies because there are many differences in products, technologies, manufacturing processes, competition, and market conditions. Notwithstanding this, we shall be looking for commonalities lurking among the differences. All of the companies are seeking market opportunities and access to them; they display greater or lesser skill in designing and developing products and bringing them to potential users; they are attempting to marshal large numbers of people and suppliers toward common goals; and they need to understand the changing world economy and adapt their logistical schemes to its requirements. These, of course, are not simple or easy tasks in the changing international environment.

The globally dominant position of IBM in computers and semiconductors less than a decade after the appearance of transistors in 1947 makes it the unquestioned choice for scrutiny in that industry. Nevertheless, the second leading company, Digital Equipment Corporation (DEC), is a highly successful 1957 start-up, and Apple Computer, the number two firm in the largest market segment, personal computers, dates from only 1976. Persistent Japanese efforts have relegated IBM to third position in Japan, but French, British, and German attempts have been less successful. IBM's lead, five times the size of its closest challenger, is formidable if not unassailable.

Similarly, Boeing is the unquestioned leader in the manufacture of commercial aircraft, although there have been more challengers than many industry analysts remember, even in the jet age. The British Comet was the first unsuccessful commercial jet, which predated the Boeing 707 by almost a decade, and the French Caravelle was too narrowly adapted to the limited European needs of the early 1960s to be useful as route systems grew. General Dynamics, Lockheed, and Douglas also made bids for a share of the market. The Russians, who enjoyed as large a subsidy from military spending as did the American builders, have never penetrated much beyond Eastern European and other Communist countries.

The General Electric Company, which has always bested Westinghouse in the United States, has found itself eclipsed in size within the electrical equipment market by the recent Asea Brown Boveri merger. It also shares this market with a group of similar-sized firms—Siemens of Germany, Compagnie Générale d'Électricité in France, and Hitachi of Japan—as well as several smaller manufacturers. General Electric's strategy of "lead or divest" is of particular interest as it has exited several segments of the electrical equipment business. Truly a conglomerate, it has moved away from a large concentration in capital goods to financial services and broadcasting, while still retaining a sizeable collection of successful capital goods products. It is the largest jet engine manufacturer for aircraft and once participated in the computer industry.

The selection of Eastman Kodak, representing the photographic equipment and supplies industry, requires some explanation. Although heavily dependent on consumer products for significant revenues and profits, Kodak makes more than half of its photographic product revenues from sales of capital goods, such as copiers, graphic arts, and business and medical imaging. In addition, technical leadership in the motion picture industry and professional photographic markets is crucial to its ability to maintain its consumer market position. Also, it has long occupied a position of dominance both in U.S. and world markets. Recently, it has been challenged by Japanese and European firms. One of Kodak's responses has been to invest further in diversification, most recently into pharmaceuticals. From its formidable position, and with this questionable strategy, it has suffered repeated inroads.

Prior to 1970, Caterpillar faced largely U.S. domestic competition in its leadership of the construction machinery industry, occasionally encountering companies operating within limited regions and protected markets abroad. That changed gradually in the 1970s, and during the early 1980s it suffered a severe buffeting from Komatsu, recession, exchange rate shifts, and labor unrest. Nevertheless, after retrenching, Caterpillar remains the undisputed global leader, but is now encountering more established competitors from Japan and Europe. Other U.S. manufacturers fared less well.

Cummins Engine faces a unique situation as an independent supplier of diesel engines for trucks and buses, other machinery, especially in construction and mining, for marine installations, and electric generating sets. The heavy truck industry, at least in the United States, is not well integrated with the large automakers. Other manufacturers requiring sources of power for installation in their own equipment represent a sizeable market. General Motors has largely left the diesel engine business and joined Volvo in a joint venture in heavy trucks. Cummins is the largest manufacturer of diesel engines throughout the world. How long can it remain so, as the industry restructures and international competition intensifies? Caterpillar ranks second in the manufacture of diesel engines.

U.S. machine tool makers lost market leadership worldwide in the late 1970s, primarily because of their lethargy in adopting new technologies and lack of aggressiveness in pursuing global markets. Cincinnati Milacron has been the largest U.S. firm for some time and has been the most forward in attempting to develop automated machines for a domestic market not yet ready for them. It was run by the grandson of the founder until recently, which is typical of the family-firm orientation of the industry. The Japanese and the German industries now vie for global leadership and along with other foreign suppliers have captured half of the U.S. market. The scale of companies in the machine tool business, both here and abroad, is much smaller than for the other industries considered, although as we have learned from the Japanese and Germans, there may be ways to compensate for this. Both GE and IBM are displaying interest in the control of automated machine tools.

Together, the industries in which these seven multinational firms participate constitute a worldwide market approaching $700 billion a year, half in computers and semiconductor chips. Within the U.S. economy, these seven industries comprise approximately one-tenth of value added and employment within the manufacturing sector. They account for about one-quarter of capital goods shipments and employment. Five of the seven companies selected are the world leader within their respective industries. Only one, however, could consistently meet accepted criteria for excellence in profit performance in the last decade, partly because of the volatility characteristic of capital goods sales, although most of them performed better than average for U.S. firms in their industries. Three suffered multiyear losses in the 1980s. Sales growth for three of the seven exceeded the gross national product's (GNP) growth significantly during the last two decades, three experienced about the same rate of growth as the GNP, and one did less well. As a group, they did not do as well in the 1980s as in the 1970s, as the growth of the economy slowed.

As might be expected for multinational companies engaged in global markets, the seven have a relatively high proportion of foreign sales from facilities in the United States and abroad, with a median of 43 percent and a simple average of 39 percent in 1989. The range was from 21 to 59 percent. All have established some manufacturing facilities or supply arrangements abroad, reflected in a lower proportion of U.S. export sales, ranging from 9 to 54 percent. Nevertheless, five of the seven have consistently been among the top ten exporters from the United States, and if automotive sales to Canada were disregarded, Boeing, GE, and IBM would be the three largest exporters. Together, the seven firms investigated accounted for 7 to 8 percent of U.S. exports in the past decade.

Capital goods industries left out of this study include telecommunications, where the chief users have only recently experienced deregulation or privatization, and where the technology is undergoing rapid change. Others include bearings, oil field and mining equipment, air conditioning and heating equipment, scientific instruments, shipbuilding, medical and dental equipment, valves and pipefittings, and farm and other specialized industrial machinery. The companies examined are participants in several of these industries, although their primary attention is focused elsewhere.

A special comment about the automobile industry is appropriate. Autos are not included in the Commerce Department definition of capital goods because they are not used chiefly in the creation of other goods and services. They do provide a flow of services to consumers and have many technologies in common with the capital goods industries. General Motors engaged in the manufacture of construction machinery for more than twenty-five years without marked success, finally withdrawing in 1981. About that time Volvo and Fiat increased their interest in the industry. General Motors had an even larger involvement in the manufacture of diesel engines and only recently withdrew from that field. Moreover, a large share of the demand for machine tools comes from the automobile industry.

The labor situation for the seven firms illustrates the variety of organizational activity. Two have no unions. Two are organized by the International Association of Machinists, one faces a number of electrical unions, one is organized primarily by the United Auto Workers (UAW), and one has an independent company union representing its workers.

MACRO FORCES INFLUENCING CHANGE

Economic, political, and social forces and events have affected the competitive performance of U.S. capital goods companies in a variety of ways, depending on industry peculiarities and adaptability of the firms. This section sets out the environment in which the companies have operated during the last two decades and indicates the effects on the capital goods industries. Largely, the factors investigated are economic aggregates or developments shaped by the political realities of administrative and congressional action or reaction. In the cases of the level of aggregate savings and productivity change, however, social choices also are at work.

Economic Policies and Effects

The most conspicuous and dramatic economic change during the last quarter century has been the slowing in economic growth following the first

Table 1.1
Annual Growth in Industrial Production, Seven Industrial Countries (Average Percentage per Year)

Country	1960 to 1970	1970 to 1980	1980 to 1989
U.S.	4.9	3.3	2.8
Canada	6.2	3.3	3.1
Japan	15.9	4.0	3.9
France	6.1	3.0	1.2
Italy	7.3	3.3	1.4
U.K.	2.9	1.1	2.0
W.Germany	5.2	2.3	1.5

Source: U.S. Department of Commerce.

Note: Percentages calculated.

oil crisis in 1973. Its effects on the capital goods industries are especially pronounced because the demand for capital equipment is dependent on the rate of growth in output as well as replacement requirements. This retardation in growth in industrial production in the large trading countries is shown in Table 1.1, where annual rates of increase are presented in each of the last three decades. Japan has enjoyed the most rapid industrial expansion throughout the period, and Canadian and U.S. growth has been more rapid than Europe's in the last two decades.

The effect of the slowdown in growth on the capital goods industries was masked by three factors that buoyed their sales into the early 1980s. First, the two oil crises boosted earnings of oil producers, enabling them to acquire huge quantities of equipment. Second, the decline in the value of the dollar during the 1970s made U.S. exports attractive, an effect that lagged into 1981–82 because of the lead time for such trade, even after exchange rates had begun to reverse the advantages. Third, external debt of the less-developed countries (LDC) grew rapidly in the late 1970s—by 18 percent annually from 1975 to 1982. This enabled Latin American, African, and Asian customers to make large purchases of capital goods. The last of these supporting influences was gone by late 1982.

Attempts by governments to achieve maximum (or optimal) economic growth consistent with full employment and price stability are not always successful. Heads of state of the seven large industrial nations have met annually since 1974 in an effort to coordinate economic policies, and the finance ministers meet even more frequently. Nevertheless, two major reces-

Table 1.2
Annual Rates of Consumer Price Inflation (Average Percentage per Year)

Country	1970-75	1975-80	1980-85	1985-90
U.S.	6.7	8.9	5.5	4.0
Japan	11.5	6.5	2.8	1.4
W.Germany	6.1	4.0	3.9	1.3

Source: U.S. Department of Commerce.

Note: Percentages calculated.

sions occurred, one in 1974–75 and another in 1981–82, both more severe than other postwar recessions and the second more severe than the first. Price inflation also got out of control in the 1970s, and U.S. policy relied heavily on monetary measures as opposed to fiscal changes in taxation or government spending.

In order to curb the double-digit inflation then taking place, credit was tightened by the Federal Reserve authorities in late 1979. Economic activity in the United States began to fall in 1980 and turned down sharply in late 1981. The ensuing contraction was brief, but capital spending continued to decline into 1983. Although the U.S. recession was over by then, the overseas environment had changed adversely for U.S. manufacturers. The slowdown continued abroad, and the dollar appreciated, undermining the competitive position of U.S. exporters. Commodity prices fell, reducing the export earnings of the developing countries, the LDC debt crisis had begun, and oil prices and earnings were falling. As a result, the markets for many U.S. capital goods industries suffered extensive retrenchment and were slow in recovering fully from the 1981–82 recession. Tighter monetary policy brought higher interest rates, depressed profits, and reduced the demand for capital equipment. Consumption was maintained at a high level, savings and investment suffered, and the government deficits made investment dependent on funds from abroad.

Price inflation also ran higher in the United States than in Japan and Germany, America's principal export competitors throughout most of the last twenty years. Annual rates of increase in consumer prices for the three countries are shown in Table 1.2. Only in the early 1970s did the Japanese inflation exceed that in the United States. The story changes if unit labor costs in national currencies are compared. U.S. labor costs increased less than in Germany during the 1980s, but in Japan unit labor costs actually declined, indicating that the fruits of productivity improvements were distributed in lower prices or higher business profits. Floating exchange rates also made a difference in effective export and import prices as the following section reveals.

Figure 1.2
Foreign Exchange Value of the U.S. Dollar Relative to the Currencies of Ten Industrial Countries, 1980–90

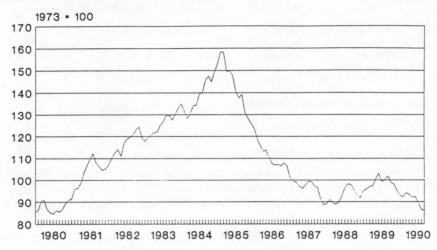

Source: Board of Governors of the Federal Reserve System, *Federal Reserve Bulletin*, 1981–1990.

Fluctuating Exchange Rates

Since the breakdown in the Bretton Woods fixed exchange rate system in 1971–73, rates of exchange among the major currencies have been free to float relative to one another, subject to the periodic intervention of central banks at the discretion of their governments. The U.S. dollar lost approximately 20 percent of its value relative to other major currencies in the 1971–73 devaluation and fluctuated thereafter, losing another 15 percent by mid–1980. At that point the credit tightening and anti-inflation measures adopted by the Federal Reserve the previous September were taking effect and the United States began to attract a flow of investment and speculative funds from abroad. This continued for four and one-half years, causing the dollar to appreciate by 87 percent by February 1985 as shown in Figure 1.2. This shift made U.S. exports progressively more expensive for customers abroad and made imports more attractive in this country.

A massive realignment of trade flows resulted from this change in exchange rates, reinforced by the fact that the recovery in the United States was greater than in other major industrial nations. Exports fell from 1981 to 1983 by 15 percent and then recovered slowly, while imports fell only one year during the recession and by 1985 were 28 percent larger than in 1981. Because of the delayed response to the rise in the dollar, the trade deficit did not reach its peak until 1987. By then, the effect had been to sacrifice a portion of the output and employment of U.S. capital goods industries. Some U.S. companies increased their sources abroad, and some foreign companies acquired markets and facilities in the United States.

A reversal of the appreciation of the foreign exchange value of the dollar began in March 1985, as shown in Figure 1.2, and in the following three years the dollar depreciated almost to the mid–1980 level. Once large movements have occurred, however, things do not necessarily revert to the way they were before the change. When companies have acquired a share of the market they do not surrender it readily, despite lower profits.[4]

Beginning in September 1985 with the Plaza Accord, the United States in conjunction with several leading countries sought to lower the dollar relative to other key currencies through exchange rate intervention by their central banks. Later, in 1989, these countries tried to limit the renewed appreciation of the dollar. While such actions may have some effect for short periods, their lasting effect is questionable because the magnitude of foreign exchange trading is so vast it is likely to overwhelm their efforts.

The effect of these wide swings in the foreign exchange value of the dollar has been to expose large segments of manufacturing sales and employment, dependent on foreign trade, to the vagaries of fluctuation in the foreign exchange market. To maintain flexibility in their operations, companies have had to adapt their sources of supply by currency area. Part of the supply of U.S. and foreign markets for capital equipment was ceded to foreign sources during the 1980s.

The Cost of Capital

Throughout the 1980s, U.S. capital costs appeared to be higher than in the home countries of its chief competitors for international markets, Germany and Japan. The simplest and most direct manifestation was in interest rates. For example, during the 1986–89 period, in the United States short-term interest rates averaged 2.4 percent higher (more than 50 percent) than in Germany and Japan, and long-term interest rates averaged 2.1 percent higher (33 percent) than in Germany and 3.7 percent higher (80 percent) than in Japan. Nevertheless, the unity of international capital markets for the same currency is demonstrated by the similarity of U.S. and Eurodollar short-term rates. Business people are cognizant of other possible international differences in capital costs, including taxation, leveraging of capital structures, and inflation premiums. Obviously, this is a complex question, and the whole picture must be considered.

Capital costs are especially significant to capital goods manufacturers because of their need to invest in research and development and plant facilities. In addition, some form of financing the purchase of the equipment they sell is usually required.

A recent study by the staff of the Federal Reserve Bank of New York for the period 1977–88 found significant disadvantages regarding these factors in the United States and Britain relative to Germany and Japan. Their findings are not surprising. They reject income tax structures as determinants and point to higher household saving in Japan and Germany, as well as practices and policies encouraging the greater reliance on debt financing in those countries. Other differences were attributed to greater success in promoting growth in Japan and stable prices in Germany and in the relationship of banks and governments to corporations in responding more favorably to private business distress. These differences were not small. The required rate of return in 1988 for machinery and equipment with a life of twenty years was found to be more than 50 percent higher in the United States than in either Germany or Japan. In financing a research and development project with a ten-year payoff lag, the authors found 1988 U.S. costs to be more than one-third higher than they were in Germany and more than twice as high as in Japan.[5]

The extent to which these extensive differences in the cost of capital can be avoided or offset is debatable. By virtue of their access to international capital markets, the larger companies may be able to skirt some but not all of the higher costs. The ability to move funds internationally is no solution because forward foreign exchange premiums and the uncertainty of future interest and exchange rates may more than offset interest rate differentials. Large firms capable of operating in many foreign markets have more opportunities to offset capital cost differences, but it is doubtful that they can make more than a partial compensation vis-à-vis the German or Japanese-based company. During the 1980s, U.S. multinationals and their U.S. employees were hostages to a greater or lesser extent to U.S. monetary and fiscal policy.

Oil Prices and the LDC Debt Crisis

Other factors affecting the world economy and the contour of trade among nations during the 1970s and 1980s were the two oil crises and the independent but related debt crisis in LDCs. Beginning with the Arab oil embargo in late 1973, the thirteen members of the Organization of Petroleum Exporting Countries (OPEC) quadrupled the price of crude oil by early 1974, where it largely remained for the rest of the decade. A second shock occurred following the Iranian revolution in 1979 and the beginning of the Iran–Iraq war, which pushed oil prices to thirteen times the early 1970s' level. This raised revenues of the OPEC countries to almost $400 billion in 1980 (in 1982 dollars). These huge revenues distorted price, cost, and income patterns, contributing to the recessions of 1974–75 and 1980–82 and the inflation that accelerated in the 1970s. Much of the increased OPEC revenue was either spent or deposited in banks in the industrial countries, and a portion of these deposits were invested by the banks in the form of loans to the LDCs to enable them to continue to purchase oil and other imports at the higher prices. This recycling of petrodollars by U.S. banks, with their implicit guarantee to depositors, increased rapidly during the late 1970s, as mentioned earlier, without sufficient caution by the banks about the ability of the LDCs to generate enough export earnings to meet their debts.

The industrial countries gradually reduced their consumption of oil, non-OPEC oil production increased, and discipline within the OPEC cartel weakened. Oil prices and revenues fell and by 1986, when Saudi Arabia sought to maintain its revenue by raising production, OPEC revenue was less than $100 billion (1982 dollars), close to the 1973 level. Long before that, however, the debt crisis of the LDCs broke when Mexico, one of the newly expanded oil producers outside OPEC, found it could not meet its debt payments in August 1982, as its oil revenue declined. The crisis quickly spread throughout much of the developing world. By then, the United States was deeply into the most serious recession of the postwar period, and when economic growth slows in the industrial countries, the effects are soon apparent in the LDCs. The International Monetary Fund (IMF) index of dollar prices of thirty-four commodities (excluding gold and oil), which contribute importantly to LDC export earnings, fell 20 percent from 1980 to 1982, recovered less than 10 percent during the U.S. recovery of 1983–84, and then declined to less than 70 percent of its 1980 level by 1986. LDC export earnings and their ability to finance imports and amortize debt decreased sharply.

Under the leadership of the IMF, the World Bank, and the U.S. government, technical default was averted, but in the 1982–85 interval Latin American countries made net foreign payments of interest, dividends, and principal of $100 billion only by drastically reducing their imports, including capital goods. Although commodity prices and export earnings revived later in the 1980s, the burden of outstanding LDC debt remained unrelieved and continued to limit the resumption of economic growth, especially in Latin America and Africa.

Labor Costs, Productivity, and Educational Achievement

Two developments in labor productivity are mentioned frequently with special relevance to the U.S. competitive position. One is the slowdown in productivity growth after 1973, although it had picked up again in the 1980s. The other points to America's less favorable performance relative to Japan and Germany. Annual increases in output per hour in manufacturing shown in Table 1.3 indicate that in these measures the United States has been losing ground by significant margins to the Japanese, while the earlier losses to Germany appear to have been arrested in the 1980s. The slowdown after 1973 was general throughout the industrial countries, but it was particularly marked in the United States. As mentioned earlier, com-

Table 1.3
Annual Productivity Increases in Output per Hour in Manufacturing (Average Percentage per Year)

Country	1960 to 1970	1973 to 1980	1980 to 1989
U.S.	2.9	1.3	3.5
Japan	10.8	5.7	6.1
W.Germany	5.9	3.7	2.2

Source: U.S. Department of Labor.

Note: Percentages calculated.

parative unit labor costs in the 1980s reveal the intensity of the Japanese export drive, inasmuch as they actually declined. Japanese workers have not shared as fully as their counterparts elsewhere in productivity gains. Depreciation of the dollar against the yen and the mark from 1971 to 1990—except for the rise in the early 1980s—alters the picture still further.

Efforts to interpret what has been happening to productivity have been tardy and show no unanimity of opinion among those who measure it. A consensus may be emerging that relates the decline in productivity increase to the oil price shock and to the slowdown in economic growth associated with the two major recessions that followed.[6] There are measurement problems. The MIT (Massachusetts Institute of Technology) Commission on Industrial Productivity suggests broadening the discussion to "productive performance," which would include other factors not in the economic measures. These would embrace such concepts as quality of product, timeliness of service, and technological innovation and effectiveness. They also suggest U.S. shortcomings may rest in organizational structures and social attitudes.[7]

A continuing study of the productivity question sponsored by the Brookings Institution that explores measurable aspects of these broader questions suggests that the prime difficulty may reside in slowed innovation, particularly in missed opportunities within U.S. industry. The authors do not reject such factors as educational attainment and work effort but find insufficient evidence to label them as quantitatively important. Throughout the 1970s, the possible decline in quality of labor force entrants, as measured by SAT scores (after refinement for changes in the population being tested), could not have had more than "a minor effect on productivity."[8]

There were mounting indications in the 1980s, however, that whatever the productivity effects of the past, the United States may well be generating a problem for the future through the inadequacies of its primary and secondary education. The MIT Commission cites the evidence on international comparisons of science and mathematics achievement by ten-, thirteen-, and seventeen-year-old students and other information that indicates substantial problems are being encountered as young people enter the work force.[9] The problems lie not only in the comparative levels of average achievement but also in the wide variations that exist in the United States and the numbers of work force entrants lacking basic skills needed in an increasingly technological society.

Trade Policies

Since the end of World War II, the twenty-four Organization for Economic Cooperation and Development (OECD) countries have moved steadily toward freer trade and the exposure of larger portions of their economies to worldwide competition. One exception has been the negotiation of voluntary export restraint agreements for products in several industries. A mechanism for negotiating the reduction of trade restraints was established in the 1947 General Agreement on Tariffs and Trade (GATT), and there have been eight rounds of negotiations, including the Uruguay Round scheduled for completion in 1990 but prolonged by disagreement over agricultural policies. After the first one, the most important have been the Kennedy Round, which ended in 1967 and took effect in the following five years, and the Tokyo Round, completed in 1979, which became effective over seven years. Nominal tariffs are now less than 8 percent (in many cases zero) for capital goods in the United States, Japan, and the European Community, and the Uruguay Round of negotiations deals with intellectual property rights and services as well as tariffs and other matters.

Many U.S. corporations responded to the establishment of the European Economic Community and the evolution of its common external tariffs and removal of internal tariffs from 1959 to 1968, by establishing new facilities and expanding existing ones in Europe to have greater access to the Common Market. The initial six member countries have now grown to twelve, including the accession of Britain in 1973 and Spain in 1986. Efforts are currently underway to complete the economic union by 1992 through the negotiation of almost 300 new Community laws covering subjects from customs procedures to labor policy. A unified market of 330 million people is emerging. It is expected to be liberal or free market oriented, as are its principal member nations today, but there is some concern that it will become more exclusive.

With its traditional concerns for self-sufficiency and protectionism, Japan came later to the liberal trading community of Western nations. The postwar political ascendency of business classes has given it a strong drive for economic growth, and much of its success has depended on gaining access to the markets and technology of the United States and Europe. It joined GATT in 1955, on a limited basis, but true trade liberalization was not promised until the end of 1968, when the decision was made to implement it over the next three years. The liberalization of business investments into Japan was further delayed until the late 1970s. There have been many subsequent complaints by outside businesses that liberalization has actually been meaningless, often because of administrative delays in gaining approval for imports or investments, or because of difficulties in penetrating markets resulting from Japan's inefficient distribution system. Most economists attribute the overall U.S. current account deficit to the budget deficit, the fall in the personal saving rate, the rapid growth of U.S. output, and the appreciation of the dollar. The question is why 45 percent of the trade deficit is with Japan. The concentration of the trade deficit with Japan and the newly industrialized countries of East Asia is due to conditions and policies in those countries. Many Japanese blame the large and persistent U.S. trade deficit on the U.S. budget deficit and ineffectual business efforts to cater to Japanese buyers. Many Americans argue that in much of the 1970s and most of the 1980s the Japanese government deliberately prevented the yen from appreciating enough to reflect its strong international economic position. There is some truth in all of these arguments, although future success by U.S. multinationals will require more consistent efforts than many have made in the past two decades.

The United States has resorted to voluntary export restraint agreements to limit foreign competition in steel (1969), automobiles (1981), semiconductors (1986), and machine tools (1986). For most of the period since 1969, some form of restraint has been imposed on U.S. steel imports, raising the cost of steel to domestic users, an action not conducive to improving the competitive position of U.S. capital goods exports, many of which use steel as a raw material. The automobile restraint agreement, only with Japan, is a quantitative one based on units and has had the effect of raising auto prices, inviting Japanese competition in the larger car market, and acting as a protection for U.S. auto industry wages and compensation, which are approximately 50 percent higher than the average for all U.S. manufacturing. Negotiated with Japan in 1986, the semiconductor agreement was intended to gain access for U.S. chip makers to the Japanese market, but it has been the source of controversy almost from the day it was concluded. Later that year, restraints on the importation of machine tools were negotiated for five years with Japan and Taiwan, and then the government applied similar controls on the basis of national security to Germany, Switzerland, and a number of other countries.

The whole question of limits on imports from Japan is complicated by the failure of the yen to appreciate sufficiently. Had the yen been permitted to rise more fully, the bilateral trading experience between the United States and Japan would have been different.

Another form of trade restraint is exercised by the government through the Coordinating Committee for Multilateral Export Controls (COCOM), a sixteen-nation group that has existed since World War II to prevent sensitive technology from getting into the hands of adversaries. U.S. restraints, however, have been more stringent than those of other allies in the group. This has led to squabbles with the other NATO nations and Japan, as it did when the United States tried to limit pipeline equipment sales to the Soviet Union in 1981. These types of control have given rise to business criticism because competitors in other member countries often made the sales instead of U.S. firms. Capital goods makers, in particular, have often had export licenses denied, although the volume was probably seldom crucial to their long-term success. As a result of the Cold War thaw, these restrictions are being modified significantly.

World trade expansion for many decades has progressed at a rate from one-third to one-half again as fast as the GNP growth. Inasmuch as the United States has more export trade than any other nation, followed by Germany and Japan, and because more than one-third of its exports are capital goods, it follows that capital goods makers have a vital stake in future trade expansion. If, as seems likely, a number of Eastern European nations will be increasing their trade with the West, and if the developing countries adopt more open trading policies in order to hasten their own progress, then U.S. capital goods manufacturers will find many new opportunities and challenges in future global competition.

NOTES

1. The Standard Industrial Classifications, 35, 36, 37 less 371, and 38.
2. William F. Finan, Perry D. Quick, and Karen M. Sandberg, "The U.S. Trade Position in High Technology: 1980–1986" (Report prepared for the Joint Economic Committee of the United States Congress, October, 1986), app. A, p. 70.
3. Robert E. Lipsey and Irving Kravis, "The Competitiveness and Competitive Advantage of U.S. Multinationals, 1957–83" (National Bureau of Economic Research Working Paper No. 2051, Cambridge, Mass., October 1986).
4. A recent study finds that only 50 to 60 percent of exchange rate appreciation is reflected in higher import prices and that "Japanese firms appear to absorb a higher proportion of exchange rate fluctuations into their profit margins on sales to the United States" than do other countries (Peter Hooper and Catherine L. Mann, "Exchange Rate Pass-through in the 1980s: The Case of U.S. Imports of Manufactures," *Brookings Papers on Economic Activity* [1989–1]: pp. 297–337). A similar conclusion was reached by Richard C. Marston, "Price Behavior in Japanese and U.S. Manufacturing," Working Paper No. 3364, National Bureau of Economic Research, Cambridge, Mass., May 1990. He uses a sectoral approach within manufacturing to examine behavior by industry.
5. Robert N. McCauley and Steven A. Zimmer, "Explaining International Differences in the Cost of Capital," Federal Reserve Bank of New York, *Quarterly Review* (Summer 1989): pp. 7–28.
6. Stanley Fisher et al., "Symposium on the Slowdown in Productivity Growth," *The Journal of Economic Perspectives* 2, no. 4 (Fall 1988): pp. 3–97.
7. Michael L. Dertouzos, Richard K. Lester, Robert M. Solow, MIT Commission

on Industrial Productivity, *Made in America: Regaining the Productive Edge* (Cambridge, Mass.: The MIT Press, 1989), chap. 2, pp. 23–45.

8. Martin Neil Baily and Alok K. Chakrabarti, *Innovation and the Productivity Crisis* (Washington, D.C.: The Brookings Institution, 1988), especially chap. 2, pp. 13–45.

9. Dertouzos, Lester, and Solow, *Made in America*, p. 84, and Richard Kazis, "Education and Training in the United States: Developing the Human Resources We Need for Technological Advance and Competitiveness," MIT Commission on Industrial Productivity, *Working Papers*, vol. 2 (Cambridge, Mass.: The MIT Press, 1989), p. 17.

2

COMPUTERS AND CHIPS: IBM ATTEMPTS TO IMPROVE ITS RESPONSES

The last twenty years have been a revolutionary period in the computer and semiconductor industry. When the revolution began in 1970, the mainframe was king and IBM was introducing its System/370. The Radio Corporation of America (RCA) and GE promptly gave up and exited the industry. The following year, Intel announced its triple whammy—the DRAM memory chip, the EPROM software storage, and the microprocessor—little more than a decade after the introduction of integrated chips. This laid the groundwork for the microcomputer later in the 1970s and much more. The technology was in place for progressive compression of integrated circuits of ever increasing complexity onto a single silicon chip. About the same time, Digital Equipment Corporation (DEC) and others were perfecting minicomputer designs to replace the smaller mainframes. Japan mounted its Very Large Scale Integration Project in the late 1970s in preparation for its challenge of the world's semiconductor markets. And IBM endured the protracted thirteen-year antitrust suit brought by the U.S. Department of Justice and a concomitant inquiry by the European Community into complaints of violation of the antimonopoly articles of the Rome Treaty.

That is a quick summary of a much more complicated story. If IBM's recent performance has been disappointing to some observers, that is to be expected. Its position has eroded, but IBM is still the highly dominant firm in a rapidly changing industry, with aspirants at home and abroad goaded by enormous private profits and intense governmental pressures. The question is: How much better should it have done, given the competition, the industry situation, and its unwieldy size? This chapter is a selective outline

Figure 2.1
IBM Revenues and Profits, 1979–89

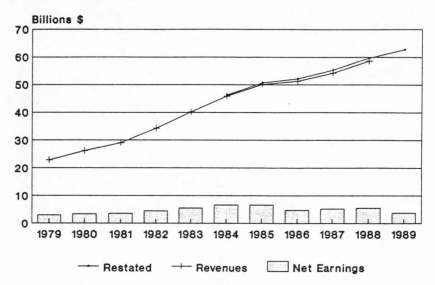

of developments in the complex computer and semiconductor industry and an evaluation of the salient events in the evolution of the world's most critical business activity during the period 1970–90.

RECENT PERFORMANCE DISAPPOINTING

Success carries its own price; people expect it to continue. IBM's spectacular performance during the decades leading up to the mid–1980s led stockholders, employees, and users to expect much. Growth in revenues from 1970 to 1984 raced along at an average of 13.8 percent per year and then in the last half of the decade fell to less than half that rate, to 6.5 percent annually. Net profits peaked in 1984, as shown in Figure 2.1, a level not reached again in the 1980s. Computer industry growth slowed after 1984, and IBM lost share to U.S. and foreign competitors, both developments tending to overshadow its outstanding accomplishments. Opportunities within the industry existed for even greater adversity because of size and inertia, rapid technological shifts, and exchange rate volatility. Early in the growth retardation, *The Wall Street Journal* took an intensive look at IBM, and one of its writers observed that "to some extent, IBM is just lucky.... Powerhouses in other industries once played similar roles, only to stumble before foreign competitors, tempestuous unions, bureaucratic management or economic forces beyond their control."[1]

IBM's loss of market share is most clearly shown relative to its five leading U.S. mainframe and minicomputer competitors—Digital Equipment (DEC),

Unisys, Hewlett-Packard, NCR, and Control Data—in the period from 1983 to 1988. As a percentage of IBM sales, the five rose from 63 to 70 percent, although only three of the five—DEC, Hewlett-Packard, and NCR—grew faster than IBM. Unisys and Control Data sales rose only slightly. The loss reflects the continuing success of the minicomputer, first introduced in the 1960s, outside the mainframe market. Two other developments that were occurring are not revealed by these data. First, the Japanese were moving into world markets in computers and in semiconductors. Second, in 1977 the microcomputers appeared with an explosive impact. Although IBM made an impressive response with the introduction of its personal computer in 1981, it ultimately yielded more than 80 percent of this market segment to Apple Computer and the IBM clones, or compatible makers. By 1988, Apple's sales were exceeding those of Control Data.

The Japanese competition in the mainframe area came initially through Fujitsu's minority ownership of Amdahl in the mid–1970s and U.S. distribution of plug-compatible machines. Other foreign competitors followed, but the loss of market share was chiefly by other U.S. firms, not IBM. The later capture of the merchant semiconductor business, again by the major Japanese computer manufacturers, affected independent semiconductor makers in the United States and led to concern by IBM about the adequacy of outside U.S. suppliers.

The protracted U.S. antitrust case and associated private lawsuits against IBM, which extended throughout the 1970s, did not result in findings against the company, but did cause a major diversion of top management attention. The last of some twenty-five cases in the United States came to an end in the early 1980s, and a final settlement of the European Community Statement of Objections was made in 1984. No major changes in operating practices were required, but two effects did follow. IBM became more cautious about product announcements and their timing, in order not to appear to preempt the sale of competitors' products, as claimed by a number of plug-compatible manufacturers. More importantly, the settlement of the European Community complaints necessitated the provision for some technical information about new IBM products, to enable compatible peripherals to be adapted within a short period.

Among the twelve leading computer companies in 1989 were six U.S. firms, three Japanese, and three European, as shown in Table 2.1. Not included because of the size of the industry are a like number of computer and semiconductor manufacturers with multibillion dollar sales, distributed geographically in about the same way, plus thousands of smaller firms. These estimates probably overstate the importance of the Japanese companies, inasmuch as current exchange rate values are used in accounting translations, rather than the relative purchasing power of the sales revenues. (There is ample reality to the translated financial data, however, because that is the basis on which companies are bought and sold in international

Table 2.1
World Computer Market Share Estimates, 1989

Company	Revenue Bill. $	Percentage
IBM	60.8	23.8
DEC	12.9	5.0
NEC	11.5	4.5
Fujitsu	11.4	4.5
Unisys	9.4	3.7
Hitachi	8.7	3.4
Hewlett-Packard	7.8	3.0
Bull	6.5	2.5
Siemens	6.0	2.3
Olivetti	5.6	2.2
Apple	5.4	2.1
NCR	5.3	2.1
Other	104.5	40.9
Total 100 firms	255.8	100.0

Source: *Datamation*, June 15, 1990.

Note: Percentages calculated.

capital markets.) The figures are probably surprising to those accustomed to thinking of IBM as dominant in the mainframe market in the United State and Europe. But the world market includes Japan, the smaller machines, and myriad smaller software and service companies.

Because IBM is almost five times as large as its closest rivals and has led the field for thirty-five years, no other firm participates as fully in all market segments as it does nor can claim the installed customer base. DEC, the second largest U.S. firm, and also the number two company in world markets until Fujitsu's acquisition of ICL, has performed extremely well by concentrating on minicomputers and the possibility of upgrading capacity by networking with common architecture. During the 1980s, DEC sales grew twice as fast as IBM revenues. In 1990, it entered the mainframe market. Unisys, the merger of Burroughs and Sperry in 1986, struggled to combine dissimilar architectures and was not helped by softening markets in 1989. Hewlett-Packard offers a strong midrange line and has been active in establishing foreign alliances. NCR is especially oriented toward point-of-sale machines and banking. Apple's growth in the past decade has been phenomenal, despite a stumble in 1985. In marketing personal computers it has emphasized user accessibility and has been particularly successful in educational markets. Control Data Corporation, which concentrates on large systems and compatible peripherals, has been struggling since the mid–1980s to refocus and restructure. Other multibillion dollar U.S. companies include troubled Wang Laboratories (midrange systems), Compaq Computer (IBM-compatible personal computers), Amdahl (IBM plug-compatible mainframes using Fujitsu components), Tandem Computer (a niche player, using a fault-tolerant redundant processor), Tandy (personal computers), AT&T (which developed UNIX software and moved back into computers in 1984), Sun Microsystems (workstations), and others, plus the semiconductor manufacturers and the software and service houses.

The Japanese computer industry was developed with the protection and assistance of the government. Imports and foreign investment in computer facilities were rigidly controlled in the 1960s until domestic manufacturers were established and supplying more than half of Japanese needs. That occurred in 1966, and IBM's share of that market continued to shrink until recently. Four of the Japanese companies helped by the government have become major factors in world competition. They also make their own chips, supplying a major portion of U.S. and European needs. Fujitsu was assisted by Gene Amdahl, who left IBM in 1970 to establish his own company, in developing IBM-compatible machines. It holds a large interest in Amdahl in America and supplies Siemens with mainframes for resale in Germany and components to ICL in Britain. Hitachi also makes IBM plug-compatible machines. It acquired National Advanced Systems (NAS) in the United States in 1988 in a joint venture with GM's Electronic Data Systems division. It supplies mainframes for resale to NAS and also to Olivetti in Italy. Nippon Electric (NEC) has aimed at specialized applications for both midrange computers and microcomputers. It supplies mainframes to Bull in France for distribution in Europe. Toshiba withdrew from the mainframe market but is especially strong in personal computers. Other Japanese computer manufacturers include Mitsubishi Electric, Oki Electric, Seiko Epson, and Nippon Telephone and Telegraph, which has done much to foster semiconductor technology in Japan.

IBM is almost three times as large as Siemens Nixdorf, its closest competitor in the European market. DEC is third, followed by Bull and Olivetti. The recent acquisition by Bull of Zenith, the leader in battery-powered laptop computers, improved Bull's position. Others playing significant roles in Europe are Hewlett-Packard, Unisys, Philips of the Netherlands, and ICL of Great Britain, recently acquired by Fujitsu.

A product-line breakdown of IBM revenues, excluding "other" (largely financing), is presented in Figure 2.2. This breakdown roughly parallels recognized industry market segments and also the U.S. lines of business divisions established by IBM in 1988. The discussion in the next five sections follows an organizational outline by product: (1) mainframes, (2) midrange computers, (3) personal computers and workstations, (4) semiconductors, and (5) software and services. The definitions of mainframes, midrange computers, PCs and workstations are arbitrary and usually made on the basis of price or capacity. Semiconductors and software change with product improvements and enhancements. Midrange computers in the late 1980s could

Figure 2.2
Estimated Breakdown of IBM Revenues, 1989

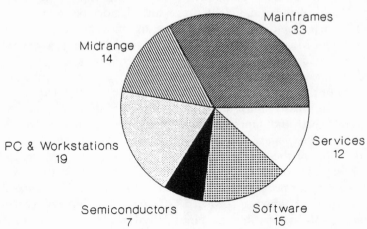

perform the operations a mainframe had ten years earlier, and personal computers had the capacity that a mainframe had twenty years before. Another distinction is IBM's maintenance of three separate architectures for the three classes of machines.

MAINFRAMES

By the end of the 1980s, mainframes still accounted for roughly half of IBM's total revenues and perhaps as much as two-thirds of its net income. This becomes evident if an appropriate portion of software, service, and semiconductor revenues as shown in Figure 2.2 is allocated to the market giving rise to it. Here the size of the installed base, the prior customer investment in software, and the large-scale advantages in manufacturing costs are greatest for IBM. The company cannot be criticized for wanting to defend and not disturb this market, where its lead in North America (about 70 percent of the market) and in Europe (more than half) has remained a commanding one. The problem is that since 1984 IBM's growth has slowed, and the future potential for expansion of large systems appears limited. This is because the imputed growth rate in the productivity of computer output has been so phenomenal, 26 percent per year from 1965 to 1985 according to an estimate based on data for computer output and prices provided by the Department of Commerce.[2] That source indicates computer output has risen by 37 percent annually during the period, and real prices of computer output have dropped by 21 percent per year. With these tremendous rates of change and the equally impressive rise in capability of the smaller machines, the market for mainframes is approaching maturity.

Obviously, with different classes and families of machines, the targets are moving ones. Products evolve and are replaced but leave strange legacies of architecture and software to influence future designs. When IBM introduced its System/360 in 1964, demand was underestimated by a factor of one to two. It was replaced six years later by the System/370, which remains the architectural standard for many large computer systems, inside and outside IBM. The onrush of minicomputer competition from the late 1960s through the next two decades was not adequately met by IBM's midrange small business systems. There appeared to be enough market for all—IBM grew with its existing customer base and found new ones, and the mini-computer makers found many new buyers to serve—until growth slackened in 1985. Nevertheless, the large system market was well defended by IBM with the 308X series beginning in 1980, the still larger 3090 in 1985, and the entry level 9370 in 1986. The replacement System/390 was announced in 1990 and when fully implemented will embrace the two prior systems as well as the 4381 small mainframe.

Other established mainframe manufacturers did not fare well in the last twenty years. Honeywell was in the business for twenty-nine years, from 1957 to 1986. It acquired GE's interests in 1970 and those of Xerox in 1975 but slipped from second to eighth in the U.S. industry between 1973 and 1982. Sperry, which had a running start over IBM with its UNIVAC in the early 1950s, did not initially support its machines with adequate services, and its position gradually weakened. It acquired the remnants of RCA's computer business in 1971, which helped little, and was acquired itself by Burroughs in 1986, which had fared somewhat better. But the merged company, called Unisys, which ranks second in the U.S. mainframe market, is troubled.

IBM's stubborn competition in the mainframe market has come in the form of "plug-compatible" equipment, first in peripherals—tape and disk drives, printers, memory devices, and so on—and later in complete machines. Components that could operate with IBM machines were introduced in the late 1960s by Telex, Memorex, Control Data, Storage Technology and others, sometimes based on technology provided by ex-IBM employees. These companies acquired perhaps 25 to 30 percent of the peripheral market and have been difficult to dislodge without destroying pricing structures and profits.

In 1970, Gene Amdahl left IBM, where he had been prominently involved in design work, and founded a company to produce IBM-compatible mainframe machines. Lacking adequate financing, he turned to Fujitsu, which assumed almost half of the equity in the new company in exchange for cross licensing and other technical information. Amdahl Corporation delivered its first machine in 1975 and now markets Japanese-designed machines in the United States. Amdahl eventually left his new company to found another, but the Amdahl-Fujitsu share of the mainframe market has continued to rise to an estimated 9 percent worldwide.[3] As mentioned earlier, Fujitsu mainframes are marketed in Europe through other companies. Hitachi, which at one time had a technology-sharing agreement with Fujitsu, also uses the IBM-compatible approach and is fourth in the global mainframe market.

The Japanese government has taken an active interest in promoting the computer industry through projects sponsored by the Ministry of International Trade and Industry. The first major project was in response to the introduction of IBM's System/360. It began in 1966 as the five-year Very High Speed Computer System program sponsoring Fujitsu, Hitachi, and Nippon Electric in a cooperative effort. A project followed that was twice as large and included nine companies: it started in 1971 and was known as the Pattern Information Processing System, aimed at developing various aspects of artificial intelligence. A third large joint undertaking was the Fifth Generation computer project, begun in 1981 to further work achieved in the earlier project and to design new computer architecture.

Together with governmental procurement policies, these projects played an important role in enabling the Japanese companies to gain 80 percent of their domestic market and to be in a position to move aggressively abroad. As a participant in all of these projects, Nippon Electric (NEC) emerged as the third Japanese mainframe manufacturer, with the strategy of developing specialized computers for integration with communications, a concept it continues to pursue as the second largest Japanese computer firm.[4]

Supercomputers, used primarily for scientific and engineering problems, are made by several American and the three Japanese mainframe manufacturers, none of which has yet penetrated the other's, largely governmental, domestic market to any great extent. Seymour Cray designed several models for Control Data and then left to found Cray Research in 1974, now the leading company in the field. Cray left that company in 1989 to establish another one to pursue the design of the Cray 3 supercomputer, judged to be too ambitious by Cray Research. About the same time, Control Data announced that it was leaving the field. After being out of the supercomputer market since the early 1970s, IBM reentered it in 1985 with the general purpose 3090. It also has invested in Supercomputer Systems, Inc., founded by Steve Chen after he left Cray Research. Present technology trends favor the development of massively parallel computers in the future, embodied in Chen's work and in computers made by Thinking Machines and Intel, among others.

As the breakup of the AT&T monopoly approached in 1984, IBM intensified its interest in telecommunications equipment. However, the time was not yet ripe for a convergence of computer and telecommunications technology, despite numerous overlaps. Robert Crandall and Kenneth Flamm wrote in 1989 that "the recent attempts by AT&T and IBM to invade one another's markets have been remarkably unsuccessful."[5] IBM divested itself of its interest in Satellite Business Systems in 1985, and the development and manufacturing segments of Rolm, which it had acquired in 1984, were taken over by Siemens in 1988. IBM's interest in telecommunications continues in some products, such as communication controllers, and in services offered. AT&T's interest in computers has been chiefly in smaller machines that the company sought to improve through a relationship with Olivetti, which was terminated in 1989 after five and one-half years. Late in 1990, AT&T launched an unfriendly $6 billion takeover bid against NCR, the sixth largest U.S. computer company, signalling its continuing interest in the computer industry, despite having suffered heavy losses in computers since 1984.

The minicomputer or midrange market, the other market niche that became an avalanche in the 1970s and 1980s, spawned another mainframe challenge in 1990. Digital Equipment Corporation (DEC), the most formidable minicomputer manufacturer, introduced a line of mainframe computers. Tandem Computers also launched a new low-priced mainframe series at the same time.

THE MIDRANGE CHALLENGE

Eight years after its founding by MIT-educated Kenneth H. Olsen, DEC introduced the PDP 8 in 1965, priced at only $18,000 and aimed at academic, scientific, and industrial users. It was an immediate success and acquired the descriptive designation "minicomputer." DEC offered the first time-sharing machine the same year; the PDP 11 series ran from 1970 to 1977. Fifty-thousand machines were sold, many to new users who were installing their first computer in a small organization or in a department or specialized operation of a larger business. The next update, the VAX 11/780 model and its successors, enabled midrange computers to take over many general purpose applications formerly reserved for mainframes and enabled DEC to aggressively market the concept of a single architecture with interactive computing, networking, and upgradability.[6]

As the years advanced, DEC's phenomenal rate of growth in sales also slowed, from 34 percent annually in the second half of the 1970s to 18 percent per year in the late 1980s. The midrange market, never as large as that for mainframes, however generously defined, also may be approaching maturity. The larger question for DEC eventually may be who will replace the company's sixty-four-year-old founder, who has no successor identified. More intent on growth and share of market as opposed to return on shareholders' equity, DEC nevertheless has returned more than 15 percent on equity in half of the years since 1974; this compared to IBM's 20 percent-plus return from 1977 to 1985. Now DEC is a large company, one-fifth the size of IBM. It, too, encountered the necessity for retrenchment in 1989 and experienced its first quarterly loss in

1990 in conjunction with a $400 million charge for severance pay and other costs associated with its cutbacks.

Hewlett-Packard started as a maker of scientific test instruments and still receives more than one-third of its revenue from that activity, giving it from the beginning a significant volume of business unrelated to computers. Its first midrange computer was introduced in 1966, and it has developed into one of the principal manufacturers of small business systems. Always close to the cutting edge in technology, it recently acquired one of the pioneer workstation producers, Apollo Computer, thrusting it into the forefront of that burgeoning market.

Other important suppliers of midrange computers are Unisys, Sun Microsystems, Toshiba, and Fujitsu. Nixdorf of Germany, recently acquired by Siemens, introduced a minicomputer in 1968 and became significant in the midrange market throughout Europe and in the United States as well. In the last decade, however, its fortune waned.

Ease of entry made the market more diffuse for midrange computers than for mainframes, although the entrances and the exits have not been as frequent nor as dramatic as in personal computers. Specialized machines for science and engineering, process monitoring, and other purposes such as banking or point-of-sale are more important. Other firms in the industry include Wang, NEC, Unisys, and NCR, which by their diversity have made it difficult for IBM to stay abreast. Characteristics of the market originally included less software support, sale as opposed to rental, and limited function.

IBM's response to this midrange competition was inadequate for more than twenty years. It introduced the System/3 series of small business computers in 1969 and followed it later with the S/34, S/38, and S/36 machines, utilizing separate operating system software and application packages. In 1979 the 4300 series of small mainframes was introduced using S/370 architecture, requiring a conversion to upgrade from the S/3X models. Although one observer lauded the competitive pricing of the 4300 as a bold choice of sacrificing profits to retain market share,[7] IBM was progressively losing position to DEC, Hewlett-Packard, NCR, NEC, and others. Not until the AS/400 was introduced in 1988 did IBM adequately defend itself with an appropriate product in the midrange size. Either IBM did not perceive the seriousness of the midrange challenge by DEC and others, or it could not find the right technological response in a timely way. System/370 architecture was a more difficult entry for the emerging customer than the systems offered by DEC and others.

By the late 1980s growth rates in the midrange market signalled that the action was shifting to the proliferation of products in the personal computer, workstation, and supermicro market, where entry was still easier, more niches existed, and the entrepreneurs were quickfooted. How fast can an elephant run, and how maneuverable can one become?[8]

PERSONAL COMPUTERS AND WORKSTATIONS

The most revolutionary development in the computer industry since its founding at the end of World War II occurred in 1977 with the successful commercialization of the microcomputer. The groundwork had been laid with the invention of the microprocessor in 1971. Apple Computer brought the first commercial quantities to market in 1977, and ten years later there were tens of millions of them in use throughout the world. Initially headed by Stephen Wozniak, Mike Markkula, and Steve Jobs, the latter then twenty-two-years old, Apple was one of those brilliant successes that led to immediate emulation by others hoping to capitalize on its achievement. Scores of models appeared, creating a confusion of incompatible languages. This babel continued until IBM, having once failed with a small entry model, finally decided in 1980 to approach the market again. By the time it entered a year later with its highly successful rationalizing standard, the Personal Computer, or PC, Apple had more than 300,000 machines in the hands of users. Eventually, there would be more than one standard.

Apple continued its extraordinary rates of increase in sales through the first four years of IBM's entry. It introduced an improved model and a new model in 1983, the first well received, the latter not. From the beginning, Apple catered to the uncertain user and targeted the educational market, where many first-time users gained familiarity with its machines. The Macintosh, designed and produced under the direction of Jobs, achieved new levels in ease of use, but it was not highly successful initially. In 1985, the entire personal computer market ran out of steam. Apple was forced to restructure and closed three of its six plants. Jobs resigned and was replaced by a marketing executive who had been brought in earlier from Pepsico. Eventually, continued elaboration of its basic strategy with improved models of the Macintosh and the earlier Apple II won renewed acceptance for Apple products.

Apple's early competition came from Tandy Radio Shack's TRS–80 and a host of lower tier companies, many of whom did not survive a short flush of prosperity. The market awaited definition and expansion by IBM.

With strong support from CEO John Opel, in 1980 IBM's crucial Corporate Management Committee approved an iconoclastic approach to the new computer market. In little more than a year, a team at the Entry Systems Division plant in Boca Raton broke long company traditions by designing a personal computer that employed an Intel 16-bit microprocessor chip as the central processing unit, and by using a software and operating system written by upstart Microsoft and disk drives supplied by Tandon, with the computer itself to be distributed primarily by Computerland and Sears stores. This was a wild departure for a decades-old, staid company. While not nearly as risky as the System/360 had been in 1964, the PC was the break necessary to establish a new class of com-

Table 2.2
Percentage Share of U.S. Personal Computer Market

	1983	1988
IBM	25.4	15.7
Apple	17.7	12.2
Compaq	2.0	6.9
Zenith	1.2	6.8
NEC	0.8	2.4
Toshiba	–	1.9
Epson	0.2	1.9

Source: The Economist, August 19, 1989, p. 54, from Dataquest.

puters with millions of potential customers. It was designed with an open or nonproprietary architecture so that other applications software could be written to widen its use. It was an immediate sensation. Within three years three additional models were introduced, one of which, the bottom-of-the-line PC Jr, proved to be a disappointment and was dropped after a year and a half. IBM reentered the home or low-end PC market in 1990.

The PC's open architecture had the advantage of attracting an abundance of user programs and ancillary equipment, but it also attracted the clone makers, the compatibles, and the cheaper look-alikes. Some companies quickly added improvements not available on the PC. By 1985 Compaq Computer, which was founded in 1982, had more than a half billion dollars in sales by making a portable unit and adding features. Three years later it had quadrupled sales again and ranked third in the market after IBM and Apple, as shown in Table 2.2. Other important participants in the personal computer market include Olivetti of Italy, Tandy, Zenith (now part of Bull), especially in laptops, Japan's NEC, which has half of the Japanese market, and Toshiba, a world leader in laptops.

IBM's second generation personal computer, the PS/2, was introduced in 1987, six years after its first entry. This series of models featured a 32-bit Intel microprocessor with greater memory, Micro Channel architecture, and an optional new operating system, OS/2, jointly developed by Microsoft and IBM. Sales of the OS/2 were initially rather slow; only 200,000 copies were sold in the first two and one-half years.[9] Many of the earlier clone makers led by Compaq formed a consortium utilizing Extended Industry Standard Architecture (EISA) to challenge IBM's new standard. Hewlett-Packard and Compaq announced the first machines with the competing architecture, which probably points toward multiple standards in the future. Most of the new models can handle the older MS-DOS standard as well, which will remain predominant for a lengthy transition period, especially since the introduction of an improved version of easy to use Windows software in 1990.

Another 1982 start-up firm, Sun Microsystems, pioneered the emerging workstation market, by developing desktop computers with both greater power and the capability (usually) of interaction in networks. (Definitions differ; IBM calls any terminal for the end-user a workstation.) It based its designs on Bell Laboratories' UNIX software system, which is popular with the scientific and engineering community, and followed an open strategy to encourage easy access. Sun licensed Fujitsu and Hitachi to offer its designs in Japan. Hewlett-Packard is seeking a leadership position in this market segment, especially since acquiring Apollo Computer. DEC is also active in this arena. IBM, however, has been slow in getting established, not entering with machines that could compete effectively until 1990, despite having developed fifteen years earlier the Reduced Instruction Set Computing (RISC) simplified designs used to speed computation. These models threaten larger midrange machines because of their capacity.

By the end of 1989, 109 million personal computers had been sold world-wide.[10] U.S. companies still supply about 80 percent of the American market, half the European, but only 10 percent of the market in Japan. The Japanese market is expanding rapidly, after a slower start than the markets in North America or Europe.

SEMICONDUCTORS

Semiconductor chips have been made primarily of silicon since the mid–1950s, and the integrated circuit combining many transistors on one chip was invented in 1959. They are the driving components for computers, telecommunications equipment, automated instruments and tools, consumer electronic goods, and important military hardware. Now a $50 billion-plus industry, more than half of the semiconductor market is outside computers, although if telecommunications applications are added, the two together would account for roughly two-thirds of the applications. Integrated circuits used in computers consist of logic chips, memory chips, and microprocessors, the central processing unit on a chip.

Until the late 1970s, U.S. semiconductor manufacturers supplied practically all of the American market and more than half of the world market, although they never had more than a minority position within Japan. That changed during the early 1980s as the Japanese thrust into the American and European markets and became the largest suppliers worldwide, with approximately half of the global market. Of the top dozen semiconductor manufacturers, six are Japanese, five American, and one European. IBM is the largest maker, all for its own use. It also buys perhaps as much as half of its supply. Many computer manufacturers also sell chips to other users, but in the United States there are a large number of independent semiconductor makers, not engaged primarily in computer manufacturing. They include Motorola, Texas Instruments, Intel (recently beginning to make computers), National Semiconductor, and Advanced Micro Devices. The hundreds of U.S. semiconductor manufacturers, many quite small, often rise from sporadic schisms in the larger, more successful organizations, exploit niche markets, and result in occasional brilliant successes, which are often followed by another schism and a new start-up.

Despite this proliferation, which is one of the factors weakening U.S. merchant or independent semiconductor suppliers, the industry is highly concentrated on a global basis, with the top ten manufacturers accounting for more than 80 percent of the total. IBM is the only captive chip maker among the ten largest producers; other captive manufacturers include AT&T, DEC, Hewlett-Packard, Unisys, and GM's Delco Division.

The Japanese expansion to the forefront of global competition in semi-conductors occurred as a result of the MITI Very Large Scale Integration project (involving circuits containing more than 1,000 logic gates) with assistance from Nippon Telephone and Telegraph, whose semiconductor laboratory work somewhat parallels the early work of Bell Laboratories on transistors. The companies involved were NEC, Toshiba, Hitachi, Fujitsu, and Mitsubishi Electric. When the 1976 to 1979 effort was completed, these companies had achieved state-of-the-art proficiency in design and manu-facturing and were ready to assault world markets. They concentrated their attention on large volume memory chips, called DRAMs, where their man-ufacturing skills were most telling. They used aggressive pricing and by 1985 drove all U.S. manufacturers, except Texas Instruments and Micron Technology, out of the market. American purchasers perceived quality ad-vantages in the Japanese-made chips, which apparently had fewer rejects, a perennial problem in chip making. The profusion of chips created a glut in the semiconductor market, with multibillion dollar losses for the Japanese. The integration of computer manufacturing and financial support within the keiretsu, or family of related companies, made it possible for these losses to be absorbed. They achieved their share-of-the-market objective and cre-ated much American animosity and concern in the process.

Antidumping suits against the Japanese semiconductor manufacturers led to a U.S.-Japanese agreement in 1986 that called for Japanese government monitoring of export prices to the United States and increased access of U.S. chip-makers to the Japanese market. The first stipulation was more effective than the second. Dumping was ended in 1987, according to the U.S. Department of Commerce. Prices rose and, as the market rebounded from the 1985 to 1986 glut, shortages developed. Strong demand in 1988 was accompanied by critical shortages of chips. Smaller computer manu-facturers, including Apple, had to pay high prices for semiconductors, which affected their profits and product pricing. After the turmoil, not much was changed. *The Economist*, writing about the agreement at the time, was prescient: "All the same, the deal under consideration is unlikely to hurt Japan's microchip makers as much as they claim."[11] In 1989, the shortage disappeared again, and prices fell sharply.

The U.S. government also expressed frustration with the Japanese by denying Fujitsu the acquisition of Fairchild Semiconductor from Schlumberger (a French company) in 1987. Several months later National Semiconductor made the acquisition at half the price. Motorola tried a different tack. It made a joint venture with Toshiba to learn the one-megabit DRAM manufacturing technology by providing 32-bit microprocessor technology to Toshiba in exchange.

South Korean and Taiwanese firms also are engaged in producing semiconductors. Samsung agreed to supply Intel with memory chips in 1985, after Intel exited the DRAM business. Intel supplemented this arrangement in 1990 when it made a joint venture to market all of the chips produced by NMB Semiconductor of Japan, an outsider in Japanese business circles. The conglomerates, Lucky Goldstar, Hyundai, and Daewoo, manufacture and export significant quantities of chips. Taiwan's emerging ventures are based on expatriate engineers who learned the business in America and are returning home. Acer, Taiwan's personal computer manufacturer, has joined with National Semiconductor and Texas Instruments in semiconductor ventures.

The European producers have fared no better than the Americans, providing less than one-tenth of the world chip supply, but they are still trying. The eight-year Joint European Submicron Silicon program involving $5 billion was announced in 1989 and is financed by the European Community, the producers, and the national governments. The three leading European chip manufacturers—Philips, SGS-Thomson, and Siemens—are joining with many smaller firms in an attempt to leap from the current four-megabit chip to the development of a 64-megabit one. This project succeeds an earlier one that teamed Philips and Siemens in a catch-up effort in chip making. Siemens and IBM announced a 64-megabit chip design venture in 1990.

IBM became concerned as its independent suppliers were threatened by Japanese competition. Late in 1982, it made an initial 12 percent minority investment in Intel, the microprocessor supplier for its personal computer, in order to strengthen Intel's "research, development, and production capacity," as described in IBM's 1982 *Annual Report*. This investment was subsequently increased to more than $600 million and then disposed of in 1986 and 1987 as conditions in the industry improved. In 1987, IBM participated in the formation of SEMATECH, the Semiconductor Manufacturing Technology Institute, to improve and develop manufacturing technologies. SEMATECH is jointly funded by the U.S. government and fourteen semiconductor manufacturers. Two years later, IBM was one of seven companies that sought to found U.S. Memories and offered to license its four-megabit DRAM technology to the new consortium as well as to provide its first president. The purpose was to jointly reestablish memory chip manufacture on a broader basis in America through the experience gained in the endeavor. However, after seven months the project was abandoned for lack of support from U.S. computer manufacturers. The abundance of chips at low prices in late 1989 made it an inauspicious time to launch a venture inspired both by the earlier chip shortage and the disappearance of U.S. merchant producers from the memory market.

As if in anticipation of these difficulties, in 1989 the MIT Commission on Industrial Productivity concluded that "the traditional structure and institutions of the U.S. industry appear to be inappropriate for meeting the challenge of the much stronger and better-organized Japanese competition."[12] Problems include the higher cost of capital in the United States, the several hundred million dollar investment needed to manufacture a new memory device, the off and on nature of the market in the 1980s, and the weakness of many independent manufacturers. Design and fabrication proficiencies must be regained before U.S. chip makers can reacquire an important position in the memory market.

Chip makers in the United States still possess important assets. Intel, Motorola, and others have enjoyed a clear lead in the manufacture of microprocessors, and U.S. manufacturers have led in the custom market for logic chips. Japanese manufacturers are utilizing the skills gained in the fabrication of memory chips to move into these markets. IBM was ahead of the Japanese in the production of one-megabit and four-megabit DRAMs and eclipsed them again in 1990 in the next generation, the 16-megabit device. Its facilities and semiconductor technology are thought to be current, and it has facilities for semiconductor manufacture in the United States, Europe, and Japan, as do its leading competitors.

Research is underway on 64-megabit chips by producers in each of the three regions. Transition to the 64-megabit and 256-megabit chips, the next two generations anticipated by the latter half of the 1990s, may require X-ray technology to etch semiconductors fine enough to pack in the many small circuits. Thirteen Japanese firms are engaged in a joint project called Sortec to pursue X-ray lithography, and their effort exceeds that of IBM, the principal company engaged in this research in the United States. Two other technologies also are being explored: extension of present optical lithography and electron beam lithography. The size of the effort will not necessarily determine the successor.

SOFTWARE AND SERVICES

Software, the instructions required to get information into and out of a computer, is a vast business far overshadowing computer hardware in value. There are two types: (1) systems software including programming languages, operating systems, and networking software, and (2) applications software. The first was originally proprietary in nature, but has become more standardized and open with the evolution of the industry. The second is the larger of the two because users are constantly writing new programs or rewriting older ones to change them, to incorporate new data or arrangements, and to accommodate new needs or capabilities. Annual expenditures for software are reckoned at more than $200 billion in the United States alone: no exact data are available. Their size explains why programs often last longer than hardware, why businesses struggle to prolong the life of software investments, and why they seek to find new systems compatible with existing programs. Many businesses develop bottlenecks in programming applications and have long backlogs of programs and revisions waiting to be written. Packaged software, both proprietary and open, was estimated to be a $35 billion business globally in 1988.

The advent of personal computers in the late 1970s ended the dominance of proprietary software and professional programmers. Now anyone with inclination and ability can get into the act, and hackers are abundant. Few advantages of scale exist in program writing because so many small software firms exist, more than 25,000 in America alone. Software is a U.S. province and American leadership is unquestioned, a situation that may change with time. Japanese entry into the field was probably delayed because of the complexity of the Japanese language, their slowness in microcomputer usage, and the peculiarities of their working style.

The history of technology at IBM has endowed it with three primary architectures and software systems. The mainframe System/360 and S/370 date from the initial introductions of those models in 1964 and 1970. In the midrange computers, System/3X architecture began in 1969. MS-DOS for its personal computers originated in 1981, and OS/2 was introduced in 1987, both provided by Microsoft and available as open systems. Another schism appeared in 1990 when Microsoft introduced an improved version of MS-DOS software called Windows, which sold a million copies in the first few months. This left IBM as the chief sponsor of the struggling OS/2, which is its preference because of its greater power.

This evolution has created advantages and disadvantages for IBM. On the one hand, the legacy of proprietary systems in its mainframe and midrange models, together with the number of installations, gives it a degree of controlled access to a large volume of business for years to come. On the other hand, there is awkwardness in three systems of software, and the world is moving toward more open systems. IBM has recently tried to provide communication among the three systems with a new Systems Application Architecture.

The significance of the value of installed systems is underscored by the fact that IBM canceled development of yet another mainframe system in the mid–1970s under the growing realization that the programming costs of a totally new system would be overwhelming. The installed base is far

Table 2.3
Computer Operating Systems (Percentage of Machine Sales $)

System	1988	1993 projected
DOS & OS/2	26	29
UNIX	9	19
DEC/VMS	5	6
S/370	24	19
S/3X	3	4
Others	33	23
Total	100	100

Source: The New York Times, October 25, 1989, from International Data Corporation.

more important than software revenue, in which IBM does very well indeed; its sales are almost six times those of its nearest competitor, Fujitsu.

The most formidable competition for proprietary software in the main-frame and midrange lines is the UNIX system, capable of use on all sizes of machines. Developed by Bell Labs, a division of AT&T, in the 1960s, it languished for many years as a scientific and engineering system. AT&T was prevented from offering computers prior to its deregulation and re-organization in 1984, and the system was made available for general use. Although a number of UNIX versions evolved, its popularity gradually increased because of its adaptability for time-sharing and networking ap-plications. The attractiveness of the language, in addition to AT&T's in-creased sponsorship once it was free of the 1956 Consent Decree shackles, led to increased interest in the mid–1980s. UNIX interest was enhanced in 1985 when European governments called for adoption of Open Systems Interconnection standards in future systems, designed to enable machines of different manufacturers to communicate with one another. AT&T and Sun announced completion of the design of a standard UNIX version in late 1989, while a competing effort by IBM to develop another version, called AIX, was postponed. The latter was encouraged through the for-mation of the Open Software Foundation in 1988 by IBM and other pro-ducers who wanted to avoid being locked into an AT&T standard. Thus, the sorting out of new open standards is underway and will continue for several years. By the late 1980s, most computer manufacturers were offering machines capable of adaptation to UNIX software.

Other systems are widely used, as shown in Table 2.3. DEC offers ma-chines that operate on its own proprietary software, called VMS, and on UNIX. The largest independent software house, Computer Associates, offers software for mainframe to personal computers, especially for small business accounting applications, with sales growth of 40 to 50 percent compounded annually during the 1980s. Other software houses include Microsoft for IBM-compatible personal computers, Lotus for PC-spreadsheet analysis,

Ashton-Tate in the PC data-base market, and Oracle, which has programs capable of running on larger machines as well.

Speculation as to the future direction of operating systems is presented also in Table 2.3. UNIX systems may more than double in share and number during the present five-year period. Proprietary systems will not disappear, and the non-IBM systems are thought to be the most vulnerable. Their designers will pursue the sometimes contradictory objectives of making them more attractive and unique and, at the same time, more communicable with other systems. Several standards will coexist for the foreseeable future.

Sales of IBM software enjoyed a strong uptrend in the 1980s and now exceed maintenance services in volume. Maintenance is big business, 12 percent of total revenues excluding other services, and a highly competitive business. To an extent a double standard exists. Maintenance of IBM machinery is a highly attractive and price sensitive target for service competitors, whose failure to deliver must be reliably picked up by the primary vendor.

Rental income, a significant 41 percent of IBM sales at the beginning of the decade, rapidly gave way to outright sale or lease-purchase by the latter 1980s. This makes IBM revenues and income much more sensitive to economic conditions and to product acceptance.

BIGNESS, GROWTH, AND ADAPTABILITY

IBM can best be measured by its own aspirations. Its goals or objectives, as expressed by management in successive annual reports during the last decade, have included (1) product leadership, (2) the most efficient company or low-cost producer in all functions, (3) growth with the industry, (4) constructive partnerships or joint ventures with other companies, and (5) superior profitability. Stated differently or modified from time to time, these goals exhibit enough consistency for them to serve as useful criteria in assessing and evaluating IBM's performance. They are played out in an arena highly cognizant of the company's size and the implications that entails. Bigness merits consideration relative to its effect on efficiency, competitiveness, nimbleness, and adaptability.

Product Leadership

No decision in the last twenty years involved the kind of "bet-the-company" importance that the introduction of IBM's System/360 did in 1964. Changes in the computer industry are rapid enough, however, to render many seemingly lesser questions vital to the health of the company. The most grievous error was to leave the midrange inadequately defended to the ravages of competition from DEC, Hewlett-Packard, and others through almost two decades prior to the introduction of the AS/400 in

1988. It was not that IBM did not try—the small business S/3X and the 4300 had their merits. But the facts speak otherwise, as IBM lost significant market position reckoned in the tens of billions of dollars of installations in the 1980s alone. The problem was exacerbated by IBM's dissimilar architectures that place a particular burden on marketing representatives who must properly judge the needs of emerging business customers in order to help them avoid the costly error of changing architectures as their needs grew. DEC's single software standard had a sales appeal, and they sold it well. Although now better positioned, IBM's problem has not disappeared, but is evolving—now in transition from the AS/400 to the S/390. How well IBM can deal with it remains to be seen.

IBM's product leadership also came into question when Apple successfully introduced the microcomputer and IBM's design team was delayed three years before setting to work on the Personal Computer. The brilliance of IBM's response does not contradict the conclusion that, for all its demonstrated technological skills, it has trouble coming up with appropriate products fast enough in a field of agile minds and venturesome entrepreneurs. Similar charges of lateness have been applied to its entries in technical workstations, laptop computers, and file servers. Few would argue, however, that any single manufacturer could have dominated the entire field of small machines in the way that IBM did mainframes in the 1960s. The question is, What is good enough? The product leader ought to have models in most segments soon after their existence is demonstrated, as prior presence in and knowledge of the marketplace permits no other judgment. Niches will always exist. The relevant task becomes one of identifying the significant markets quickly enough to permit a timely response.

Upstart Apple taught the industry a lesson in product design with its emphasis on user-friendly machines. Now that the entire industry has emulated Apple, the advantages of keeping the customer foremost in product conceptualization are once again clear. Apple's Macintosh enabled many more people to feel competent to operate personal computers.

IBM sought to expand and adapt its products and services to meet customer needs soon after John Akers took over as CEO in 1985. By 1989 the company was claiming in its *Annual Report* "more than 10,000 joint marketers, systems integrators and Business Partners" worldwide for its personal and midrange computer customers. There was an accompanying large expansion of software development employees to assist customers with applications programming. The belated but effective introduction of the RISC/System 6000 provides another example of product adaption to customer needs.

Low-cost Producer

IBM's second goal is to be the most efficient company in the industry—in manufacturing, marketing, service and maintenance—in all aspects of the business. Crude measures, such as revenue per employee, suggest that IBM is in fact more efficient than comparable companies, with an occasional exception for one of the Japanese computing firms, again complicated by the foreign exchange translation problem. Expert comment supports the cutting edge technology and productivity of IBM's manufacturing plants.[13] This is further underscored by its ability to compete in semiconductor manufacture of the latest DRAM chips and in the arena of manufacturing technology, capabilities it acquired in the 1970s, according to Kenneth Flamm.[14] When demand is either growing rapidly or contracting or failing to grow as fast as anticipated, manufacturing efficiency is difficult to control, adjustments IBM has managed with equanimity when considered in juxtaposition to its full employment or no-layoff policy. In the marketing of capital goods, IBM has few peers. Either market research failed at crucial times, or management failed to weigh and act on it promptly.

One seldom-mentioned IBM strategy, made possible by its size and international deployment, is its policy of balancing its exports and imports by major country or currency area. This has afforded two benefits, different in purpose and effect. In an era of fluctuating and occasionally erratic movements in exchange rates, IBM has greater ability to shift temporarily to lower cost sources of supply if sufficient production capacity exists. In recent years, IBM has reported that approximately 90 percent of non-U.S. revenue has originated within the currency environment in which its foreign subsidiaries operate. Of greater importance than this advantage is its ability to counter economic nationalism by removing the requirement for external funds in many important areas of operation. Obviously, this cannot work everywhere in the 130 countries in which it has operations. In addition, IBM's policy of wholly owned subsidiaries has necessitated that it withdraw or curtail operations in India, Brazil, and Nigeria because of requirements for local ownership participation. Overall, the policy of balancing payments has conferred significant advantages to IBM, especially during the 1980s when the appreciation of the dollar cost many U.S. capital goods producers lost sales in foreign markets.

Growth with the Industry

IBM has not met its goal of growing with the industry. The failure has been chiefly in the midrange and personal computer markets, and in the case of the latter, it was probably unrealistic to assume that it could have done so because of ease of entry into microcomputers. Of major consequence was IBM's failure to bring forth appropriate products in the midrange market, and the company paid the price of foregone sales for its mistakes in market judgment. Along with others, it grossly overestimated U.S. sales growth after 1984. While IBM eschewed issuing forecasts, it shared the general exuberance of the industry as late as 1986 that its sales would grow in excess of 15 percent annually, which implied sales of almost $100 billion in the early 1990s and $200 billion by the latter part of the decade.[15] Many of the sales lost to others were in midrange computers, prior to the introduction of the AS/400. Cumulative revenue losses of more than 1 percent per year were experienced for at least a decade ending in 1988. The long gap in offering scientific computers was another niche left open until the RISC/System 6000 was made available in 1990.

The miscalculations were costly too. Investment spending on plant expansion for the wrong products was allowed to run up for another year after 1984, by one-third to $6.1 billion, before cutbacks were made. Subsequently, nine plants were closed and four successive employment reductions were announced, utilizing attrition and early retirement to lower the work force by approximately 11 percent. Many displaced manufacturing employees were redeployed into marketing and service functions. The company's tradition of no layoffs has remained. The morale benefits from the full-employment policy probably outweigh the temporary savings by abandoning it. Stock market analysts expressed surprise at the size of the $1.3 billion special plant write-off, announced in late 1989. Relative to equipment investment at the time, however, the charge was less than 5 percent of the total. Second guessing about the magnitude of the reductions and criticisms of the no-layoff policy were extensive. With these latest efforts, however, there can be little doubt of the company's willingness to tackle its problems.

Partnerships

Since the beginning of the 1980s, joint ventures and other cooperative alliances have abounded in the industry, and IBM has been no exception. Business partnerships with suppliers, remarketers and applications specialists, as well as with customers and employees, became an expanded feature of IBM's strategy in the late 1980s. These range from Sears and Nippon Telephone and Telegraph to individual entrepreneurs. Software houses and value-add vendors make up an important component of the "business partner" approach, numerically and symbolically, because they help connect the colossus with the environment of personal and midrange computer users, struggling to adapt standard packages to unique situations. By 1989, seventy-five equity alliances had been established. Many joint ventures have crossed national boundaries. Some have failed to develop, such as the interest in Satellite Business Systems, disposed of in 1985, or the reshaping of the Rolm telecommunications investment in 1988, which became a marketing joint venture with Siemens after selling the development and manufacturing properties to Siemens. It is much too early to judge the success or failure of this new emphasis on business partnerships. Intended to improve responsiveness to customers, it is sorely needed by IBM and could have great promise in humanizing the giant bureaucracy if allowed to do so.

Profitability

IBM CEO John Akers has indicated a target of 18 to 20 percent return on stockholders' equity, a goal consistently achieved by the company until 1985, but not reached since then.[16] The slowdown in revenue growth combined with heavy price discounting has been primarily responsible for this result. Return on equity in the last four years of the 1980s was just under 14 percent, a performance that might be viewed with envy had it been for any company except the paragon, IBM, and the disappointed anticipations held by investors. The stock price fell to less than one and one-half times book value in late 1989, as low relatively as at any time in the decade. Much of the last five years, IBM stock has sold at a price-earnings ratio substantially below that for the market as a whole, as measured by the Standard & Poor's 500 stock index. Because the stock is widely held and the company extensively watched and studied, the market price must be viewed as the evaluation resulting from an efficient market, one that has all relevant information carefully weighed. The company used the period since 1985, with the reduction in investment spending, to buy back almost 10 percent of the stock previously outstanding.

IBM entered the 1980s as a large, centrally controlled, corporate bureaucracy and ran into difficulty as markets shifted toward the midrange and smaller computers and the competitive environment quickened. Somehow the arrogance of the mainframe mentality of Armonk and Endicott needed to change. In 1988, IBM management revised the organization of its U.S. operations along product lines, pushing responsibility into seven lines of business and a U.S. marketing and services division. Each of the seven divisions has worldwide responsibility for development and U.S. responsibility for manufacturing its products and services; revenue and profit goals also are assigned at this level.

Earlier in the decade, IBM experimented with the creation of independent business units, such as Academic Information Systems, Information Services, IBM Instruments, Industrial Automation, Science Research Associates, Financial Services, Low End Storage, and Biomedical Systems. Most of these— at maximum, fifteen in number—had been phased out by the time of the 1988 reorganization, which is much more basic and comprehensive in coverage and intent. Whether or not this delegation of operating responsibility will succeed depends on how quickly IBM people can learn a completely new style. They cannot continue to field platoons of specialists, with little understanding of small business, often armed with what seem like incomprehensible questions, to deal with the segments of the market that have become increasingly important. Bigness has its advantages and disabilities, and in order to minimize the latter, extraordinary efforts are necessary to improve maneuverability and customer responsiveness.

SUMMARY

Like other organizations, IBM's future will depend on its people and their cooperation in achieving common goals. Its employment and ethical policies should encourage morale if its management can find ways to encourage an increased sense of participation.

The demise of the large machines appears to be an oversimplification of technological trends in the industry, although the open or nonproprietary systems remain as the biggest issue and problem confronted by IBM. Stories of the replacement of mainframes by midrange computers, file servers, workstations, and even personal computers are true, although they exaggerate the extent of the transition. Users like the flexibility, cost, and immediate responsiveness of smaller systems. There is little likelihood that they can replace mainframes in handling large data bases involving continuous activity. Use of mainframes in conjunction with smaller systems is increasing. Fewer mainframes are being added, but upgrading continues.

The company has the potential to grow considerably faster than the economies of the 130 countries in which it does business. Industry growth of 7 to 10 percent annually is a widely accepted expectation in the next decade.

Any company as large and successful as IBM, having made mistakes as it has and surrounded by a number of smaller, rapidly growing companies, inevitably has its full share of detractors. The stock market evaluation of the late 1980s and early 1990s shows their influence and appears to be excessively negative. Based on the assumption that the entire industry is becoming a commodity market, this judgment is too facile. Parts of the industry have moved toward standardization, but it is still a highly complex business overall with proliferating tentacles still growing in many directions. A large company still leading in all five principal product lines, that learned to adapt, may surprise even the well informed.

NOTES

1. John Marcom, Jr., "Behind the Monolith: A Look at IBM," *The Wall Street Journal*, April 7, 1986, p. 25.

2. Nestor E. Terleckyj, "Growth of the Telecommunications and Computer Industries," in *Changing the Rules: Technological Change, International Competition, and Regulation in Communications*, ed. Robert W. Crandall and Kenneth Flamm (Washington, D.C.: The Brookings Institution, 1989), pp. 354–355.

3. Flamm has called this "a turning point for the Japanese computer industry."

Kenneth Flamm, *Creating the Computer: Government, Industry, and High Technology* (Washington, D.C.: The Brookings Institution, 1988), p. 195.

4. Flamm, *Creating the Computer*, pp. 185–202. Also Kenneth Flamm, *Targeting the Computer: Government Support and International Competition* (Washington, D.C.: The Brookings Institution, 1987), pp. 125–153.

5. Crandall and Flamm, *Changing the Rules*, p. 3.

6. Flamm, *Creating the Computer*, pp. 127–131.

7. William H. Davidson, *The Amazing Race: Winning the Technorivalry with Japan* (New York: Wiley, 1984), pp. 208–209. Also Bro Uttal, "How the 4300 Fits IBM's New Strategy," *Fortune*, July 30, 1979, pp. 58–64.

8. According to the authors of *Blue Magic*, Frank Cary, former IBM CEO, was reported as having once said that Independent Business Units "might even teach an elephant how to tap dance." James Chposky and Ted Leonsis, *Blue Magic: The People, Power and Politics Behind the IBM Personal Computer* (New York: Facts on File Publications, 1988), p. 2.

9. Andrew Pollack, "IBM and Microsoft Promote OS/2," *The New York Times*, November 14, 1989, p. 50.

10. "Business This Decade," *The Economist*, December 23, 1989, p. 79.

11. Ibid., "America and Japan Stack the Chips against Their Customers," July 12, 1986, p. 61.

12. Michael L. Dertouzos, Richard K. Lester, Robert M. Solow, and the MIT Commission on Industrial Productivity, *Made in America: Regaining the Productive Edge* (Cambridge, Mass.: The MIT Press, 1989), study F, p. 261.

13. Prepared by Commission Working Group, "The U.S. Semiconductor, Computer, and Copier Industries," MIT Commission on Industrial Productivity, *Working Papers*, vol. 2 (Cambridge, Mass.: The MIT Press, 1989), pp. 28–29.

14. Flamm, *Creating the Computer*, p. 236.

15. John Marcom, Jr., "Tomorrow: $200 Billion by 1995? Maybe But Obstacles Loom," *The Wall Street Journal*, April 7, 1986, p. 18. "IBM talks of the total industry quadrupling to more than $1 trillion in revenue in the 1990s." At the 1990 annual stockholders meeting, Chairman John Akers spoke of an industry of $400 billion at that time.

16. John Markoff, "10,000 Jobs to Be Cut by IBM," *The New York Times*, December 6, 1989, p. C1.

3

GOVERNMENTS AND CONSORTIA: BOEING'S COMPETITION

Since the beginning of commercial jet airline transportation, two dozen jet airliners have been designed and built.[1] Boeing has produced six jet airliners, including the most successful. Most others have failed, however, for one reason or another, including the first ones placed in service in the early 1950s. Two of de Haviland's Comets disintegrated in midair because of metal fatigue. As a result of timing, Dassault found buyers for only ten Mercures. Lockheed sold 249 of its well-designed 1011 Tristars, but the company had to be assisted with a loan guarantee by the U.S. government. The engine builder went bankrupt, and Lockheed withdrew from the manufacture of commercial aircraft following the experience, as did General Dynamics after one try. Only Boeing, the European consortium Airbus Industrie, and McDonnell Douglas remain as major commercial aircraft manufacturers. Boeing has produced more than half of the 11,000 airliners delivered in the West since the jet age began thirty-eight years ago.

Revenue passenger miles (RPM, paid passengers times miles traveled), the airline's measure of demand served, grew by just over 15 percent annually during the 1960s and has since declined to half that rate. Growth is expected to fall further, to approximately 5.5 percent per year through the year 2000. Demand is projected to increase more rapidly outside the United States than within, and more than half of the commercial aircraft sales will be required to supply the demand for expansion, as opposed to replacement of the existing fleet.

A large part of the expansion in airline RPM in the 1960s was due to the displacement of surface transportation by rail and ship. The first jet engines were fuel intensive, and higher fuel prices lay just ahead in the early 1970s, followed by a marked slowdown in economic growth. Apparently oblivious to these possibilities, Boeing forged ahead with the design of a huge aircraft, the wide-bodied 747 jumbo jet, still the largest passenger aircraft in use. It almost ruined the company: two-thirds of its work force was laid off from 1969 to 1972. According to John Newhouse, in 1966 three major U.S. airlines recommended to Boeing that the design of a smaller, two-aisle, two-engine jet, suitable for 250 passengers for distances of less than 2,100 miles would better fit their anticipated markets.[2] One of them, American Airlines, went so far as to provide specifications for this short- to medium-range jet. Airbus took the projected market considerations seriously and designed to meet them, not the least of the reasons it became a major player in the industry.

Meanwhile, others were committing their own follies. The French were obsessed with leapfrogging into supersonic technology and developed the Concorde, an engineering achievement and commercial disaster. Nevertheless, they were successful in drawing the British into the project. Lockheed and McDonnell Douglas brought forth more traditional jets, somewhat smaller than the 747, but they were so similar in design characteristics that neither one succeeded.

Eventually the market grew large enough for the 747, and Boeing recovered its vitality. Now it faces an increasingly robust Airbus Industrie and a restructuring McDonnell Douglas, the latter still primarily devoted to a shrinking military aircraft market. The three principal jet engine builders have gone through their own realignment, and the airlines are changed and changing, following more than a decade of deregulation in the United States and increasing international competition abroad. The Japanese and others are determined to acquire a place in the industry. These and other considerations are examined in this chapter as they impinge on the fortune of the leader, Boeing.

BOEING

Boeing owes its entry into the jet airliner business to its prior production of military transports and bombers, plus its willingness to "bet the company," to engage in what those in the industry refer to as the "sporty game."[3] The 707 was a descendant of the prototype 367–80 (called the Dash Eighty) and the B47, the first jet bomber.[4] First delivered in 1958, almost a thousand of the long-range, four-engine jets were produced before it was phased out twenty years later. Even greater commercial success awaited Boeing with the short-to-medium-range 727, introduced in 1964, of which there were 1,832 delivered before the production run ended in 1984. A third and smaller two-engine 737 jet was introduced in 1969 and is still, in its subsequent derivatives, in production today. All of these designs shared the same fuselage cross section and other common features. These well-crafted planes and their acceptance by air carriers and passengers accounted for Boeing's initial success in competition with other manufacturers both in the United States and Europe. They fulfilled a range of needs from domestic to intercontinental travel and were well supported by Boeing in use throughout the world.

Flushed with this success, the chief executive officers of Boeing and Pan American World Airways, William Allen and Juan Trippe, decided in 1966 to design and build a large two-aisle airliner capable of seating nine or ten abreast. They felt no need to consult other airlines for potential need and made the launch decision based on fifty firm and certain orders, half from Pan American, which agreed to pay half of the purchase price before delivery. As the design progressed, the airplane grew. Two of the three engine suppliers dropped out of the project, leaving Pratt and Whitney struggling to meet the increasing thrust requirements for an expanding aircraft. Weight was increased by one-quarter during the design, but Boeing insisted on keeping the original delivery schedule. Many of the early engines failed in testing, and problems multiplied, but they were eventually overcome. The difficulties for Pan Am, however, were just beginning, and they were increased when it acquired eight more of the large planes in addition to its original order. Boeing soon faced a major readjustment. Beginning in 1969, no orders for 747s were received from U.S. airlines for three years.[5]

Almost a decade of turmoil and recovery lay ahead for Boeing. Massive layoffs of more than 60,000 of its 100,000 Seattle-area employees were made in the next three years. With the help of the 727 business, it managed to stay in the black, although profits were marginal until the late 1970s. By then, it was time for the company to consider the next generation of new aircraft. Pan American, however, never fully recovered. The market variability in the demand for commercial aircraft is illustrated in Figure 3.1, where U.S. shipments are shown.

Sales volume reached its nadir in 1972, from which it gradually recovered, until a resurgence of buying recurred at the end of the decade. Sustained for several years largely by foreign orders, Boeing fought to control costs and gradually turned the 747 into a successful venture. The company is generally credited with being the industry's low-cost producer, and it continues to pursue cost reduction aggressively with design-built teams, computer-assisted manufacturing technologies, including the generation of three-dimensional structures, and total quality control for itself and its vendors.[6]

While not without turmoil and drama, Boeing's labor relations have been amazingly positive for a company subjected to such wide fluctuations in employment. The company has paid profit-sharing Christmas bonuses to workers since 1983, a popular practice with younger workers. This precedent was continued in the three-year labor agreement with its principal union, the International Association of Machinists, in 1989, although in

Figure 3.1
U.S. Shipments of Transport Aircraft, 1969–89

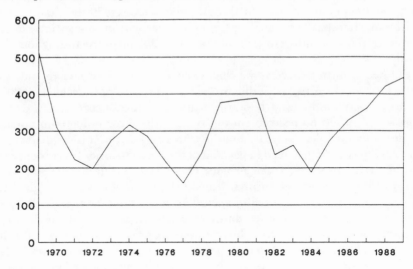

Source: Aerospace Industries Assn., *U.S. Industrial Outlook*, 1990.

addition it granted 10 percent wage increases over three years plus cost of living adjustments. This was the first wage increase since 1982 and followed a forty-eight day strike, Boeing's longest, avoiding larger increases sought by the union in the face of the company's record order backlog.

Planning for the ramp-up in the late 1970s began in 1976 with discussions on the 767, a seven-abreast, two-aisle airplane somewhat smaller than the 747. Initial orders in 1978 came from the large U.S. carriers and first deliveries were made in 1982. About the same time, the 757 was developed as a narrow body utilizing the fuselage cross section of the 727–737 family. It was intended to be smaller than the 767, but the design was expanded following discussions with British Airways, one of the launch customers. Powered by two engines, it produces less drag because of its narrow body. Sales were slow initially—only two were ordered in 1984—but they picked up by the end of the decade. That left a hole in the 150-seat size range after the 727s were phased out, especially as both McDonnell Douglas and Airbus moved to fill the gap. Boeing's response was to modify the 737 to increase its capacity for that need, which was attractive to the airlines because of commonality with existing fleets. (By early 1988, the various configurations of the 737 had outsold the impressive record of the popular 727.) This was a wise move, given the decreasing fuel costs in the mid–1980s.

Boeing's efforts to share costs through joint ventures with European aircraft manufacturers were largely unsuccessful, and the result was that Boeing did not forestall the Europeans' collaboration in the Airbus program. An attempt to involve the French came to nothing, according to Newhouse, because Boeing had in mind a subcontracting relationship, not full partnership. This approach would continue to discourage true risk-sharing.[7] An arrangement with the Italian firm, Aeritalia, fell through for similar reasons, although eventually the firm became a supplier of some wing and tail sections of the 767.[8] A still more ambitious proposal involving the British raised negotiations to the head-of-state level in 1978 in the person of Prime Minister James Callaghan.[9]

This plan would have given the British, through a wing designed by British Aerospace and engines produced by Rolls-Royce, a 55 percent contribution to the new 757 program. Callaghan met with all the principals, including McDonnell Douglas, which had a competing proposal, and Frank Borman of Eastern Airlines, who had tried the Airbus 300. The prime minister then made a typically British decision: British Airways preferred the 757 to the Airbus and would be permitted to purchase it, despite French opposition. The Boeing arrangement was rejected, partly because Boeing was treating British Aerospace as a subcontractor rather than a partner. Boeing probably did not try harder because it was apprehensive that British aircraft manufacturing costs were substantially higher than its own. Most important, Britain cast its lot with the Airbus program. Airbus needed the wing technology at British Aerospace, the Germans were urging their participation, and Britain, then a member of the European Community, would become more European by joining the consortium. Newhouse wrote in 1982: "They drew lines that lock Europe and Boeing in direct competition. The pattern is likely to last for a generation."[10]

Collaboration with the Japanese was more forthcoming. After their own costly failure in commercial aircraft design in the 1960s, the Japanese were willing to take a subordinate role in order to learn the business. A consortium of Mitsubishi Heavy Industries, Kawasaki Heavy Industries, and Fuji Heavy Industries became a subcontractor for 15 percent of the development and production of the 767, mainly parts for the fuselage, financed by a government loan. In 1984, the same group became a quarter partner with Boeing in the design of the 7J7, the new 150-seat airliner, which was placed on hold in 1987 as fuel prices remained low and the 737–400 series continued to be viable. Late in 1989, Boeing proposed the design of a new aircraft to be called the 777, larger than the 767 but smaller than the 747, with Japanese suppliers assuming a slightly larger role than in 767 production, but still not in a partnership role. First delivery is planned for 1995.

Despite the enormity of Boeing's occasional mistakes, its leadership is impressive and based on solid advantages. These include its global strategy in viewing the world market as its target rather than some regional fraction, engineering excellence throughout its product line for most of the years since 1958, a full line of aircraft to serve airline needs at home and abroad, and a reputation for delivering reliable and unremitting after-sale product support. There is a tendency for observers to forget the number of competitors who have failed since the 1950s in challenging the company or in exploiting temporary advantages they may have had. Boeing's dominance for more than thirty years in jet airliners is not founded on good fortune, but on correctly performing the tasks that others did less well. Now, however, its failure to circumvent the organization of the Airbus consortium is giving the Europeans an opportunity to demonstrate their own technological superiorities, to develop a full line of aircraft, to utilize governmental support in defraying huge development costs, and to find a partial "hole in the market" for its 150-passenger A320 as it did with its initial A300.

AIRBUS INDUSTRIE

Following the failure of several individual country and company jet airliner projects, the Airbus program had its origins in discussions between the French, Germans, and British in the mid–1960s regarding joint efforts to enter an industry in which their separate efforts were clearly inadequate. Britain soon withdrew when the other two parties rejected the Rolls-Royce engine in favor of one jointly produced by GE and SNECMA (Société Nationale d'Étude et Construction de Moteurs d'Aviation). There were other reasons as well, including the exclusion of the British from the European Economic Community by President Charles de Gaulle of France and the difficulties encountered in the Concorde supersonic jet project, also a joint undertaking of the French and British.

The Germans and French were determined to carry on and the program continued in 1969 as a fifty-fifty venture. The wide-body A300 carrying 260 passengers for middle distances was designed and first delivered in 1974. Resort was had to Britain's Hawker Siddeley (later merged into British Aerospace) for wing design because the Continentals were lacking in that technology. The project did not get off to an auspicious beginning. In the first four years only thirty-eight planes were sold; sixteen more were built without buyers and were parked near Airbus factories.[11]

In 1978, the situation improved decisively for Airbus. Within two years several hundred orders had been received; one of the most significant was from Eastern Airlines, signaling entry into the North American market. Eastern was afforded the use of four planes for a trial period, which led to an order for twenty-three in the spring of 1978. Discussions between Eastern President Frank Borman and Prime Minister Callaghan also helped reassure the British of the viability of the Airbus program. Later that year, the French and German governments decided to authorize a second Airbus model, the smaller A310. Callaghan's calculated risk that British Aerospace was needed for its wing design capabilities paid off, and the British, since 1973 a member of the Common Market, rejoined the Airbus consortium as a 20 percent participant. (The Spanish later took a 4.2 percent interest through Construcciónes Aeronáutica SA (CASA), making the consortium 37.9 percent Aerospatiale, 37.9 percent Messerschmitt-Bölkow-Blohm (MBB), in addition to British Aerospace.) The timing was propitious with the upturn in Airbus orders, many of which came from Middle Eastern and other Moslem countries, some flushed with oil revenues and several pleased to have a non-American source.[12]

Subsequently, Airbus has announced three additional models in its product line, giving it a full family of aircraft to compete with Boeing and introducing technology not yet available from any other supplier. Design of its 150-seat short- to medium-range aircraft, the A320, was begun in 1984 and included new "fly by wire" features such as electrical controls and a computerized cockpit system. Orders were more numerous than for any other aircraft prior to the beginning of deliveries four years later. A stretch version is to be available in 1994. Larger and longer range aircraft, the A330 and A340, are being designed and are to be shipped in 1992.

Airbus exists because of the political determination of the sponsoring governments to be involved in aircraft manufacturing as a high technology, export activity. Much debate and many allegations have been made regarding the size of the subsidy, which at least has covered all design and development costs until recently. Because of its organization as a French *groupement d'intérêt économique*, with unified management and participating companies responsible for its obligations, no data are published. Airbus reported an operating profit in 1990, but dependence on government subsidies continues. *The Economist* quoted a 1988 Coopers & Lybrand estimate: "Airbus has swallowed up $13.9 billion in unpaid loans and guarantees."[13]

It is obviously difficult for a private company like Boeing to meet this kind of competition, and it is equally true that Airbus is now well established and will be a force to be reckoned with for the foreseeable future. The more imminent U.S. question is whether or not McDonnell Douglas will be in the commercial aircraft business after the next downturn in the market.

McDONNELL DOUGLAS AND OTHERS

As the aircraft manufacturers entered the 1990s with relatively full order books for civilian planes, McDonnell Douglas, the third major producer, struggled to reorganize its transport aircraft division to lower production costs and improve performance on deliveries. The company is America's number one defense contractor, chiefly for transports, trainers, fighters, and missiles, although the boom in airline orders has thrust its Douglas Aircraft division, acquired in 1967, to the forefront as the military budget is pared back. At present it offers only two basic models, both of which are derivatives of planes launched more than twenty years ago.

Douglas dominated the U.S. commercial airliner business from the 1930s until the late 1950s when the jets arrived. The DC8 trailed the Boeing 707 in introduction and never caught up, despite the fact that it is an excellent aircraft. Shortly after it introduced its second and smaller model, the DC9, and stretched the DC8, the company ran into financial difficulties and became a merger candidate. Unfortunately, Douglas has not flourished under McDonnell's guidance. The life of the DC8 derivatives was truncated with the introduction of the larger DC10 and its competition with the Lockheed L–1011, which had similar performance characteristics. Again, the DC10 is a well-engineered aircraft, but sales were disappointing.

Lockheed's fortunes in the commercial aircraft business, of course, were far worse. The company's sole entry into the jet market carried it to the brink of disaster. The L–1011 was designed for use with the Rolls-Royce RB.211 engine, whose initial design counted on the use of cost-saving composite turbine blades. They did not work and had to be replaced by more expensive titanium blades, severely stressing Rolls-Royce financially. Through Herculean effort, the L–1011 project was completed, and in several ways it introduced a technologically superior aircraft. The bankruptcy of Rolls-Royce almost carried Lockheed down as well; however, it did survive, but only with a government loan guarantee of $250 million.[14] Partly because of the difficulties surrounding its introduction and partly as a result of its direct competition with the DC10, L–1011 sales were limited. Lockheed announced its termination in 1981 and departed the commercial aircraft business. Its reentry as a subcontractor, or as an affiliate with one of the other airframe manufacturers, has been discussed on occasion, as with Fokker in 1989, but no substantive arrangements have evolved.

The phoenix-like rebirth of interest in the 1980s in derivatives of the two McDonnell Douglas aircraft has been as phenomenal as the company's inability to persuade potential joint venture partners of its dedication to the manufacture of commercial aircraft. The turnaround owed much to cheaper fuel prices, as became apparent in the 1982 lease of MD80s on very favorable terms to American Airlines.[15] For the remainder of the decade, orders continued to accumulate for the aircraft in various configurations seating about 150 passengers. Success with the MD80 was partially responsible for Boeing's later decision to modify and continue its 737 model.

McDonnell Douglas's failure on three occasions to develop affiliations with foreign companies illustrates its shortcomings in pursuing alliances. First, it was a serious participant in the 1978 negotiations with British Aerospace and was rejected because its proposal lacked concreteness.[16] Second, a memorandum of understanding with Fokker in the early 1980s regarding joint development of a new 150-seat aircraft came to nothing.[17] Third, joint venture talks with Airbus in 1986 were soon abandoned. The company did succeed in 1985 in arranging a co-production agreement with China for MD80s, now extended to 50 aircraft through 1994.

Typical of its procrastination was the long delay, until late 1986, in the decision to move forward on the modification of the DC10 into the MD11, to increase both capacity and range. The result is a production gap between the two versions of two years. The MD11 was first delivered in 1990, and much of McDonnell Douglas's future hinges on its success. One observer refers to McDonnell Douglas as "a marginal player" and another as "a niche player" in the market.[18] These judgments could be excessively negative if the company seizes the opportunity afforded by full-order books to remedy its production and profitability problems. Early in 1989, a reorganization of the Douglas transport aircraft plant was initiated to compress eleven layers of management into five and to improve quality. More than a year later the division was still losing money, and a 16 percent layoff was announced. The company has another chance to get its house in order and to solve these longstanding difficulties. Greater dedication to the commercial aircraft market than McDonnell Douglas has displayed in the past will be required if it is to succeed.

Both British Aerospace and Fokker make successful commercial jet aircraft in the 70 to 100 passenger size. British Aerospace owns 20 percent of Airbus for which it makes wing sets and is also heavily involved in military aircraft and other weapons production as well as automobiles. Fokker of the Netherlands is an associate member of Airbus, participating in development work and as a parts supplier. The BAe146 and the F100 overlap with the smallest version of Boeing's 737 series.

THE ENGINE BUILDERS

Jet engine manufacturers are three in number—two American and one British—plus several European and Japanese affiliates. Engine design and development is costly and generally takes longer to evolve than a new aircraft. Airframe builders are obviously dependent on engine performance for design characteristics; the two must move forward hand in hand. Most, but not all, aircraft are offered with more than one engine option. The genesis of the wide-body jet aircraft in the late 1960s and early 1970s was so beset with engine problems that airframe and engine builders alike found it very costly—as recounted earlier, one went bankrupt and one left the business. Each of the engine makers participates extensively in the military, as well as the civilian, sector of the market.

For almost three decades of jet age transportation, the Pratt and Whitney division of United Technologies was the largest supplier, and still has the biggest base, of installed engines. The current derivative of its workhorse JT8D series, still generating more orders than any other engine, was first produced in 1964. Although Pratt and Whitney now has engines available in all sizes, it had lacked a new small engine for several years because of problems encountered by the consortium developing it. Worse still, it allowed service and other problems to accumulate in the 1980s to the point that it lost business. The telling order occurred in 1987 when Japan Air Lines, which had been an exclusive Pratt and Whitney customer for thirty years, shifted to GE for powering its new 747s.[19] By then, General Electric had assumed leadership in aircraft engines. (JAL is Boeing's largest 747 customer, with approximately 10 percent of that model aircraft delivered or ordered since 1966.)

GE got into the commercial engine business as the result of experience acquired in World War II in military aircraft engines.[20] Its first success was in powering the DC10, and it eventually became the largest supplier to several wide-body models. In competition with Pratt and Whitney, it won the French joint venture with SNECMA for powering Airbus models and also became the exclusive supplier of Boeing's popular 737–300 series. The GE-SNECMA venture is currently seeking additional partners to help develop a new engine for Boeing's proposed 777 at a cost estimated between $1.2 and $2 billion. The engine business has become one of GE's most important product lines and has been a leading generator of profits for several years.

Rolls-Royce occupies a distant third position in the engine market with a 10 to 12 percent share.[21] Its aspiration for a larger position led it to commit a leap of faith in the new composite blade material for the new engine that was to power Lockheed's L–1011 in the late 1960s. That would have been serious enough, but it wanted the business so badly that it made a fixed price contract for the untested technology, which proved to be its undoing. After bankruptcy, Rolls-Royce became a government entity in 1971 and did not emerge into private ownership again for sixteen years. Fortunately, Boeing avoided this fate in its 747 project by writing in cost escalation clauses. The Rolls-Royce debacle and Lockheed's dependence on their engine almost carried the latter company under as mentioned earlier. Subsequently, Rolls-Royce has been able to reestablish itself as a reliable engine supplier technologically abreast of the two larger manufacturers in most respects.[22]

Rolls-Royce and Pratt and Whitney each assumed a 30 percent ownership interest in International Aero Engines, a consortium formed to design a new small engine for the Airbus and McDonnell Douglas planes, first produced in 1989. Others in the consortium are Japan Aero Engines (Ishikawajima-Harima, Kawasaki, and Mitsubishi Heavy Industries), 19.9 percent; Motoren-und Turbinen Union (MTU), now part of Daimler-Benz, 12.1 percent; and Fiat, 8 percent. General Electric and Rolls-Royce made an agreement in 1984 that eventually gave the other partner a quarter of the work on a large GE engine and a medium to large Rolls-Royce engine. Two years later, it was terminated because of product overlap, but a modified agreement for the joint supply of engine components was made. Along with the cooperative agreement emerging on a GE engine for the 777 mentioned earlier, the use of joint ventures on these expensive engine projects appears well established.

Everyone wants to be involved in the technology, but few can justify the multibillion dollar costs alone.

Both GE-SNECMA and Pratt and Whitney-GM are developing unducted fan or ultrahigh bypass engines. Neither of these engines has been selected for powering an aircraft, partly because they are new technologies and partly because they are not economically attractive as long as fuel prices stay close to the low levels of the late 1980s. If prices escalate again as a result of turmoil in the Middle East, there will be renewed interest in these projects.

SUBSIDIES, DEREGULATION, AND LEASING

Extensive argument exists about the effects of governmental subsidies on the success of commercial aircraft manufacturers, much of it fired by the nationalistic rivalries of the participants. Boeing was undoubtedly helped initially in the development of its 707 by its bomber and military transport business. Its production run of 707 derivative KC 135 tankers was almost as numerous as the 707 and the cargo 720 version. Similarly, Airbus was dependent on sizeable direct subsidies from the participating governments to the joint venture partners. The magnitude of the $10 billion-plus subsidies during the past two decades in developing the first three Airbus models leaves little doubt of their significance in getting these planes to market, whatever their future role. Beyond these two historic facts, the controversy is less clear. One astute observer believes the claims and counterclaims are exaggerated, which they probably are.[23] President Giscard d'Estaing may well have used his office to promote Airbus sales in the Middle East and elsewhere, but these countries probably needed little encouragement at the time to buy other than U.S. aircraft.

The requirements for military and civilian aircraft have moved in divergent directions for many years, so that development costs no longer share common usefulness. To the extent that military work supports civilian aircraft development, it can be argued that most airframe and engine makers in the major countries are involved in both. The companies are not islands of proprietary technology; the industry is in fact very fungible. When one company becomes a prime military contractor, its competitors are likely to become its subcontractors, and each is served by many hundreds of suppliers. Technical employees move steadily from one firm to another as their work ebbs and flows; there are few well-kept secrets. Although the same mobility does not apply internationally, foreign alliances are becoming more and more common.

NASA's funding of civilian aircraft research and development is quite modest and has been for some time. In 1990, it initiated a five-year $248 million project to explore the feasibility of developing a supersonic airliner, probably to carry 250 to 300 passengers 7,000 miles at perhaps as high as Mach 3 speeds (approximately 2,250 miles per hour). MITI has invited all of the major jet engine manufacturers to participate in developing an engine for a hypersonic plane, tentatively involving the expenditure of $195 million.[24] The three larger firms in the Airbus consortium, together with Boeing and McDonnell Douglas, have announced a study of the possibility of a Mach 2.5 plane to replace the Concorde, which might cost more than $10 billion to develop.[25] Congress ended earlier euphoria for U.S. governmental funding of a supersonic transport in 1971—the name remains for the Seattle basketball team.

Deregulation was legislated for civil air transportation in the United States in 1978 and is anticipated in Europe in 1992. The initial effect was an expansion of traffic and competition followed by a consolidation of airlines. The hub-and-spoke pattern of operations developed—a more efficient system than earlier—and fares have declined (after inflation) on most routes, according to the Department of Transportation.[26] Eight domestic airlines now provide 90 percent of the traffic, in contrast to sixteen in 1984, concentrating the acquisition of equipment as well, and further consolidation is likely. The effects in Europe, coming fourteen years later, are likely to be less rapid and less traumatic, although there is already evidence of small country airlines seeking alliances, for example, SAS, Sabena, KLM, and Swissair. Hub-and-spoke patterns preexist to a greater extent in Europe, and there may be greater reluctance on the part of passengers to give up national carriers.

One effect of the increased U.S. competition has been to remove participation in aircraft engineering and design from the carriers, to thrust it back upon the manufacturers, and to cause new technology to compete for acceptance against existing technology on the basis of cost. Another effect has been to enhance the leasing of aircraft by removing the risk of ownership obligation when route patterns are subject to change from competitive forces. A number of major leasing companies have emerged and now play an intermediate role in aircraft purchase and finance, increasing airline equipment flexibility. Although this may not alter underlying equipment needs, it changes the way they are expressed and probably results in more efficient equipment utilization.

ASPIRATIONS: JAPANESE AND OTHERS

The Japanese are now looking into a third civil aircraft project following the failure of their first two. In the 1960s they designed and built a limited number of small turbo-prop airliners. Most recently, the government spent $210 million over twelve years developing an 80 to 100-seat plane, which was quietly put to bed after test flights ended in 1989. The latest undertaking is reported to be a 75-passenger jet for which they are seeking European assistance.[27] These efforts demonstrate their determination to eventually produce aircraft on their own rather than as suppliers or joint venture participants.

The failures have been embarrassing enough to impress on them the need to learn by assuming subordinate roles, and several manufacturers have thought it wise to establish alliances. As mentioned earlier, three Japanese firms have supplied about 15 percent of Boeing's 767 airframe requirements. They would have had a larger role in the 7J7 had it gone forward, and they are to have a role in the 777, for which the launch orders were received in 1990. McDonnell Douglas has purchased trailing edges of the MD80 wings from a Japanese firm. International Aero Engines, a small jet engine consortium, is composed of three Japanese companies in addition to three from Europe and one from the United States. Finally, MITI is financing an international consortium for supersonic engine development.

Manufacturers from Europe and elsewhere are aggressively seeking to participate in the industry, although no complete large aircraft projects other than Airbus, British Aerospace,and Fokker have been forthcoming. Boeing is using Aeritalia and Canadair for components of the 767, and Samsung is supplying some parts for other models. For the MD80, McDonnell Douglas has secured components from Aeritalia, Swiss Federal, Hawker de Haviland (Australia), SAAB-Scania, and Shanghai Aviation Industrial of China.[28] The latter provides China with hard currency earnings to offset a portion of the costs of assembly kits it is importing from McDonnell Douglas. None of these companies, except perhaps Aeritalia and SAAB-Scania, is a serious contender in larger civil aircraft projects. The advantages offered are participation in high technology in exchange for some leverage in obtaining airline orders.

A more likely contender is, of course, the Soviet Union, although several of its assured customers in Eastern Europe are beginning to buy from the West, and those markets will probably provide more sales for Boeing, Airbus, and McDonnell Douglas than Western airlines will for Russian planes in the immediate future. Aeroflot is also buying token numbers of aircraft from the three Western firms, but the lack of hard currency will prevent any significant sales from occurring. The world's largest airline, Aeroflot will provide a sufficient market for continued Soviet airframe and engine development, even with the loss of some Eastern European business. Aeroflot flies 25 to 30 percent as many jets as the Western countries together. Soviet technology is close enough to provide potential competition, if lack of confidence in engines could be overcome, in addition to dissatisfaction with such important features as comfort, safety, and noise control. Talks were reported to have taken place in 1990 among the Soviets, Israel Aircraft, United Technologies, and others to adapt Ilyushin 96 and Tupolev 204 aircraft for sale worldwide.[29]

VOLATILITY, PROFITABILITY, AND COMPETITION

Transport aircraft are expected to find a growth market for the next decade or two relative to GNP expansion, albeit somewhat less than in the

first four decades of the jet age. As a postponable capital good with a fifteen-
to twenty-year life, aircraft demand will probably continue to be volatile
and to fluctuate widely from one five-year period to another, as has been
the case in the past. Slower growth in air travel and aircraft fleet expansion
is being joined by increasing airport congestion, air traffic control problems,
the ever-present threat of terrorism, and public demand for safety, all of
which present manufacturers and system designers with tasks of increasing
magnitude and complexity. High speed railroad travel in Europe and Japan
may limit air travel expansion between major cities less than 500 miles
apart, perhaps a boon to longer flights.[30] Boeing will be seriously challenged
by the Europeans and the Japanese to maintain its 53 percent share of the
market, especially with its present extended delivery schedules, but it is in
an excellent position to meet its competitors.

Two trends indicate that the future may not be as favorable for Boeing
as the past. One is that the U.S. market for jet airliners was larger than
foreign markets in the early decades of jet air transportation. Now foreign
markets are growing faster than those at home, making them more significant with the passage of time. The second is that formerly there was no
full-line producer abroad capable of serving airline needs for various types
of aircraft with ready access to a large market. Now Airbus has these
qualities, backed by the interest and support of the British, French, German,
and Spanish governments.

Boeing alone has made profits primarily from the manufacture and sale
of jet airliners while others have tried and failed. Profitability is problematic
in more years than it is not. The company aims for a 20 percent return on
stockholders' equity, but in the best years it tended to gain little more than
half that level until 1990. The prestige of the business is such that it appears
as if some authority confers on participants the privilege of losing money.
Through its more than three decades of civilian jet plane manufacture,
Boeing has mixed in a significant portion of defense work—it has consistently been among the top five to ten defense contractors—but airliners have
tended to comprise about two-thirds of its sales revenues. It has not eschewed
military work; in fact, in 1985 it sought to acquire Hughes Aircraft for
almost $5 billion, only to be outbid by General Motors. Sometimes, it has
sought government work too assiduously and unlawfully, as it did in obtaining unauthorized documents, for which it pleaded guilty in 1989 and
paid fines of more than $5 million.[31] Nevertheless, its core business is build-
ing passenger planes, something it has done well.

Despite government-to-government discussions of charges and counter-
charges of subsidies and other assistance under the auspices of the General
Agreement of Tariffs and Trade (GATT), no satisfactory agreement has been
forthcoming. In the original agreement, Article XIV, which proscribes subsidies, was poorly worded as a basis for corrective action, and another, Ar-

ticle XXI, which permits security exceptions, has been easily stretched to cover the ambiguous mix of military and civilian aircraft manufactured by companies, often in the same plants. An agreement negotiated in the Tokyo Round completed in 1979 stating that "civil aircraft prices should be based on a reasonable expectation of recoupment of all costs" was not accepted by five nations (including Spain) aspiring to aircraft manufacture.[32] It has had little effect. Negotiating efforts were broken off in 1991 by the United States, which announced that it would file a complaint with the GATT. The greatest likelihood is that two of the partners in the Airbus consortium, Germany and Britain, will become weary of the costs and will expect their now privately owned companies to carry these burdens after two decades of subsidies, although Germany recently guaranteed to underwrite foreign exchange risk in excess of $2 billion to Daimler through 1999.

The circumstances of the three primary Airbus participants are indicative of internal problems, despite the consortium's achievements. Aerospatiale, a French government-owned enterprise, has operated recently with nil profits and huge research and development outlays. Each partner may do design work on any part of the aircraft in competition with the others. Aerospatiale does the final assembly in Toulouse, except for the new A321, which has been assigned to Germany. In January 1990, its chairman was carping about strike delays in the receipt of wing sets from British Aerospace.[33] The latter became privatized in 1981 and is expanding as a conglomerate; it acquired the Rover Group (automotive) in 1988, and announced a joint venture with Honda the following year. The company is Britain's largest exporter and had been a takeover target until the government raised the limit on foreign shareholdings from 15 to 29.5 percent, broadening ownership opportunities.

Control of Messerschmitt-Bölkow-Blohm was recently acquired by Daimler-Benz, Germany's largest industrial company and another conglomerate. Three German states will continue to hold a minority interest. This concentrates practically all of German aircraft manufacture within one company, including Dornier (military and commuter aircraft) and MTU (engines). The German press labelled it "the elephant's wedding" and *The Economist* expressed the opinion that it would be good for German aerospace, but probably not for Daimler-Benz.[34]

While all of this shuffling is taking place, Airbus management is trying to assert greater control and seeking to reorganize as a corporation. Under the present arrangement, decisions on important issues require unanimity, permitting one partner to block choices of planes or work division.[35]

Because of the wide fluctuations in aircraft industry shipments, shown earlier in Figure 3.1, the MIT Commission on Industrial Productivity is concerned about the quality of people that can be attracted to the industry with its recurrent layoffs and ramp-ups. Another concern is that European workers have a three-year apprenticeship training,[36] while in America only three-quarters of the young people complete high school. Boeing shares this problem with other U.S. aircraft manufacturers, which may become increasingly difficult if not reversed.

World competition in aircraft will intensify in the years ahead, and the risks will continue to be high; the sharing of them has become the new art to be mastered. Boeing has many assets, including its tremendous lead, which if wisely used ought to yield many advantages.

NOTES

1. Only completely new aircraft are counted, not "stretches" or modifications of models. For example, Boeing offers twenty versions of its existing four models.

2. John Newhouse, *The Sporty Game* (New York: Knopf, 1982), p. 122.

3. Ibid., p. 3.

4. Artemis March, "The U.S. Commercial Aircraft Industry and Its Foreign Competitors," MIT Commission on Industrial Productivity, *Working Papers*, vol. 1 (Cambridge, Mass.: The MIT Press, 1989), p. 22.

5. Newhouse, *The Sporty Game*, pp. 161–169.

6. March, "The U.S. Commercial Aircraft Industry," pp. 46–50. "By the mid–1990s, [Boeing] may be as well positioned as a private company can be to meet the challenges from Europe and the Far East." p. 50.

7. Newhouse, *The Sporty Game*, p. 197.

8. Ibid., p. 198, and "Boeing versus Airbus: Forget Miles-per-Gallon," *The Economist*, January 30, 1988, p. 51.

9. The full negotiations are described by Newhouse in *The Sporty Game*, pp. 201–211.

10. Ibid., p. 213.

11. Ibid., pp. 28, 124–126, and 192–195.

12. Ibid., pp. 30–31 and 40–43.

13. Paul Markillie, "All Shapes and Sizes: A Survey of the Civil Aerospace Industry," *The Economist*, September 3, 1988, p. 10.

14. Newhouse, *The Sporty Game*, pp. 173–183.

15. March, "The U.S. Commercial Aircraft Industry," p. 70.

16. Newhouse, *The Sporty Game*, p. 210.

17. M. Y. Yoshino, "Global Competition in a Salient Industry: The Case of Civil Aircraft," in *Competition in Global Industries*, ed. Michael E. Porter (Boston: Harvard Business School Press, 1986), p. 532.

18. Yoshino, "Global Competition," p. 537, and March, "The U.S. Commercial Aircraft Industry," p. 8.

19. March, "The U.S. Commercial Aircraft Industry": "Although it is sometimes alleged that United Technologies has underinvested in Pratt, some managers of both GE and Pratt locate the problem differently: poor management, inefficient manufacturing, and not having the right product at the right time." p. 9.

20. Ibid., p. 9.

21. Ibid.

22. Newhouse, *The Sporty Game*, pp. 173–184, and March, "The U.S. Commercial Aircraft Industry," pp. 9–10.

23. Newhouse, *The Sporty Game*, p. 29.

24. "Role for U.S. on Japan Jets," *The New York Times*, December 1, 1989, p. D5; David E. Sanger, "GE, Pratt Expected to Aid in Designing 'Hypersonic' Engine," *The New York Times*, January 4, 1990, p. C1; and Edmund L. Andrews, "Technology: Mach 3 Passengers? No Simple Formula," *The New York Times*, January 14, 1990, p. F8; Jacob M. Schlesinger, "American, European Companies to Work with Japanese Concerns on Jet Engine," *The New York Times*, February 19, 1991, p. A13.

25. Rhonda L. Rundle, "Five Aircraft Firms in U.S., Europe Join Study on New Jet," *The Wall Street Journal*, May 24, 1990, p. A5.

26. John H. Cushman, Jr., "Support for Airline Deregulation," *The New York Times*, February 14, 1990, p. C1.

27. "Aerospace Takes Off," *The Economist*, April 8, 1989, p. 72, and "Jet Joint Venture," *The Wall Street Journal*, November 20, 1989, p. A11.

28. "Boeing versus Airbus: Forget Miles-per-Gallon," *The Economist*, January 30, 1988, pp. 50–51.

29. "Russian Airliners: Jumboski," *The Economist*, August 5, 1989, pp. 61–62; Eric Weiner, "Aeroflot Buys First Airliners from West," *The New York Times*, January 25, 1990, p. D22; Charles W. Stevens, "Aeroflot Goes on Shopping Trip in West, Opening Huge Market to Aircraft Firms," *The Wall Street Journal*, February 5, 1990, p. A9B; and Susan Carey, "U.S.-Soviet Plan for Plane Venture Faces Obstacles," *The Wall Street Journal*, September 13, 1990, p. A11.

30. "High Speed Travel in Europe," *The Economist*, February 3, 1990, pp. 19–22.

31. Andy Pasztor and Rick Wartzman, "The Clique: How a Spy for Boeing and His Pals Gleaned Data on Defense Plans," *The Wall Street Journal*, January 15, 1990, p. 1.

32. Congressional Budget Office, "The GATT Negotiations and U.S. Trade Policy," (Washington, D.C.: U.S. Government Printing Office, 1987), quoted in March, "The U.S. Commercial Aircraft Industry," p. 18. A discussion of the negotiations and an outline of the 1979 GATT agreement are contained in Irene L. Sinrich, "Airbus Versus Boeing (A): Turbulent Skies," rev. ed., Case 9–386–193 (Boston: Harvard Business School, 1988), pp. 15–17 and 25.

33. "Aerospatiale Expects Rise in 1990 Revenue," *The Wall Street Journal*, January 16, 1990, p. C10, Midwest edition.

34. Ferdinand Protzman, "Approval Seen for Daimler on Messerschmitt Merger," *The New York Times*, September 7, 1989, p. D1; idem, "Messerschmitt's Sale to Daimler Approved," September 9, 1989, p. 30; and "Daimler and MBB: Indigestion," *The Economist*, September 16, 1989, pp. 75–78.

35. Susan Carey, "Airbus Industrie Seeks Its Independence," *The Wall Street Journal*, August 10, 1989, p. A12.

36. March, "The U.S. Commercial Aircraft Industry," p. 51.

4

ELECTRICAL EQUIPMENT: GE KEEPS ONLY THE WINNERS

General Electric is a diverse company, and its diversity has been increased by actions taken in the last decade. This is so notwithstanding the efforts of its CEO, John F. Welch, Jr., to concentrate the company into thirteen key businesses or clusters from a less-focused group of dissimilar enterprises. Since assuming the leadership role in 1981, Welch has undertaken an extensive program of divestitures and restructurings involving almost 200 enterprises, and an even more ambitious program of acquisitions. Acquisitions during the 1980s totaled $19 billion, mostly for seven large businesses, and dispositions were a little more than half as large. The strategy is simple—to be first or second in the key businesses worldwide or to exit and redeploy resources elsewhere.

The larger acquisitions have emphasized financial services, broadcasting, synthetic materials, and medical diagnostic imaging equipment, each of which is thought to be a newer, more rapidly expanding activity than those left. The departures were from consumer electronics and small appliances, natural resources, and some electrical gear. There is a movement to shrink the number of key businesses (fifteen in 1985, thirteen in 1989), although the classification of businesses into clusters is somewhat arbitrary. Also, the score keeping on firsts and seconds is subject to interpretation.[1] The results have been good, if not spectacular—a decade of quarterly increases in earnings per share. Return on stockholders' equity was never lower than 16.5 percent, and performance in the 1980s clearly was superior to that of the 1970s, despite product sales declines in 1982 and 1988.

The company is complex, and analysts have exhibited confusion. Moreover, its strategy has not been without its critics. One of these, Professor Michael E. Porter of the Harvard Business School, points out that investing in businesses that are first or second leads to emphasis on size rather than competitive advantage, that rather than being a strategy, restructuring "is a means of dealing with the failure of past strategies," and that GE has "divested a very high percentage of its acquisitions" in the 1950–86 period.[2] GE's power systems and electrical distribution businesses have moved from being one of its cardinal fields to one of restructuring and partial divestiture in the past decade.

The peak in power systems sales and profits occurred in 1984. During the first half of the 1980s, they were the largest of GE's business groups, accounting for one-fifth of both revenue and earnings. Following the second energy crisis in 1980, electric power expansion in the United States stagnated, and sales and earnings from this activity decreased. Foreign markets in other industrial areas have been of limited significance to U.S. electrical equipment makers, providing little cushioning for the downturn. As a result, the industry has faced a painful restructuring. Despite the decline from earlier levels, power systems is still one of GE's larger activities among its thirteen key businesses, as shown in Table 4.1, and together with electrical distribution and control equipment, the production and distribution of electricity ranks among its leading markets. Complementary or related businesses are lighting, motors, locomotives and electric wheels, and aircraft engines.

This discussion is limited to the power systems and electric distribution segments of GE's activities as they fit into the company's overall strategy. These segments are where GE started more than one hundred years ago. The relevant question is, how well did the company manage adjustment and decline in its traditional industry?

THE DEMAND FOR EQUIPMENT TO SUPPLY ELECTRICITY

At the end of the 1980s, the ten largest free-world producers of power generation, transmission and distribution equipment were providing approximately $60 billion in aggregate revenues. (See Table 4.2.) All are large companies engaged in the manufacture of other highly engineered products, from railroad locomotives to computers. The smaller manufacturers or niche players probably account for less than 20 percent of new equipment. As a result of mergers and joint ventures and the slowdown in the growth of U.S. demand for electricity, GE is no longer the leader; instead it is closer to the middle of the group.

The demand for electricity in the United States increased at a rate of 7 percent annually from 1950 to 1968, slowed slightly in the ensuing five years, and then decreased by half to 3 percent per year in the 1973–78

Table 4.1
GE's Thirteen Businesses,* 1989 Estimates

	Billions $	% of Total
*Financial Services	12.9	23.2
Financing	(7.3)	(13.2)
Insurance	(2.7)	(4.9)
Securities	(2.9)	(5.2)
Industrial (incl. GE Supply)	(7.1)	(12.7)
*Lighting	4.1	7.3
*Motors	1.1	2.0
*Elec.Dist.&Controls incl.		
Factory Automation	1.2	2.2
*Transportation Systems	.7	1.3
*Aircraft Engines	6.9	12.3
*Major Appliances	5.6	10.1
*Aerospace	5.3	9.5
*Power Systems	5.1	9.2
*Materials	4.9	8.8
Technical Prod.&Services	(4.5)	(8.2)
*Medical Systems	2.1	3.8
*Communications & Services	2.4	4.3
*Broadcasting	3.4	6.1
Total#	55.8	100.1

#Before Corporate Items and Eliminations

Table 4.2
Estimated Revenues from Electrical Equipment, 1989

Company or Joint Venture	Billions of $
ABB	9.1
Siemens 9/89	8.3
Hitachi 3/90	8.3
GEC-Alsthom	
(Incl. RR equipment) 3/90	7.4
GE	6.2
Toshiba 3/89	6.0
Mitsubishi Electric 3/89	5.1
Framatome	3.1
Westinghouse	2.6
Fuji Electric	
(Incl. RR equipment) 3/90	1.4

period. Since then, growth has averaged less than 1.5 percent annually. The electric utilities failed to perceive this declining trend for a time, which resulted in a substantial buildup of excess capacity, particularly in the 1973–75 period when the economy was struggling to adjust to higher energy prices brought about by the OPEC cartel. Martin Baily and Alok Chakrabarti calculate this excess capacity to be in the neighborhood of 20 percent in the 1975–80 years.[3] The adjustment process required of the utilities was complicated by the passage of the Clean Air Act amendments in 1970, just before the first energy crisis, which added significantly to the cost of new generating plants. After 1978, Congress required the installation of expensive scrubbers to eliminate sulfur dioxide emissions from steam plants. Initially the utilities moved toward the construction of nuclear facilities, but they did not perform as well as expected.

Operating availability of nuclear units in the United States still averages less than two-thirds of the time. The Three Mile Island accident in 1979 followed by the one at Chernobyl in 1986 sealed the doom of the nuclear energy option in America, at least for a decade or more. No new orders for nuclear power plants have been made since 1978, and many cancellations have taken place.

As a result of all of these developments, the price of electricity rose relative to other prices by the 1980s rather than declining as it had for decades before. The demand for electricity rose very slowly, excess capacity continued to exist, and additions to electric plants dwindled. These reactions were not duplicated as fully abroad, although the purchase of electrical equipment by the developing countries was interrupted by the debt crisis after 1982. U.S. turbine generator shipments, which had averaged 46,550 megawatts annually in 1972–74, fell to 3,422 in 1986. Transmission and distribution equipment sales did not fall as much, but power transformer shipments declined from a peak in 1975 to less than one-third that level in 1986–88. The turndown in global equipment buying was less abrupt, although severe.

Additions to new capacity will rebound during the 1990s, but there is much disagreement about when, where, and how much. In the United States, this is further complicated by what portion of new capacity may be added by independent power producers, many operating cogeneration plants, as opposed to electric utilities. The independents were enfranchised by the Public Utility Regulatory Act of 1978, which required utilities to purchase power from them, and they now provide about 2 percent of the total. Already isolated shortages of electricity are beginning to develop. The Department of Energy anticipates a need for about 19 percent additional capacity during the 1990s. The utilities have plans currently for less than half that much, while a private engineering firm in the industry sees a need for more than a one-quarter increase in capacity.[4] Gauging the demand for new capacity is further complicated by how much existing capacity will be retired, and that in turn is partially dependent on clean air policy decisions.

Current estimates of retirements by the year 2000 are small—5 percent or less of existing capacity. Outside the United States, the provision for new capacity has been more consistent in Europe and Japan. Backlogs of need are accumulating in the developing countries, but the mood of confusion and indecision is widespread.

General Electric has spent much of the past decade restructuring its power systems and transmission and distribution businesses in the face of the radically contracted market. Five of nine turbine plants were closed. GE's installed base of all U.S. steam turbine generators is an impressive 50 percent plus, and its share of large gas turbines worldwide is close to one-half. Attention has been shifted to maintaining and servicing the 12,000 steam and gas turbines the company has operating throughout the world and to the design of its new 7F gas turbine, which was first installed in 1988 and will ultimately become a part of an integrated gasification combined cycle plant. Efficient small-increment plants of this type suggest the direction of technology and demand in the immediate future. Orders in 1989 indicated a turnaround is occurring. GE is continuing its interest in boiling-water nuclear systems, pending a possible revival of that business. Nevertheless, it has left some businesses, including the manufacture of large power transformers, sold to Westinghouse in 1987, and high voltage direct current transmission equipment, sold to CGE-Alsthom of France in the same year. Now it sells extra-high voltage circuit breakers made by Hitachi in Japan. It also ended its experimentation in fuel cells and geothermal equipment as alternative fuel sources when energy prices fell in the early 1980s.

Markets for electrical equipment in the three principal industrial regions of the free world—North America, Europe, and Japan—have been dominated by their indigenous suppliers. Markets elsewhere in Latin America, Africa, and Asia have been shared by the eight major suppliers—two American, three European, and three Japanese—with the proximate suppliers having the advantage. These patterns may change with the competitive realignments that are occurring and the technological developments underway. The United States is already a little more open than the other two regions. The following discussion is organized the way things are today in the industry—by region. The concluding section explores GE's likely place in the equipment markets of the future.

NORTH AMERICA

The U.S. market for power generation and transmission and distribution equipment is larger than for all of Western Europe combined and almost four times that of Japan. Electricity generation per capita is larger only in Canada, which sells a sizeable volume of hydroelectric power to the United States. As in other categories of goods and services, the U.S. market for electrical energy and the means of producing it is vast. That is why the retreat from certain segments of the market by GE and Westinghouse is viewed with disbelief by some European and Japanese businesses, which would sacrifice much just to have access to such a large market. The decline from past volumes has been exceedingly painful for the major producers, but they should remember and know from the 1930s that long cycles of feast and famine occur and that once the recent excess capacity is absorbed, demand for new equipment will reappear. The question is, Are GE and Westinghouse pruning lines to concentrate on their strengths, or are they leaving too much of the business to others who can better demonstrate their concern for total customer needs? In addition to the two large companies, Combustion Engineering and Babcock and Wilcox, a part of McDermott International, are each engaged in supplying nuclear reactors as well as boilers.

General Electric's dominance in the steam and gas turbine businesses, the heart of power generation equipment typically custom designed for specific installations, is unquestioned in the United States and those areas of Latin America, Africa, and Asia to which it has easy access. According to a recently reported comment of a GE official, the company has been unable to book a European steam turbine order for twenty-five years, although one-tenth of new U.S. turbine purchases have gone to overseas manufacturers.[5] Limited GE access to the European market for gas turbines may be gained through GE's 10 percent stake in a joint venture with GEC-Alsthom (a combination of General Electric of the United Kingdom, unrelated to American GE, and Compagnie Générale d'Électricité of France [CGE]), announced in 1989. Negotiations have been underway for several years to open government procurement procedures and continued in the Uruguay Round of GATT negotiations. GE clearly intends to stay in the turbine and generating business following restructuring write-offs of $783 million in the 1983–87 period and plant and equipment additions during the same period in excess of that amount. Similarly, its commitment to electric distribution and control equipment over a five-year period ending in 1988 exceeded $300 million on plant and product improvements.

Westinghouse Electric follows a business strategy similar to that of GE— keep the winners, sell the others—with the result that it has exited from a larger part of its electrical equipment business than has GE. It has had an affiliation with Mitsubishi Electric for seventy-one years and now has its gas turbines supplied under license by Mitsubishi Heavy Industries in Japan. Its line of power circuit breakers was sold to Siemens in 1985 and a joint venture was formed with Mitsubishi Electric the following year for the supply of large breakers made in Japan. U.S. distribution was taken over by Mitsubishi in 1990 following disposition of Westinghouse's transmission and distribution business. It was sold to Asea Brown Boveri late in 1989 after a brief joint venture between ABB and Westinghouse. The sale was to include power generation equipment as well, but that effort was blocked by the U.S. Department of Justice because of ABB's prior involvement in the electric generating business in America. Westinghouse has a pressurized water-nuclear reactor under development, which at 600 megawatts is about half the size of most earlier nuclear reactors. It is sponsored by the Department of Energy, the Electric Power Research Institute (EPRI), and others. Both Westinghouse and GE have nuclear fuel supply units.

With the acquisition of Westinghouse's transmission and distribution equipment business and also Combustion Engineering, which was completed in 1990, ABB now has electrical equipment sales in the United States of approximately $7 billion, larger than General Electric and more than twice Westinghouse's remaining business. Combustion Engineering had been the largest U.S. supplier of boilers. Asea also has a joint venture with Babcock and Wilcox, another large U.S. boiler manufacturer. Asea and Brown Boveri formed their fifty-fifty joint venture in 1987 and rationalization of their subsequent Combustion Engineering and Westinghouse acquisitions will require time, but few would question the formidable competition ABB will offer in the future. Both Asea and Brown Boveri had been in the electrical equipment business in North America for many years; the former is recognized as a world leader in high voltage direct current systems and the latter was a pioneer in gas turbines.

The Canadians have pursued an independent course with a unique technology in a heavy water reactor design using natural uranium. Ontario Hydro generates half its power from CANDU reactors and a number of units have been sold to developing countries. In all, Atomic Energy of Canada, a government agency, has made more than 5 percent of the world's reactors. Their program is ongoing, and the approach is particularly attractive where there is access to natural uranium.

Other participants in the North American market include Siemens of Germany, which produces switchgear in the United States; McGraw Edison (a subsidiary of Cooper Industries); Square D in the transmission and distribution equipment business; Foster Wheeler, boilers; Merlin Gerin of France (a division of Schneider), one of the world leaders in switchgear; and Hitachi, also in transmission and distribution equipment. Siemens acquired Allis Chalmers' transmission and distribution equipment business in 1978–85 and has yet to turn a profit in its North American operations.

GE has not sold a nuclear reactor in the United States since 1974. U.S. orders for about sixty-five reactors were cancelled during the late 1970s and 1980s, while construction has continued in Japan, France, and elsewhere.

After a visit to Japan in early 1990, members of the team of observers organized by the National Science Foundation expressed concern about the ability of U.S. firms to compete. The chairman of the group stated that "the infrastructure required to build nuclear plants in the United States is slowly dwindling. Without more projects, our ability to build them as cheaply as others will suffer."[6] Part of the concern arises from the fact that Japanese governmental research and development expenditures on advanced reactors are several times that of the United States. The Tokyo Electric Power Company is building two advanced boiling water reactors, to be completed in 1996 and 1998, in which GE is participating in a joint venture with Hitachi and Toshiba. In 1989, this project provided a $750 million GE order for the largest combined cycle plant yet built, one that will incorporate several passive safety features new in reactor design. The company is also working to design a smaller unit, comparable in size to the experimental Westinghouse model, sponsored by the Department of Energy and EPRI. Whether or not additions to nuclear power have a future in the United States is as yet undecided, but if they do, GE clearly intends to play a role.

EUROPEAN TOGETHERNESS

Europe is the second largest regional market for electrical equipment. Further integration of the European Community after 1992 holds forth the prospect for more rapid economic growth than in North America during the next decade or two, especially through opening public procurement to wider competition, and the promise of a closer economic relationship between the six Eastern European countries and Western Europe. Until mid–1989, there were five principal firms supplying power-generating equipment, and pending the success or failure of the GEC-Alsthom joint venture and the Rolls-Royce–Northern Engineering Industries merger, there may be four or five future players, exclusive of any significant penetration by American or Japanese firms, which now seems unlikely. Each of the European companies has moved to enhance its competitive position through major joint venture or merger activity within the past five years.

Next to ABB, Siemens appears to be best positioning itself as a major global competitor. GEC-Alsthom claims to be the largest supplier within the European Community, but Siemens is not smaller globally, and its position outside Europe is more developed. That does not mean that it is well developed globally. In fact, *The Economist* asks, "Why didn't Siemens push more firmly abroad before?"[7] In 1989, it made a fifty-fifty joint venture agreement with Framatome of France to market nuclear reactors abroad. Framatome is partially owned by CGE, owner of half of the GEC-Alsthom joint venture. Siemens also acquired 40 percent of Plessy, a weapons maker also in nuclear equipment, along with GEC, which acquired a 60 percent interest. GEC holds the other half of GEC-Alsthom. Siemens's largest interest abroad is in the United States, where it acquired its first gas turbine orders in 1988. A joint venture with ABB's German subsidiary in nuclear reactors was formed about the same time.

The fifty-fifty joint venture between British GEC and French CGE, called GEC-Alsthom, became effective in the second quarter of 1989, and merged the power systems and railroad equipment sectors of the two companies. Ostensibly, the combination was triggered by the ABB combination a little more than a year earlier. CGE had just been shifted back into the private sector in mid-1987 after five years of public ownership at the instigation of the socialist government. France has the highest proportion of electricity supplied by nuclear plants, and Alsthom, the CGE part of the merger, has supplied more than sixty nuclear units in conjunction with Framatome. More than half of the sales of the GEC-Alsthom joint venture are outside Britain and France. GEC is still delivering nuclear power units inside and outside Great Britain, and in 1988 it made a joint venture with Westinghouse for the supply of components for the latest British nuclear plant, a pressurized water reactor. In early 1989, four agreements were made with GE, two involving power generation and transmission and distribution equipment. The joint venture mentioned earlier (in the discussion of GE), between GE and GEC-Alsthom, gave GE a minority interest in the new European Gas Turbine Company. The other established a fifty-fifty joint venture between subsidiaries of GE and GEC for European electrical distribution equipment.

Framatome produces nuclear steam supply systems and has the capability of furnishing all of the principal components for pressurized water reactors. The French government's Atomic Energy Commission, its electric utility company, and a government controlled bank now hold 52 percent of the company. CGE sought to acquire a controlling interest in 1990, but was opposed by the government in doing so.

The boldest move in the electrical equipment industry was the merger of Asea of Sweden and Brown Boveri of Switzerland effective at the beginning of 1988. Fortunately, the companies had available a young executive commensurate to the task, forty-seven-year-old Percy Barnevik, who had headed Asea since 1980. There he had pursued a "Nordic strategy" by expanding the base of operations through acquisitions in Norway, Denmark, and Finland and by extending marketing efforts in the developing countries. With ABB, he is evolving a global strategy with initial attention to shrinking the central staff, rationalizing the operations of the two companies, and improving its presence in the European Community and North America. The most important acquisitions have been the additions of Westinghouse's transmission and distribution business and Combustion Engineering. Asea Brown Boveri had transmission and distribution equipment sales in 1988 in excess of $6 billion, making it by far the largest global supplier. It has a way to go to catch GE in the power systems business, but it has solid components if it combines them appropriately. The addition of the last two acquisitions in 1989 and 1990 augments an already burgeoning company as bent on cost containment as is GE.

None of the other European electrical equipment manufacturers promises to be a major player in all lines on the world scene at this point. AEG was acquired by Daimler-Benz in 1985, the steam turbine operations were sold to ABB in 1989, and AEG Kanis was sold to European Gas Turbine later the same year. AEG continues in the transmission and distribution equipment business. Rolls-Royce acquired Northern Engineering Industries, a small provincial power systems company, also in 1989. Merlin Gerin, a subsidiary of Groupe Schneider of France, is a global firm in transmission and distribution equipment, and just acquired a Canadian company in that business. Schneider launched an unfriendly bid for Square D in 1991. Sulzer Brothers, the Swiss firm, includes large power station pumps in its varied product line and recently acquired a U.S. company that is the leading maker of feedwater pumps.

JAPAN AND THE EAST

Japan and the East are the smallest of the three major geographical areas in the market for electrical machinery and also the most rapidly growing as would be expected from its overall economic expansion. Its future potential is vast because of the growth rate and the numbers of people to be served. Should China, the Indian subcontinent, or Indonesia achieve more rapid economic growth, large markets would be opened. Unfortunately, after the student repression in 1989, China is not likely to show the promise it demonstrated in the preceding decade for some time to come. Each of these three areas has an income level of less than $500 per capita. Among them, Indonesia and Pakistan have shown the most indication of economic expansion recently. Japan will remain the third largest national market for some time in the future, and other immediate opportunities lie in Australia, South Korea, Taiwan, Malaysia, Thailand, and Singapore. Japan is committed to build sixteen more nuclear plants and is contemplating further additions. As a supplier of electrical equipment, Hitachi clearly leads, followed by Toshiba and Mitsubishi Electric. Fuji Electric is a smaller participant. Ironically, GE and Siemens fostered the early development of Toshiba and Fuji Electric, respectively.

Hitachi not only is the largest Japanese manufacturer of power systems and transmission and distribution equipment, but at present exchange rates it is larger than GE in the aggregate in these lines. Currently, it is supplying both nuclear and thermal power plant units. Along with Toshiba and GE, it is a supplier of the two-unit advanced boiling water reactor project for Tokyo Electric Power Company. The prototype fast breeder reactor of the Power Reactor and Nuclear Fuel Development Corporation also will utilize significant components from Hitachi. Thermal units have been supplied or are in the process of being supplied to Tokyo Electric and Kyushu Electric Power. Up to this time, Hitachi's participation in the U.S. market has been in high voltage circuit breakers and other transmission and distribution equipment.

Toshiba, another GE licensee, has gained in the supply of heavy electrical apparatus with the delivery of a boiling water reactor to Chuba Electric in 1987 and sponsorship of the current Tokyo Electric Power project. Recently, Toshiba supplied thermal plants to Kuwait, Australia, and China, as well as Japanese utilities.

Mitsubishi Electric is a Westinghouse licensee and builds pressurized water reactors as well as thermal units. It supplied a thermal unit to Thailand in 1989 and earlier furnished components for two nuclear units in Japan. Fuji Electric and GE signed an agreement in 1987 for the exchange of manufacturing and engineering technology in the development of new electrical distribution and control products and announced a joint sales venture in the Middle East and Southeast Asia the following year.

GE'S PROSPECTS IN THE INDUSTRY

Chief executive officers of large corporations seldom have the opportunity to turn their vessels more than a few degrees; tenure is too short and the bureaucracy too stifling. Opportunities to do so are frequently lost by inaction. The halcyon days of takeovers in the late 1980s were an exception, enabling folly to be committed overnight.

ABB and GE are exceptions, where Percy Barnevik and Jack Welch have served for the past decade. They have revealed themselves to be strong leaders, and each has an extended period in which he may continue to exert influence on his company. Both espouse a global strategy, as in fact do an increasing number of corporate executives, but they have demonstrated that they know what it means. Both indicate that they want to be the low-cost producer. Both stress decentralized responsibility within their sprawling empires. No intellectual, Welch nevertheless wrote a doctoral dissertation on nuclear reactors. Barnevik came from a rock drill and specialty steel company (Sandvik). Perhaps the chief challenge for Welch is his long-range commitment to a troubled industry, which will require perseverance and patience. For Barnevik, there are already those who are asking whether he is overreaching in taking over Combustion Engineering only two years after joining together Asea and Brown Boveri to become the world's most comprehensive maker of power systems.[8] It will be an interesting contest, joined by Siemens, GEC-Alsthom, and the Japanese. Westinghouse is not likely to be inactive. How are they likely to fare?

GE will not be displaced easily from leadership in the steam and gas turbine fields. Its dominance of the installed base of U.S. steam turbines is impressive, and GE clearly leads in the newer gas turbine field, where it has been obtaining three-fifths of new U.S. orders recently. It appears to be the largest global supplier as well, despite a smaller share. GE's in-house access to whatever benefits flow from the smaller jet aircraft engine technology is a plus inasmuch as that division is also the leader in its field. Siemens has had an alliance with United Technologies since 1988, and Rolls-Royce acquired Northern Engineering Industries the following year. GE's European window through its recent alliance with GEC is just beginning, and similarly ABB and Siemens are establishing themselves in the U.S. market. Mitsubishi is sharing the Westinghouse business by building its large turbine under license.

The nuclear reactor business, however, may be a different story. Between 1970 and 1990, the U.S. suppliers moved from a position of near monopoly to a minority position. Framatome announced discontinuance of its Westinghouse license for pressurized water reactors in 1981, once it had mastered the technology. GE is still involved, as is Westinghouse, in the design of the next generation of reactors. If there is a ten-year hiatus in U.S. installations, as seems likely, or even worse, should there be no additional U.S. reactors installed, the future for the American manufacturers is bleak. Competition in the field can be retained through determination and investment, but leadership is unlikely without a home market to serve. In that case, combined cycle plants based on thermal technology would expand, and the industry would be different. GE will have a role if it is determined to stay the course.

As other revenues have grown and electrical equipment sales have shrunk, power systems has declined from one-fifth to one-tenth of GE's activities. Capital goods sales, however, including aircraft engines, aerospace, factory automation, transportation systems, medical systems, communications, commercial lighting, heavier motors and some plastics, in addition to electrical equipment, still constitute roughly half of GE's business. With respect to its frequently stated policy of redeployment of resources, it is hard to quarrel with apparent success. The company squeezed increasing profitability from limited revenues during the 1980s. Sales growth was less rapid than GNP expansion, although profits increased by almost 11 percent annually. This is what is called "harvesting" the business, and the problem is that the season ends and growth may still be elusive.[9] Profitability in 1989 was high, at about 19 percent of stockholders' equity, but the growth in equity investment during the past decade also has been rapid, with the result that GE is back at the return on equity of a decade ago. The recently announced massive stock buyback of $10 billion, which could amount to as much as one-fifth of the outstanding shares, implies that no substantial new investment projects or acquisitions are contemplated, although it could easily be aborted if something came up during the five years of the buyback period.

In electrical generating and distribution equipment, GE management handled the contraction well. Operating profits from power systems declined, but were never negative. Disposals to date of electrical equipment lines—large transformers, high voltage direct current equipment, and high voltage circuit breakers—have not been crucial to GE's position as a supplier, although the sword of Damocles pronouncements relative to unprofitable lines probably does the company image little good among its customers. It's not their fault that the market fell apart. Management is right in stressing the smallness of business disposals overall relative to its aggregate business. The most significant change in capital goods was the exit from computers, and that was twenty years ago. Many critics objected to GE's sale of its consumer electronics businesses. Nevertheless, the company still occupies a coveted position in electrical equipment, whose future is clouded by the protracted market recovery, the nuclear power question, and increasing competition. It's largely up to GE.

NOTES

1. See the *Fortune*, March 27, 1989, ranking of twelve GE businesses.

2. Michael E. Porter, quoted in "Combative Chief: GE Chairman Welch, Though Much Praised, Starts to Draw Critics," *The Wall Street Journal*, August 4, 1988, p. 1; also Michael E. Porter, "The State of Strategic Thinking," *The Economist*, May 23, 1987, pp. 17–22; idem, "From Competitive Advantage to Corporate Strategy," *Harvard Business Review* (May-June, 1987): pp. 43–59.

3. Martin Neil Baily and Alok K. Chakrabarti, *Innovation and the Productivity Crisis* (Washington, D.C.: The Brookings Institution, 1988), pp. 77–78.

4. Theo Mullen, "Unseating the Electrical Utilities Monopoly," *The New York Times*, March 11, 1990, sec. 3, p. 12.

5. Taylor Moore, "The Rise of International Suppliers," *EPRI Journal* (December 1988): p. 10. A similar comment was attributed to GE's vice chairman, Lawrence A. Bossidy, in Clyde H. Farnsworth, "Shift Urged in Control on Exports," *The New York Times*, November 30, 1989, p. D6.

6. Kent F. Hansen, professor of nuclear engineering at the Massachusetts Institute of Technology, quoted in Matthew L. Wald, "Japan Now Ahead in Nuclear Power, Too," *The New York Times*, February 27, 1990, sec. C, p. 1.

7. "Siemens: Kaske as Siegfried," *The Economist*, January 21, 1989, p. 71.

8. William Dullforce, "Risking Corporate Indigestion to Remain a Leading Player on the World Stage," *The Financial Times*, March 21, 1990, p. 17.

9. Comments of Professor Michael E. Porter of the Harvard Business School in regard to Westinghouse, which has followed a similar policy: "You are harvesting your way out of business. It's not a strategy that produces buoyant growth." Quoted by Gregory Stricharchuk, "Westinghouse Relies on Ruthlessly Rational Pruning," *The Wall Street Journal*, January 24, 1990, p. A6.

5

Kodak's Lethargic Reaction to Competition in Photographic Equipment and Supplies

Photography celebrated its 150th anniversary in 1989 with many exhibits presenting the richness of visual imagery made possible by the technology and its proliferating forms. Black and white, cinema, color, video and other electronic media—each has established a new horizon for artistic expression and in practical applications as the potential unfolds in heretofore unexplored dimensions. For most of the years since its founding in 1879, Eastman Kodak has been in the forefront of these developing media, uncovering new possibilities and providing the products and services that have enabled widespread and multidimensional growth. Kodak is the dominant firm in a troika of global suppliers that emerged in the last quarter century. Its leading position worldwide is still intact, but it has yielded leadership in Japan to Fuji Photo Film in addition to a share of the market elsewhere. Agfa-Gevaert, a part of the Bayer Group of Germany and the third member of the trio, is the leading European firm and is also engaged in world distribution. The position of each of the three is strongest in its home region, although Kodak claims about half of the European film market.

The role of the three firms is depicted graphically in Figure 5.1 (subject to the distortion of wide exchange rate swings during the past decade). Kodak's growth in photographic sales during the 1980s was 5.6 percent annually, roughly matched by Agfa-Gevaert either in dollars or deutsche marks. In the 1970s, Agfa sales growth had lagged a bit because of a large and progressive appreciation of the deutsche mark. About 80 percent of its sales are outside its home markets in Germany and Belgium. The Japanese yen also appreciated during the two decades, not enough, however, to pre-

Figure 5.1
Imaging Sales by Leading Companies

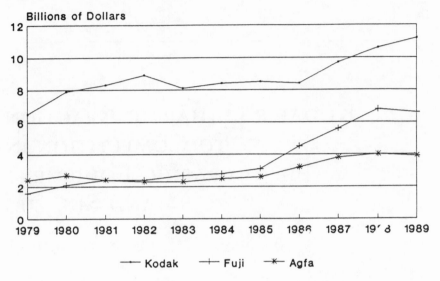

vent Fuji Film from growing considerably faster than Kodak. One of Kodak's most serious failures during this period was the degree to which it allowed its position to be eroded by Fuji.

Other things were also going wrong for Kodak. Polaroid sued for infringement of its instant photographic patents in 1976 and obtained a judgment against Kodak late in 1985, which forced Kodak out of the instant photo market. Kodak's public statements minimized the significance of the impact of the judgment, which affected only 3 percent of its sales volume and failed to acknowledge the threat of potential damages and the burden of litigation in the district and U.S. Supreme courts on management time and attention. The acquisition of Sterling Drug at a cost of $5.1 billion in 1988 involved additional debt of similar magnitude and was negatively received by investors. Since 1983 there have been several reorganizations and restructurings, the inadequacy of each necessitating further action later.

Most serious was Kodak's inattention to costs relative to its two principal competitors. Agfa's sales per employee are slightly larger than Kodak's but Fuji's sales are more than three times as much, even though Kodak sensed the need to begin cutting back excessive employment costs in 1983. Successive employment reductions were made—10 percent in 1983–84, 6 percent in 1986, and another 6 percent in 1989 in two separate actions. Twenty-four business units were created in 1984, including seventeen within the imaging sector, followed by two further restructurings later, not counting the rearrangements necessary to accommodate the Sterling Drug acquisition.

Performance data reflect the troubled state of the company during the last seven years: high costs, flat profits, and disappointing return on equity.

KODAK AND THE PHOTOGRAPHIC MARKET

Because of its size, Kodak has the broadest product line in photography and related products, but all three major firms are represented in the following seven categories: (1) consumer and professional imagery, including films, paper, and equipment, (2) photofinishing, (3) motion picture and television supplies, (4) business imaging systems and magnetic products, (5) medical imaging, (6) graphic arts, and (7) office copiers. Kodak does almost half of its business outside the United States and leads in most markets except Japan. Imaging, including information systems, which was included in the imaging division before 1989, now accounts for 61 percent of sales. By the 1980s, sales growth in imaging slowed to less than two-thirds the rate of GNP expansion. Divestitures of as many as twenty smaller businesses are being made, chiefly within the troubled information system segment. The other divisions are chemicals and health products. Diversification by large-scale entry into the health field occurred in 1986 and more than tripled with the acquisition of Sterling Drug in early 1988.

Consumer and professional films and papers are the cash cow of the imaging business. Kodak sales of these products in 1989 were in excess of $3.5 billion and constituted more than half of worldwide industry sales. Its hold on the U.S. market is an impressive 75 percent plus, although this is down from the market share held in the 1970s. The U.S. market is roughly one-third of the global total. Most sales are for color film and prints, although black and white has made a comeback, especially in professional circles. Fuji Photo Film has pushed its way into 11 percent of the U.S. film market, Polaroid entered the conventional film business in early 1989, and Konica started exporting to America in 1985. Others in the market include Agfa-Gevaert, Ilford (now a subsidiary of International Paper), and 3M (Scotch brand). Electronic imaging is making its way into commercial applications, but the traditional silver halide technology is likely to dominate amateur markets for some time to come.

Cameras and other photographic equipment are a more diffuse business. After a seventeen-year absence, Kodak reentered the 35 millimeter (mm) camera market about the same time it was forced to drop its instant photographic products in early 1986. Half the number of cameras and three-quarters of the value of camera sales are in the 35 mm format. In three years, Kodak claimed to have regained the lead in non-single-lens reflex (SLR) cameras in the United States. Reentry into the 35 mm market was a belated recognition by Kodak that its disc cameras, introduced in 1982, had been rejected by customers. They were phased out in 1988.

The 35 mm camera market expansion from high-end amateur and professional photographers to wide consumer popularity was engineered by Japanese manufacturers—including Canon, Minolta, Olympus, and Nikon. Kodak estimated that there were 354 million cameras in use throughout the world at the end of 1989, and that only one household in four was using a camera. Few observers are predicting rapid growth in the image market, because of adequate supplies in the high-income areas. The spread between pessimists and optimists ranges from 5 to 7 percent growth per year.

Electronic imaging is progressing and is still relatively expensive, relegating its use to applications that can justify its cost. As its technology progresses, silver halide may gradually be challenged in more uses. Kodak is making a major commitment to electronic imaging, as are several Japanese electronics companies. However, a large-scale transition from one technology to the other is believed to be more than a decade away, or longer.

Photofinishing is a low-margin business engaged in by the film manufacturers in order to maintain their market share in amateur film sales, which have high operating margins of around 50 percent. Representation in photofinishing also helps to establish standards for picture quality. Kodak performed rather poorly in this segment of the business in the late 1970s and early 1980s, at considerable cost in lost photographic paper sales. It entered the minilab business late, after Japanese and French manufacturers had sold more than 800,000 units in the United States.[1] Now it has left the minilab and photoprocessing business in the United States. Its U.S. processing operations were folded into the Qualex joint venture with Fuqua Industries in 1988. This venture is managed by Fuqua, which operates ninety-four laboratories and does more than one-third of this $5 billion business.

From the beginning of cinematography, Kodak has led as a supplier of motion picture film. Once as important as cartridge film sales, sales of motion picture film attained a near monopoly position in supplying the motion picture industry. This served Kodak well in the later evolution of other commercial and eventually home movie markets.[2] The advent of television and videotape techniques was closely followed by Kodak, carrying it from film to the unfolding electronic media. The contemporary adaptation to high-definition video is illustrative. The company has announced a process for converting conventional 35 mm motion pictures to HDTV, which enables existing programming to be made available without loss of quality to the new television format. A process is also to be made available in 1992 that will convert film images onto compact disks for display on television screens.

Kodak's extension into electronic and magnetic products has provided an array of business in excess of $1 billion sales in business imaging systems, mass memory, and other closely related divisions. These include microfilm products, printers, diskettes, imaging systems, and optical systems and disks, among others. Some of these were subject to sorting and divesting in the more intensive restructuring instituted in 1989, including the professional videotape businesses and the floppy disk unit. The company is attempting to integrate the storage, retrieval, and transmission of electronic images in anticipation of rapid growth of products capable of these functions within the next decade.

One special application group within the health sciences division produces X-ray films, equipment, and processing units for medical and dental uses, and has annual sales of $1.2 billion. Kodak claims to be the world leader in radiographic imaging and has enjoyed rapid growth in this area. Market share for the segment in Japan is particularly high, and more than half of the sales are made abroad.

Another billion dollar photo-related Kodak business is in graphic arts. Kodak's special attention to the printing and publishing industries dates from 1930, and the evolution of technology has carried it more deeply into these activities. Film usage in printing extends from small in-house applications to commercial and large-scale publishing operations. The microelectronic revolution of the 1970s opened the opportunity for film usage in the manufacture of semiconductors, and the sale of photosensitive materials to coat wafers for use in semiconductors has added growth to an otherwise mature market.

Finally, Kodak is a significant participant in the copier business, which it reentered very successfully in 1975 with the Ektaprint copier with new features. Kodak had pioneered the copier market in the early 1950s with its wet Verifax process but the Xerox dry copier in 1959 introduced a new technology that led to explosive growth. The Kodak Ektaprint copier is in the high volume (more than thirty copies per minute) segment of the market, but Xerox remains the leader. Kodak probably did not challenge Xerox sooner because it regarded the wet process as superior. Users felt differently, and Kodak belatedly accepted their verdict.

Revenue growth in copiers at Kodak was at double-digit rates through the 1980s with the help of the acquisition of the IBM copier business in 1988. Japanese copier manufacturers—Canon, Minolta, Ricoh, and others—invaded the copier business worldwide in the late 1970s by attacking the low-volume, smaller products. They seriously eroded the American makers' position in that end of the market where Kodak does not participate. Xerox successfully fought back, but has left the smaller models to the Japanese, who have used them as an opening to continue to attack the market for the larger models. Xerox copier volume is still several times that of Kodak, which became the second largest producer with the acquisition of IBM's copier business. In 1988, Kodak agreed to supply large copiers to Canon for sale in Japan under the Canon label.

Late in 1990, both Kodak and Xerox introduced machines to combine

computers, copying, and printing. Initially aimed at in-house printing operations, the new technology is expected to eventually result in smaller
machines and intense competition for new office systems.[3]

AGFA-GEVAERT

Agfa-Gevaert is a fifty-fifty joint venture formed in 1964 by the film
subsidiary of the large German chemical company, Bayer, and a Belgian
photo supply manufacturer, Gevaert.[4] Each company owns half of the two
prior companies. The German shares are owned by Bayer, and the Gevaert
company is owned by many shareholders in Belgium where the stock is still
actively traded on the Brussels market. Bayer is one of Germany's three big
chemical companies, which are the largest in the world. The joint venture
was a defensive move stimulated by Kodak's size and growing dominance
as internal tariffs were eliminated within the European Community. It was
also complementary; Bayer was primarily engaged in amateur photographic
products and Gevaert was chiefly devoted to commercial and business users.

At the time the joint venture was established, Kodak's research and development spending was as large as Gevaert's sales, which were somewhat
greater than those of Agfa. Both had been pioneer photographic companies
dating back into the nineteenth century as Kodak did. Together they were
engaged in all seven product lines of their chief competitors, Kodak and
Fuji. In 1970, *The Economist* estimated Agfa-Gevaert's market share worldwide at 10 to 12 percent.[5] The joint venture failed to gain market share in
its early years and had to cope with a strengthening deutsche mark in seeking
export sales in the 1970s.

Initially, the European Community provided Agfa-Gevaert with about
half of its sales, and the now expanded Community is still its principal
market, although Kodak still claims approximately half of the European
photographic business. Fuji Film made incursions there in the 1970s and
1980s, as it did in the United States, mostly at Kodak's expense. Competition
within Europe comes largely from Ilford in Great Britain, formerly a part
of Ciba-Geigy and acquired by International Paper in early 1989. Agfa
discontinued manufacturing its own cameras and other amateur photographic equipment in 1983 and concentrated its Munich plant on products
for business and professional use.

Agfa has made about one-quarter of its sales in North America during
the 1980s and claims roughly 5 percent of the U.S. market. At the end of
1988, it established the Agfa Corporation in the United States as a Bayer
subsidiary and acquired the remaining minority interests in two subsidiaries,
one in medical imaging and the other in graphic arts. Problems with the
latter's pre-press systems pulled the entire U.S. subsidiary into a loss. Agfa
has improved its posture in the U.S. market, but it achieves its third-ranked
position by selling 27-exposure rolls against Kodak's 24-exposure standard,

an effective price discount greater than Fuji's 10 percent and less than the minor competitors' 20 percent discount from Kodak's prices.

Agfa has progressed at about the same rate as Kodak in the last two decades. Employment increased less than 6 percent in twenty years. Photographic subsidiaries existed in twenty-eight countries in 1988 compared to twenty-three in 1968.

Kodak is not being pressed by Agfa-Gevaert. Neither one has made serious inroads into the markets of the other. Each has moved to strengthen its traditional markets and broaden its worldwide distribution network. The challenge has come from the East.

FUJI PHOTO FILM

Fuji Photo Film became the second largest photographic company in the early 1980s, as shown in Figure 5.1. It got there in the Japanese way: steady progress through product and quality improvement, meticulous attention to the reduction of manufacturing costs, and aggressive selling. In 1976 and again in 1984 it successfully introduced the fastest-speed color film available, and these advances were subsequently followed by other industry suppliers. Product innovations and steadily improving quality enabled Fuji to gain market acceptance, not just in Japan but throughout the world. Today, the little green box is nearly as ubiquitous as the yellow box.

The company was founded in 1934 and for many years was led by Setsutaro Kobayashi. With the assistance of tariff protection and other trade barriers, it gained a dominant 70 percent share of the Japanese amateur film market. Kodak has 13 to 15 percent of that market but has continued to be a major supplier to professional users, to whom its quality products have retained a following. Other important film suppliers in Japan are Konica, Agfa, and Sakura. The latter was responsible for introducing the 24-exposure roll to replace the 20-exposure roll, which became the industry standard. Polaroid's products are distributed in Japan by Konica, and Minolta assumed U.S. sales of Polaroid's high-end instant camera under its own name in 1990.

In 1962 the eminently successful fifty-fifty Fuji Xerox joint venture was established with Kobayashi's son Yotaro as president. Twenty years later, it played a key role in teaching Xerox how to rebut the Japanese copier competition in the United States. The contribution of Fuji Xerox to Fuji Film's profits and sales is formidable. If half of Fuji Xerox's unconsolidated sales of $3,548 million in 1988 is added to Fuji Film's revenues, they are increased by 21 percent, and Fuji Film sales become 81 percent of Kodak's total photographic business. Also the rewards to Fuji Film for moving into copiers more than a decade ahead of Kodak have been significant.

Fuji Film's movement into foreign markets has been equally impressive. It established its first overseas office in Brazil in 1958 and organized one in

New York the following year. Its U.S. subsidiary was established in 1965, twelve years before Kodak placed its own subsidiary in Japan, although Kodak had marketed there since the 1920s. Foreign sales have grown rapidly, from 21 percent of the total in 1975 to 35 percent in 1988. The company has just opened a South Carolina plant for making photo presensitized plates used in offset printing, enhancing its U.S. presence in the graphic arts.

For the European market, a subsidiary was organized in Germany in the mid–1960s. This was supported further by the construction of a film and paper plant in the Netherlands in 1984 and a magnetics product plant in Germany in 1988.

THE INFLUENCE OF CAMERA DESIGN

The sale of film and processing has always been dependent on the instruments available for picture taking. Kodak's contribution in the late nineteenth century was the simple box camera (in 1900 the popular and inexpensive "Brownie"), which transformed photography into an amateur as well as a professional art. A generation later the E. Leitz company of Germany was responsible for introducing the Leica camera in 1924, based on the 35 mm film format of the motion picture industry. This product defined the parameters for 35 mm camera development in the following decade, with interchangeable lenses, filters, flash units, and other attachments. This roughly coincided with Kodak's major and continuing coup, the introduction of Kodachrome film in 1935. In the 1960s, 35 mm camera technology was adapted by a number of Japanese companies as they proved themselves in optics and quality precision instruments in cameras offered at prices no one else could meet.

By the 1960s Nikon had become the standard for the amateur seeking perfection in contemporary equipment. It served many professional needs as well, although Hasselblad of Sweden (in combination with Carl Zeiss optics of Germany) remained the bellwether medium-format camera maker for much of the professional market. Kodak left the 35 mm camera field. As electronic components became available, Nikon and others were alert to their potential for adding automatic features. These improvements reduced the complexity of picture taking and further expanded the number of potential users of SLR and non-SLR 35 mm photography. Fully cognizant of the emerging coalescence of optics and semiconductor technologies, Nikon moved to supply the needs of semiconductor manufacturers. Within the last decade, Nikon has become one of the principal suppliers of equipment to this expanding industry. In fact, by 1988 more than half of Nikon's $1.9 billion sales were related to semiconductors.

Kodak followed a different strategy, which succeeded for a time but ultimately failed. The company decided to appeal to the mass consumer market by emphasizing a camera format that permitted film to be easily loaded. Company sales of cartridge-loading cameras totaled 150 million units in the 1960s and 1970s. The next generation of easy to use disc cameras and film was first offered in 1982 but never really caught on with customers. By then the superior quality of 35 mm pictures was evident, and the market moved in that direction.

More than a dozen Japanese manufacturers popularized 35 mm camera photography. In addition to Nikon, Canon, Minolta, and Olympus, which were the largest, Pentax, Konica, Yashica, Fujica, Mamiya, Topco, and others also participated. The competition was so aggressive and intense that several of them were eliminated from the race along with Argus and Kodak in the United States. In retrospect, it is clear that Kodak did not foresee the implications of Japanese perfection in camera technology on film supply at the time of its withdrawal from the field at the end of the 1960s and success with cartridge cameras blinded it to the 35 mm potential as it unfolded.

The principal film suppliers—Kodak, Fuji Film, and Agfa-Gevaert—obviously have an interest in the broadest distribution possible of cameras into the hands of users. Each has sought to augment ownership and use of cameras in addition to stimulating film sales through participation in and shaping of the market for equipment and photographic systems. When Kodak reentered the low-end of the 35 mm camera market in 1986, Canon and Minolta were each credited with having about 30 percent of the U.S. market. Kodak initially offered two models largely supplied from Japan by Chinon Industries. The introduction coincided with its forced withdrawal from the instant camera and film market by Polaroid and also the fading of disc camera sales. Kodak continued to sell the 110 cartridge cameras first introduced in 1963; disposable cameras were offered in 1988. Together these types of cameras are far exceeded in value by the various types of 35 mm cameras. Similarly, Fuji Film and Agfa-Gevaert have offered cameras and other equipment to engage in the many facets of the market and to expand its potential.

Polaroid has been more than a footnote but less than a revolution in photography since its introduction of instant photography in 1947. Many special applications have been found, yet the company lagged in sales growth during the 1980s despite its success in court against Kodak, which was held to be in violation of seven Polaroid patents in the suit commenced in 1976. An injunction was finally issued in 1985, and it enforced termination of Kodak sales of instant cameras and film after more than sixteen million cameras had been sold. Discontinuance and exchange of cameras cost Kodak more than half a billion dollars in 1985; in addition, in 1990 Kodak was ordered to pay Polaroid $873 million to settle the judgment, the largest patent infringement award ever made.[6]

THE PRICE OF KODAK'S MISTAKES

Kodak's management has exhibited ineptness in solving or adapting to its problems and adversities. They were not attentive to developing foreign competition when they needed to be. They were slow in recognizing product opportunities when they were privy to the relevant technology. They skated too close to the edge of Polaroid's patents, or were poorly advised by patent counsel about the dangers of litigation. Restructuring efforts over seven years have been fumbling and ineffective in solving the problem of excessive costs vis-à-vis competition. And finally, the major acquisition of Sterling Drug to provide growth and diversification was poorly received by the investment community and seen as too costly and beset with its own problems, which Kodak was not equipped to resolve. Each of these allegations will be discussed in turn before attempting an assessment of the company's overall performance and position.

Although Kodak's position in the global film industry did not go without challenge, inattention to foreign competition ultimately carried a cost. Recently retired Vice Chairman Phil Samper indicated that, when he returned to Rochester in 1976 from assignments overseas, "no one had the responsibility" to follow market share.[7] That probably exaggerated the actual situation, but Fuji Film needed no invitation to move aggressively on a global basis. Loss of market to Fuji in film and associated technologies is sizable. Kodak also has been criticized for not organizing more effectively to approach the Japanese market. A senior manager was not assigned there until 1984.[8]

Tardiness in the recognition of product opportunities is illustrated in two cases, both mentioned earlier although there are others. In the case of copiers, Kodak made an impressive entry in dry copiers in 1975—sixteen years after Xerox pioneered improvements in the field—and has done well in the highly competitive business. Some of the later competition might have been forestalled had the entry been more timely. In the market for 35 mm cameras, Kodak's long absence left a void in its own product line that competitors demonstrated how to fill. Film sales progressively moved toward the 35 mm format, giving ample indication of customer preferences. One observer emphasized the availability of Japanese camera makers, companies or manufacturing facilities, as competition in the field intensified.[9] Kodak's absence was too long as the leading company. This may have been both because it was unable to offer the product on a cost-effective basis from its U.S. facilities, since it ultimately resorted to a foreign supplier, and because of its commitment to the cartridge camera.

The Polaroid patent infringement case was costly in prestige, management time and effort during the fourteen-year duration, and the bottom line, however mitigating Kodak's circumstances were by way of argument. The company stressed the differences in its instant process from that of Polaroid, not without justification, but did not prevail. In addition to these direct and derivative costs, the company's handling of the litigation raises disturbing questions. Most technology companies are exposed to potential patent litigation; the questions relate to the extent of the infringement—seven patents—and Kodak's legal tactics, although the judge found no support for the claim of "willful" infringement. The effects are not critical as they will erode in a short time.

The acquisition of Sterling Drug in early 1988 shocked investment analysts because of the high price, the addition of substantial debt, and unamortized goodwill, which at the end of 1989 amounted to $4.6 billion or more than two-thirds of stockholders' equity. The price to earnings ratio paid exceeded twenty-six in order to satisfy Sterling's directors and wrest the prize from Hoffman-La Roche, which had made an unfriendly bid. Diversification into the drug industry would have been more favorably received had Kodak displayed more acuity in attending to its core activities. Bayer aspirin, one of Sterling's leading proprietary products, immediately developed problems and lost one-third of its sales before bottoming out, further embarrassing the acquisition. Kay Whitmore, the new chairman and CEO, readily admits that the jury will be out for five years on the merger, until Sterling is able to introduce the new pharmaceuticals it promised. Whitmore was the architect of the purchase. In an effort to increase profits, Kodak recently announced a joint venture with Sanofi of France to share the development and marketing of pharmaceuticals worldwide.

Kodak's four attempts at restructuring since 1983 have not been reassuring that it understood its problems and knew how to solve them. The progressive paring of employment and repeated reorganizations has hurt morale without demonstrating improvement. When the new CEO was announced, the fifty-five-year-old vice chairman retired and shortly took another CEO position. Most of Sterling's top management left soon after the merger, including the former chairman, despite Kodak's need and desire for them to stay. Because of acquisitions, total employment is higher than at the beginning of the 1980s, but the imaging and information systems divisions have experienced personnel cuts of more than a one-quarter. Sales of twenty small units were proposed in late 1989, involving an additional 4,500 people with sales of $1.25 billion. According to *The New York Times*, the new CEO acknowledged that Kodak's top management "does not inspire a lot of confidence.... 'Obviously, there is a credibility problem in the financial community.' "[10]

None of the foregoing mistakes is necessarily critical to Kodak's future, but they have been serious mistakes. More than anything, they are indicative of the need for change. No matter how big and successful a company has been, competitors are always looking for opportunities to move into profitable enclaves. If managements fail to adapt to new products, production methods, market conditions, or delivery systems, they will suffer as Kodak did. One 1986 judgment was perhaps too harsh: "Nothing in Kodak's future has the obvious profit potential of those familiar little yellow boxes."[11] The company has many assets in its people, technology, and market position. It must attend to the problem of its troubled newer businesses in the information systems segment and to its core activities in imaging. It will not always succeed in all its various products and markets, but it should do better than it did in the 1980s.

Despite some loss of share in the imaging business, Kodak continues to possess the advantages of global market strength and product leadership that endow it with many future options. Manufacturing cost problems need to be squarely, fully, and promptly dealt with, and Kodak must find the coherence it is searching for in the information systems businesses. If the company concludes that it does not have a contribution to make in the recently acquired collection of health and household products enterprises, an early admission would enable it to focus resources and attention on its central activities that have contributed to its historic success and to enjoy expansion nearer to these products and technologies. With recognition and determination, the malaise of the 1980s can be ended and the future made more rewarding.

NOTES

1. Claudia H. Deutsch, "Kodak Pays the Price for Change," *The New York Times*, March 6, 1988, sec. 3, p. 1.

2. Reese V. Jenkins, *Images and Enterprise: Technology and the American Photographic Industry, 1839 to 1925* (Baltimore, Md.: The Johns Hopkins University Press, 1975), pp. 278–279.

3. Laurence Hooper, "High-Tech Gamble: Xerox Tries To Shed Its Has-Been Image with Big New Machine," *The Wall Street Journal*, September 20, 1990, p. A1; Barnaby J. Feder, "A Copier That Does a Lot More," *The New York Times*, October 3, 1990, p. C1.

4. The uniqueness of a transnational joint venture at the time led to special interest in it and a number of studies, two of which are "Agfa-Gervaert: Merger or Partnership?" *The Economist*, March 7, 1970, pp. 52–53; and Michael Whitehead, "The Multinationally-owned Company: A Case Study," in *The Multinational Enterprise*, ed. John H. Dunning (New York: Praeger Publishers, 1971), chap. 12, pp. 307–331.

5. Ibid.

6. Lawrence Ingrassia and James S. Hirsch, "Polaroid's Patent Case Award, Smaller Than Anticipated, Is Relief for Kodak," *The Wall Street Journal*, October 15, 1990, p. A3; *The New York Times*, February 8, 1991, p. C3.

7. Deutsch, "Kodak Pays the Price for Change," p. 1.

8. James C. Abegglen and George Stalk, Jr., are critical of Kodak's "delay in responding to Fuji's competitive challenge," in *Kaisha: The Japanese Corporation* (New York: Basic Books, 1985), pp. 240–241. Albert L. Sieg, president of Kodak Japan, is quoted extensively by Robert C. Christopher, *Second to None: American*

Companies in Japan (New York: Crown Publishers, 1986), including the following: "For too long, we granted our Japanese competitors a safe haven. Because we didn't give them any real solid competition in their home market," p. 23.

In 1990, *The Economist* and *The Wall Street Journal* published conflicting reports on Kodak's success in gaining share of the amateur photographic market within Japan. *The Economist* indicated that Kodak had gained "a steady 1% each year for the past six years." *The Wall Street Journal* article, obviously inspired by the one in *The Economist*, emphasized the difficulties encountered by Kodak, and quoted data from *The Japan Economic Journal* showing that Kodak had declined in share of color film shipments within Japan from 1987 to 1989. Kodak, however, stated that its share of amateur color film sales had grown since 1986. "The Revenge of Big Yellow," *The Economist*, November 10, 1990, pp. 77–78; Clare Ansberry and Masayoshi Kanabayashi, "Kodak Remains Out of Focus in Japan When It Comes to Key Color Film Market," *The Wall Street Journal*, December 7, 1990, p. B1.

9. Kenichi Ohmae, *Triad Power: The Coming Shape of Global Competition* (New York: The Free Press, 1985), p. 168.

10. John Holusha, "Click: Up, Down and Out at Kodak," quoting Kay Whitmore, *The New York Times*, December 9, 1989, p. 33.

11. Alex Taylor III, "Kodak Scrambles to Reform," *Fortune*, March 13, 1986, pp. 34–39.

6

CATERPILLAR'S ORDEAL: FOREIGN EXPOSURE BRINGS NEAR CATASTROPHE

Beginning in the middle of 1982, Caterpillar earnings turned negative for the first time in fifty years. Losses continued, with a single exception, for eleven quarters. In three years, accumulated losses totalled $1 billion, the stated equity of the company was reduced by 28 percent, and employment was cut by 40 percent.

Half of the job loss of more than 30,000 was in U.S. employment related to exports. Caterpillar, one of the nation's leading exporters—it ranked third as recently as 1979—found its foreign sales cut in half. Ten plants eventually were closed, and the stock market lowered its valuation of the company by $3.7 billion or 57 percent by late 1984.

Slow recovery began in 1985, interrupted by losses again in the second half of 1986 and early 1987, not large enough to result in an annual deficit in either year. By late 1987, sales revenues and profits were approaching the pre–1982 levels, but it had been a long and traumatic ordeal.

What had gone wrong? Had another industrial star, often lauded for superb management and steady growth, suddenly fallen? In retrospect, several lessons loom clearer in hindsight than they appeared as events unfolded. They always do, but they are lessons, nonetheless, for Caterpillar and for U.S. manufacturers in general.

WHAT WENT WRONG?

Overexpansion

The thirty-five-year post–World War II expansion in the world market for construction machinery had ended by 1980. But Caterpillar was increasing its plant capacity at a rate of more than 5 percent annually as late as 1982, when its ordeal began, even though its physical sales volume had peaked four years earlier in 1978. Expansion had been pursued too long—until less than half of existing capacity was needed to meet demand—before corrective action was undertaken.

Foreign Competition

Long before the crisis began, management warnings had identified Japan-based Komatsu as Caterpillar's principal competitor, as deadly serious in its quest to displace the company as the industry leader. It is doubtful that the full impact of this was understood by many executives, middle managers, union leaders, and others concerned. Komatsu had made steady progress as a competitor through product improvement and meticulous attention to costs, helped by Caterpillar's long strike in 1982–83 and the period of the high dollar-yen relationship in the early eighties.

International Deployment

Caterpillar was an extreme case of company dependence on ability to export from the United States. In 1981, 57 percent of its sales were outside the United States, and roughly two-thirds of those sales were supplied by American exports. Among large companies only Boeing has had a heavier dependence on exports. The portion of Caterpillar's output made abroad was not increased from the late 1960s until the crisis of the 1980s. In a period of increasing foreign competition and fluctuating foreign exchange rates, the wisdom of such heavy dependence on U.S. production was questionable.

Labor Relations

As Komatsu was creeping up on Caterpillar through its attention to product design and manufacturing costs, one key Caterpillar cost, wages and benefits, was clearly out of control. Caterpillar resolved to remedy this problem in its 1982 contract negotiations with the UAW despite a backdrop of mutual distrust and misunderstanding. A 205-day strike followed that was very costly to both sides. The resulting massive operating losses for the

Figure 6.1
Caterpillar Quarterly Profit

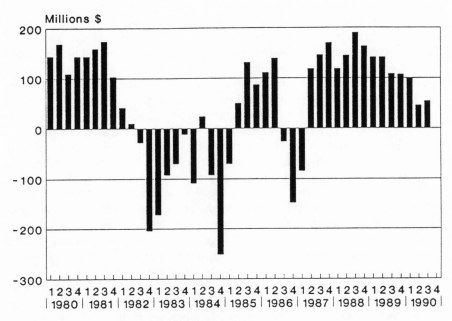

company accounted for a sizeable part of the $1 billion loss during 1982–84.

A WORST CASE SCENARIO

Managements accustomed to successful expansion are not especially tolerant of the possibility of contraction. Those who neglect adverse exposures, however, invite catastrophe. Things can go wrong, and when they do, they sometimes coincide. By early 1982, Caterpillar had accumulated a set of vulnerabilities that it could ill-afford to ignore.

Caterpillar's troubled profit performance during the 1980s is shown in Figure 6.1. Physical sales volume declined slowly at first after the peak in 1978, and then plunged in 1982 as the U.S. recession worsened. A longer interval intervened before another high in sales volume was reached than at any earlier time in the company's 65-year history. Not until the end of the 1980s did physical sales approach the previous high. Profit per share, however, was lower than a decade earlier, and sales growth in the 1980s was less than half as rapid as GNP expansion, contrary to every other decade in the company's experience.

Slower Economic Growth

When the big plunge in worldwide construction machinery sales occurred in 1982, it was probably overdue. The impact of the slowdown in global economic growth, which began soon after the first oil crisis in 1973–74, was delayed insofar as construction machinery was concerned by a number of factors, as explained in Chapter 1. First, the new-found income of the petroleum exporting countries enabled them to engage in many large-scale construction projects, for which they bought large volumes of machinery. So long as oil prices and export volume remained high—as they did through 1981—the oil exporters continued to buy equipment. Second, the recycling of petrodollar loans from the oil exporting countries to the less developed countries by the commercial banks continued into 1982 before it became apparent that they lacked the capacity to make repayments. And finally, the dollar drifted downward following the total collapse of the fixed exchange rate system in 1973, through the remainder of the 1970s, making U.S. exports of construction machinery relatively attractive in price compared to other sources. When exchange rates shift, as they did beginning in 1980, the effect tends to lag for as long as two years. All of these influences came to an end with the 1981–82 recession in the United States.

This recession was the most severe since World War II, and U.S. shipments of construction machinery fell by almost 40 percent in two years. The seriousness of the downturn was made more severe by credit tightening, which had begun in 1979 and persisted in the visible form of high interest rates through 1982, and to a degree throughout the 1980s as a result of the budget deficit and the dearth of domestic savings. The sharp U.S. recovery in 1983–84 was not matched by a similar upturn abroad, and sales of construction machinery languished throughout much of the 1980s at levels substantially less than during the 1978–81 period. By 1984, Caterpillar was achieving the dollar volume of U.S. sales it had enjoyed earlier. But that was not the case abroad, where sales continued for three more years at little more than half their earlier level.

As shown in Table 1.1, the annual growth of industrial output in most of the leading free-world economies has slowed drastically from the rates that prevailed prior to 1973. Nowhere has this slowdown been more pronounced than in the construction machinery industry, dependent as it is on construction activity associated with economic expansion. These detrimental aspects have not yet disappeared, even though Caterpillar sales recovered to roughly the physical volume of the late 1970s with the help of product additions.

Exchange Rates

Caterpillar's heavy reliance on U.S. exports to supply its foreign markets made it especially vulnerable to foreign competition as the dollar almost doubled in value during the 1980–85 period. Japanese and European competitors seized the opportunity to press for expanded sales and market shares. To a degree and for a time, they were successful, although no widespread rearrangement occurred.

Company CEO Lee Morgan called attention to the dollar-yen misalignment in 1982 and gave testimony before the U.S. Congress to the effect the next year. In the 1984 *Annual Report*, he warned that "the strength of the U.S. dollar is undermining manufacturing industries in the United States," and in an appearance the following January before the National Press Club, he called on the president to intervene in foreign exchange markets. Exchange rate intervention was undertaken by the administration in September 1985 in concert with Japan, West Germany, France, and Great Britain. Within a year, the dollar had declined by one-third against the yen and the deutsche mark, and by the end of three years, it approached the level that had prevailed in 1980 (see Figure 1.2).

Near the dollar's peak, Caterpillar embarked on a vigorous program of offshore procurement of materials, parts and components, and some production was moved abroad, something it should have done earlier. The subsequent decline and, after 1988, the renewed strength of the dollar emphasize the vagaries of foreign exchange rate fluctuation and the necessity of adaptive actions.

Labor-Management Relations

The market strength once possessed by large U.S. companies in the steel, automotive, and machinery industries, and shared by the unions in those industries, has led to wage and compensation premiums for the companies' employees not seen abroad. The premium for steel workers was most pronounced in the early 1980s, and auto and steel workers still enjoyed an average hourly compensation more than one and one-half times that for all manufacturing in 1985. Increasing concern about Japanese competition heightened sensitivity to comparative labor costs. According to the Department of Labor, between 1977 and 1985 unit labor costs in manufacturing rose in the United States relative to Japan by 39 percent. In early 1982, Caterpillar claimed its wage and benefit package was 90 percent higher than for its Japanese competitor, Komatsu.

Company managements tried to do something about these disparities as international competitive pressures intensified. In 1979, International Harvester sought to remove what it deemed were contract disadvantages, particularly in overtime and seniority procedures. A subsequent 170-day strike with the UAW cost Harvester hundreds of millions of dollars and contributed importantly to its inability to survive in three of the four industries in which it was then engaged. About the same time, Caterpillar experienced an 80-day strike initiated at its largest plant in Peoria by local UAW members who were irate over relations with the international union leadership and the company. In the 1982 bargaining three years later, an effort by the company to slow the rise in costs by eliminating the 3 percent annual improvement factor and reducing paid time off, led to a seven-month strike, the longest company-wide strike in UAW history. This inflicted heavy costs on the company in lost sales and operating deficits.

LDC Debt Crisis and Other Problems

The less developed country debt crisis, which began in 1982 and continued for the remainder of the decade (described in Chapter 1), was especially harmful to Caterpillar sales because of their sizeable dependence on construction and mining projects in the LDCs. Company sales in Latin America, Africa, the Middle East, and Asia and the Pacific regions fell by $2 billion or by 21 percent of total 1981 sales. The decline of oil prices and earnings by the producing countries also was associated with the LDC debt crisis and contributed to the longevity in the weakness of construction machinery sales.

Caterpillar inadvertently contributed to its own distress by its untimely decision to acquire the Solar Turbines division from International Harvester in 1981 for $505 million. Added borrowing costs associated with the acquisition contributed to its losses in 1982–84.

THE INDUSTRY REGROUPS

The profound effects of the difficulties reverberated throughout the construction machinery industry as sales fell and profits disappeared, employment and plant capacity were reduced, and companies were realigned or acquired. The entire industry was wracked by losses except for Komatsu, the second largest producer, half Caterpillar's size, which sells two-thirds of its products in Japan. Redeployment within the industry continued through the balance of the 1980s.

Applications of construction machinery are diverse. They include large construction projects such as dams, airports, and road building; commercial and industrial construction; residential building and forest products industries; oil production and coal mining, which have become less important as energy usage has slowed; and other mining applications.

Seven distinct product lines support these activities. Track-type or crawler tractors were the earliest specialized earthmoving tool and date back to the early years of the century. They are most frequently used with bulldozer blades, although shovel or loader buckets appeared on Caterpillar tractors in 1951. These configurations eventually became a separate product line for small and medium-sized tractors. Motor graders were developed for road construction and maintenance as auto usage spread in the 1920s. The large rubber-tired wheel tractors, which pull scrapers that scoop up earth for removal to another location, were pioneered about World War II and were much improved as the interstate highway program got underway in the mid–1950s. Industrial wheel loaders also were developed in that decade. Another product line, off-highway trucks, appeared about the same time. They are used primarily in open-pit mining but find wide application in heavy construction. Caterpillar did not pioneer any of these lines except the first, but it lagged longest in the introduction of hydraulic excavators, which it did not add until 1972. As a result, it yielded significant market share to other manufacturers in that line.

Since World War II, construction machinery sales have been growing more rapidly abroad than in the United States, and Caterpillar moved to supply a portion of this demand by investing in foreign facilities, most heavily in Europe, Japan, and Brazil. U.S. plants, however, have continued to supply more than half of foreign sales.

At the outset of the 1980s, Caterpillar strategy could be described by the following three guiding principles: (1) to provide users with quality products, in terms of superior design, reliability and durability, (2) to offer a full product line, especially for large-scale construction, open-pit mining, logging, and other target markets, and (3) to provide excellent parts and service support worldwide through independent dealers. Its 192 dealers now have facilities at 1,151 locations throughout the world, employ more people than Caterpillar does, and have invested net worth approaching Caterpillar's $4.5 billion. Parts availability worldwide is promised within forty-eight hours. As a result, its lead is still a commanding one. Only one or two of its competitors approach its comprehensiveness in products and none has comparable global distribution and after-sales support.

Komatsu exported its first tractors to the United States in 1967. Its bridgehead was expanded in 1983 when it added five additional product lines to the crawler tractors and loaders it had marketed earlier. In 1985, Komatsu announced the establishment of manufacturing operations in Tennessee, and it acquired a plant in England closed by Caterpillar, which it has expanded. During 1982–84, it gained market share outside Japan, not by massive percentages as was the case in automobiles, but the establishment of distribution channels and manufacturing facilities may prove troubling to its competitors in the future. Late in 1988, Komatsu and Dresser formed a fifty-fifty joint venture to pool their manufacturing and distribution facilities in the Western Hemisphere, adding to Komatsu's American capability. In Europe, its presence was enhanced by the acquisition of a controlling interest in Hanomag, one of the larger components of the bankrupt (1983) IBH Holdings.

Other companies in the industry hunkered down, went bankrupt, consolidated, and formed joint ventures until the seven major firms in the industry evolved as they are today. These seven—three heavy machinery

Table 6.1
Estimated Shares of World Construction Machinery Sales, 1989

```
Caterpillar (incl. Cat Mitsubishi)    44%
Komatsu                               20
Case-IH                                8
Deere                                  5
VME Group (Clark-Volvo)                5
Dresser                                4
FiatGeotech                            4

Total of seven                        90
```

manufacturers, two primarily in farm machinery, and two chiefly automotive—probably account for 90 percent of industry sales, as shown in
Table 6.1.

Dresser acquired the construction machinery business of International
Harvester in 1982, after it had suffered substantial losses in 1980–81. Once
second to Caterpillar, Harvester had declined by 1981 to sixth in the industry. Dresser also acquired WABCO in 1984, another distressed company
primarily engaged in making off-highway trucks. In addition to construction
machinery, Dresser's product line embraces a full range of mining equipment, including power shovels and air compressors, sometimes used by
contractors.

Case and Deere concentrate their efforts in the small and medium-sized
lines of construction machinery, making use of some components used in
farm equipment. Case now ranks third in the industry and has done particularly well with its hydraulic excavators and backhoes. Deere formed a
joint venture with Hitachi in 1988 to produce hydraulic excavators, to
develop and make wheel loaders, and to distribute backhoes made by Deere
in Japan.

Clark Equipment and Volvo of Sweden formed a fifty-fifty joint venture
for their construction and mining machinery businesses in 1985. Fiat and
Allis Chalmers (AC) initiated a joint venture in construction machinery in
1974 with Fiat owning the controlling share. Fiat acquired the last remaining
AC interest in 1985. By then, its American and British plants had been
closed.

Caterpillar also competes extensively in the diesel engine and gas turbine
businesses, including engines for on-highway trucks in which the leader is
Cummins. It competes, too, in the market for industrial lift trucks, in which
the Japanese and Koreans have made major incursions. These two product
lines, which constitute almost one-quarter of Caterpillar sales, also experienced serious adversity in the 1980s.

CATERPILLAR'S RESPONSE

Caterpillar's immediate reaction to the market collapse was to cut production schedules and reduce employment approximately 40 percent, largely in U.S. operations. A 22 percent cost reduction program was instituted and almost achieved in three years, a year ahead of schedule. Later, price reductions and discounting, plant restructuring, and other measures were adopted. In the meantime, steps to conserve cash were taken.

Competition from Komatsu

Effective competition and the increasing foreign exchange value of the dollar placed Caterpillar under greater pressure as the downturn in sales intensified during 1982. In the decade ending that year, Caterpillar had raised its prices an average of more than 10 percent annually, opening an opportunity for Komatsu, which had carefully controlled its costs and improved its product line, especially when the yen depreciated against the dollar from 1980 to 1985. Caterpillar commenced meeting price competition in 1983 and reduced its prices 8 percent in 1984 and 1985. When exchange rates reversed the situation, the company was able to raise its prices again, to the earlier levels, by late 1987. These price actions were clearly necessary to avoid a more serious erosion in market share.

Actually, Caterpillar was not competing effectively against Komatsu even in Japan, where its twenty-year-old joint venture with Mitsubishi Heavy Industries suffered because of higher costs and prices. Caterpillar Mitsubishi's product designs were more expensive to make; the company did not use cheaper non-Mitsubishi suppliers, its inventory costs were higher, and so were its capital costs. Within Japan, Caterpillar is still second to Komatsu by a large margin.

James Abegglen and George Stalk, Jr., observed this in 1985 in their book *Kaisha: The Japanese Corporation*, where they state: "The competition between Caterpillar and Komatsu is among the most intense ever witnessed. At Komatsu, a company slogan is 'Maru C' or encircle Cat. So far, the statistics are in Komatsu's favor."[1] They claim that labor productivity, an advantage for Caterpillar in 1976, was turned into a 50 percent disadvantage by 1982. The new Komatsu Dresser joint venture presents an even greater challenge.

Plant Restructuring

Although weakening sales became apparent in late 1981 and intensified throughout 1982, Caterpillar plans to expand capacity were still being pursued at a rate in excess of 5 percent per year and at a cost of $750 million annually, largely for facilities (85 percent) within the United States. Physical sales volume in 1981, however, already was 10 percent less than the peak in 1978, and by the time the decision was made to reduce capacity in 1983, another 25 percent increment had been added to plant capacity in the interim. Over expansion was evident: Caterpillar management was slow in recognizing the severity of the downturn in its markets.

Decisions were announced from late 1983 to early 1987 to reduce plant space one-third by closing ten plants (all but two in the United States) and by rearranging five others. A second round of cost reduction targets came in early 1986, involving the investment of $1 billion over five years in a manufacturing program called "Plant With a Future" (PWAF), aimed at a further 15 to 20 percent cost reduction. This program includes (1) identification of "core" products to be made by each plant, as opposed to outside purchase, (2) global sourcing to achieve lowest costs, (3) manufacturing space consolidation to promote efficiency and the institution of manufacturing cells to combine similar operations in one location, (4) computer monitoring of groups of machine tools, and (5) a just-in-time inventory system. Results to date are positive but fall short of the 5 percent annual cost reductions that had been anticipated from 1986 to 1989. This is partly due to the exchange rate reversal that increased costs abroad.

Subsequently, the PWAF program has grown to more than $2 billion and has been stretched out through 1992. Start-up costs are higher than estimated, and benefits are not expected to exceed costs of the program before 1991, but ultimately cost savings of 20 percent in manufacturing costs are anticipated. In the meantime, Komatsu is not standing still on cost reduction. With Caterpillar targeting equivalency at approximately 135 to 140 yen to the dollar, apprehension mounted as the dollar appreciated beyond that level in 1990.

Strategy Changes

Several basic policies were changed in response to the difficulties. First, Caterpillar reversed its policy of avoiding the purchase of finished machines for resale. Beginning in 1983, it contracted to buy lift trucks made in South Korea and Norway, hydraulic excavators from West Germany, paving machinery from an Oklahoma firm, articulated off-highway trucks from England, and logging equipment from Canada.

Second, the company began to purchase more parts and components from least-cost sources, foreign as well as domestic, instead of manufacturing its own. The company estimated that by 1990 it would "be making less than half the amount of parts items in-house" than it did in 1980. This outsourcing of parts supplies could lead to conflict with the UAW. Its labor agreements protect a certain base level of jobs in each plant, and the largest plant, in Peoria, has been under that number in recent years.

Third, it broadened its smaller product lines previously left to Case, Deere, and other manufacturers. Models designed for small contractors were expanded in 1985 when the first of a series of backhoe loaders was introduced. In 1987, the company announced the first model in a new line of agricultural tractors. Success in these product lines is uncertain; keen competition has kept profit margins slim, and Caterpillar lacks the ubiquitous distribution of its small-product competitors. Like the billion dollar plant modernization program, the test lies in effective implementation.

In the 1986 labor negotiations, both sides approached the bargaining table more cautiously. In the costly 1982–83 negotiations and strike, the company won an end to the annual wage improvement, an industry pattern since 1954, in exchange for a profit-sharing arrangement. This time, it traded limited job security for more "flexibility in the use of its work force... through a reduction in the number of labor grades and job classifications and by streamlining seniority provisions of the contract," according to the *Second Quarter 1986 Report*. The latest contract settlement in 1988 followed the usual auto industry pattern. Fuller job security and a 3 percent wage increase resulted. Despite the exposure of the construction machinery industry to global competition, and unlike the auto industry's protected position behind Japanese auto export restraints, the UAW persisted in the same pattern settlement for construction machinery.

Perhaps the latest management change will prove to be the most extensive. Caterpillar always has been a highly centralized company with more than three-quarters of its products consisting of construction machinery, and the others are closely related. In 1989, management moved to decentralize responsibility. Initially, fourteen profit centers were announced, primarily organized along product and geographic lines. Greater autonomy was given to newer product divisions such as agricultural, forest, and paving products, as well as older divisions like Europe-Africa-Middle East and Caterpillar Brasil. Later the new CEO Don Fites decided on further subdivisions and the movement of additional staff functions into each profit center. The reorganization has been extensive, and in mid–1990, the company indicated it was having some negative effects on profits. A period may be required for those named to new positions of responsibility to discover what is involved and how to deliver what is expected of them.

Caterpillar's experience illustrates the convergence of many adversities and a company's sluggish reactions to a changed marketing situation, more effective global competition, and exchange rate instability. Business intelligence and contingency planning never work perfectly, but to neglect them is perilous. The requirement for timely adjustment is constant vigilance and accurate surveillance.

One factor that helped Caterpillar measurably in weathering the long ordeal was its inherent financial strength, aided by a tradition of conservative accounting practices. Cash flow from operations was negative only in 1982.

Global Deployment

Traditionally, Caterpillar relied heavily on its ability to supply foreign sales from U.S. sources. During the first half of the 1980s, nearly two-thirds of foreign sales came from U.S. exports. IBM has a similar dependence on foreign sales (approximately one-half of sales are abroad) and has attempted to supply a much higher proportion from sources outside the United States.[2] Consequently, its foreign investments and employment are much higher relatively. In 1989, 90 percent of its foreign sales were supplied from operations within the local currency environment, in contrast to less than half that proportion for Caterpillar. Differences in scale and technology undoubtedly prevent Caterpillar from supplying as high a percentage from local sources, but in recent years it has moved in that direction. It might have benefited by doing so earlier, especially after the breakdown of the fixed exchange rate system in 1973. Its vulnerability to foreign competition once the dollar started to appreciate was demonstrated after 1980.

The question is whether or not Caterpillar's management learned the lesson well enough. In the decade ending in 1983, more than 80 percent of the company's capital expenditures were for U.S. facilities. That changed in the late 1980s by shifting a 10 to 15 percent larger share of capital spending abroad. About one-tenth more of foreign sales are now being supplied from foreign manufacturing sources. Is that enough? When a *Wall Street Journal* reporter investigated the effects of the strengthening dollar in April 1990, after a 30 percent run-up against the yen, he commented: "Caterpillar . . . has become something of a lone wolf among major U.S. companies. In the past ten years, many American corporations have built more overseas factories."[3] Massive shifts abroad in manufacturing capacity would be particularly difficult for Caterpillar, but there are probably ways to gain more flexibility in sourcing if more effort were directed to it. The costs of not having done so have been obvious for ten years and evident for twenty.

Employment and balance-of-payments effects of the recent exchange rate experience are troubling, but they are not within the ability of individual companies to influence if governments choose to ignore them. The future course for U.S. export employment by Caterpillar and other capital goods makers may depend in some cases on the collective bargaining posture of the unions involved and the extent to which they may be prepared to modify industry-wide pattern bargaining in search of more efficient solutions for individual companies. The experience since 1979 has not been encouraging for construction machinery when three of the four principal U.S. manufacturers have been involved in strikes for five months or longer. Even Deere, reputed earlier to have had excellent relationships with the UAW, experienced an extended work stoppage in 1986–87.

Although the U.S. government canceled Caterpillar's sale of 200 pipelayers to the Soviet Union in 1981 (in this case to the benefit of Komatsu), trade restraints did not play a major role in the difficulties of the early 1980s. The protection of the U.S. steel industry has not been helpful to American manufacturers, however; in Caterpillar's case one-tenth of its costs are for steel. Potential restrictions on trade, widely debated in Congress and by presidential candidates in recent years, hold large segments of U.S. exports hostage to possible retaliation.

AN EVALUATION

Will growth return for Caterpillar and the global construction machinery industry? Renewed growth, clearly beyond the peak of the late 1970s, has not been sustained as in earlier times in the company's seven-decade history. Although new highs in sales are likely in the future, they will not recur with frequency until more areas of the world experience faster economic expansion. Resolution of the debt crisis in the less developed countries and the recovery of Eastern Europe should boast construction machinery sales, in particular. In the meantime, the company appears to be taking many of the steps necessary to live successfully in a globally competitive environment.

The labor-management relationship is perplexing. Recent bargaining indicates the UAW is interested in improved job security. The company needs elbow room to deal with foreign competition. If managements and labor unions are willing to find new solutions, hard-won battles of the past need not prevent more efficient bargaining agreements.

Floating exchange rates require flexibility and timely changes in sources of supply. The company may need to move further than it has in adapting to the existing international monetary regime. Neither the U.S. government nor the G–7 nations (United States, Canada, Germany, France, Italy, Japan, and the United Kingdom) exhibit determination in greater exchange rate stability, and the company ought not expect what is unlikely.

Until Caterpillar gets beyond the learning curve in its internal management reorganization, there will be questions about its effectiveness. The creation of profit centers in a diverse organization is appropriate; how far it ought to go, based on the prior experience of those destined to carry it out, calls for the exercise of judgment. If excessive decentralization has to be rolled back after a trial period, the company will be burdened unnecessarily.

Komatsu is now well established around the world and is a force to be reckoned with in the foreseeable future. It will exert an unmistakable influence on prices and profits. Caterpillar's recent return on stockholders' equity has lagged below other periods of good business, and it is probably destined to continue to be less than the 20 percent rate frequently achieved in the past. Since recovering reasonable profitability, the dividend payout has been substantially less than earlier, reflecting the heavy cost of plant modernization and uncertainty about future returns.

Caterpillar exhibits many similarities to Eastman Kodak. Each has been the dominant firm in its industry throughout the world for many decades. Each was blindsided by a skillful Japanese competitor who gained a position as the leading competitive firm globally. Both suffered an extended time of troubles in the 1980s that required extensive restructuring, although Kodak avoided the sizeable losses experienced by Caterpillar. They both face a future with more uncertainties and less market buoyancy than either thought possible a few years ago. These are the sober realities of capital goods in the early 1990s.

NOTES

1. James C. Abegglen and George Stalk, Jr., *Kaisha: The Japanese Corporation* (New York: Basic Books, 1985), p. 117.

2. According to Michael E. Porter, "IBM ... seeks to configure its worldwide production activities so as to achieve a balance of imports and exports in each country." Michael E. Porter, *Competition in Global Industries* (Boston: Harvard Business School Press, 1986), p. 50.

3. Robert L. Rose, "Cat 22: Caterpillar Sees Gains in Efficiency Imperiled by Strength of Dollar," *The Wall Street Journal*, April 6, 1990, p. 1.

7

Cummins: An Independent Tries to Stay on Top

Cummins Engine Company is the world's leading diesel engine manufacturer, competing against an array of integrated truck and engine makers, major automobile companies, and a number of other engine builders. It is unique as a stand-alone engine company, not engaged in any other activity. Cummins management thinks they did it right during the difficult 1980s. They redesigned and expanded the product line, adapting it to new industry conditions. Plants were restructured and other steps taken to lower costs. Prices were lowered to forestall foreign competition in the prime North American market, successfully. Nevertheless, the result has been a profitless prosperity. Sales have doubled in the last ten years, but profits are nil. Like Caterpillar, the first losses since the 1930s occurred, in Cummins's case, in four of the last ten years. Return on stockholders' equity achieved the targeted 15 percent or greater level in only two years early in the decade, and in only three years during the 1970s.

Competition is intense. There are five primary contenders in the U.S. market, eight in Europe, several establishing themselves in North America, and five major Japanese firms, all locked in what is increasingly a global market. Reorganization of the industry has taken place and is continuing. The Japanese manufacturers made a pass at the U.S. truck and engine market and were largely rebuffed. General Motors has all but left the diesel engine business and placed its large truck business in a joint venture with Volvo, in which it accepted a minority position. Prior to joining with GM, Volvo acquired a U.S. truck maker. Early in the 1980s, Daimler-Benz bought another U.S. truck maker. Neither Volvo nor Daimler-Benz uses independent engines in their vehicles abroad, but they have continued to do so in North America. Volvo is forming a joint venture with Renault in Europe, and in 1990 Renault acquired Mack Trucks in the United States. Obviously, the industry is in flux.

Cummins independence is further challenged by the possibility of unfriendly takeovers. Two such threats occurred within a year of one another, beginning late in 1988. The first was removed by the willingness of the founding family to acquire the intruder's stock; the second, by the resolution of pending litigation. After an extended search, the company found three large investors in 1990, each with an interest in the company's products. These concerns, the industry regrouping, and the profit drought raise the question: can an independent producer survive and continue to lead in such a highly competitive situation?

THE NORTH AMERICAN HEAVY-DUTY TRUCK MARKET

In 1989, diesel engine sales by Cummins made up almost two-thirds of their total sales, engine component sales to others constituted 21 percent, and power systems 15 percent. The North American heavy-duty truck engines account for roughly one-third of Cummins's markets. This includes both Cummins's traditional 14-liter engine and a smaller 10-liter engine introduced in the early 1980s. A new line of medium-range engines was added in the early 1980s, along with the power systems business acquired in 1986. These are growing segments of its business, now constituting more than one-third of the total. Cummins also supplies original equipment manufacturers in construction, agricultural, and other machinery businesses, including Case (through its joint venture), Komatsu, and Komatsu Dresser. Its international business is also expanding and now accounts for 38 percent of total sales.

Cummins's traditional and principal market for heavy-duty truck engines in North America is a static and highly volatile market. Before 1980, the use of heavy-duty trucks had grown rapidly because of the shift from gasoline to diesel power to conserve energy, the increasing availability of interstate highways, and several decades of high economic growth. Afterward, these forces were either completed or lacking. Other influences were operating as well. Deregulation of the trucking industry reduced the numbers of independent and owner-operated rigs, and the intensification of competition reduced the payoff from the prestigious, powerful tractors. Preferences shifted toward lighter trucks with less horsepower. The two recessions beginning in 1980 and 1981 brought prolonged reductions in the markets for mining and manufacturing—after which there were fewer goods that required hauling for four to five years. Recovery was not followed by strong growth and the market for heavy trucks remained lackluster. Finally,

Table 7.1
Market Share of Heavy-duty Trucks, 1989

Navistar	24 %
Paccar*	24
Freightliner	16
Mack	13
Volvo-GM	12
Ford	10

*Kenworth and Peterbilt brand names.

Source: Motor Vehicle Manufacturers Association.

Table 7.2
Diesel Engines Used in Class 8 Trucks,* 1989 (Market Share, Percentage)

Cummins	50
Caterpillar	29
Mack	13
Detroit Diesel	7

*Gross vehicular weight more than 33,000 lbs.

Source: Motor Vehicle Manufacturers Association.

the slowdown in the U.S. economy in 1989–1990 brought another plunge in heavy truck sales.

The North American heavy-duty truck engine market is a derived demand, less integrated here with the manufacture of trucks than in Europe or Japan, or than in the supply of smaller trucks in the United States. Diesel engine sales are made to original equipment manufacturers on their merits or because customers demand a particular power plant. This is demonstrated in the accompanying Tables 7.1 and 7.2, where heavy-duty truck and diesel engine market share data for the United States are displayed. Navistar, formerly International Harvester, has been the leading heavy truck maker for many years. After its troubled exit from the construction and farm machinery businesses and its recapitalization in 1986, it had made progress in returning to profitability until the market declined sharply in 1989. It manufactures only a 7-liter medium-sized engine for its own trucks and other users. The larger engines are all supplied by others, principally Cummins and Caterpillar, as Table 7.2 clearly indicates. Navistar is Cummins's largest customer, accounting for approximately 10 percent of sales recently.

Paccar is an assembler of premium quality, heavy-duty trucks, with total sales about three-quarters as large as Navistar. It has maintained growth and profitability despite the difficult years in the heavy truck market. The vast majority of its engines are supplied by Cummins and Caterpillar in roughly equal proportions. Freightliner purchases engines from the three primary suppliers, despite having been owned for ten years by Daimler-

Table 7.3
Cummins and Caterpillar Engine Division, 1985–89 (Millions of Dollars)

	Cummins	Cat*	Cummins/Cat
Sales	14,038	9,181	1.53
Operating Profit	310	850	.36
Depn. & Amort.	572	698	.82
Operating Cash Flow	882	1,548	.57
Capital Spending	811	677	1.20
Ident. Assets 12/89	2,031	2,188	.93

*External engine sales only.

Benz, which has made no move to provide its own engines, contrary to its practice abroad. Mack is a troubled manufacturer, now controlled by Renault. Its policy has been to supply all of its own engines and not to offer them for sale to others. Volvo acquired White in the mid–1980s and joined with GM in 1986 to form the Volvo-GM Heavy Truck Corporation, which it controls. It supplies only a few of its own engines to this venture, as shown in Table 7.2, again contrary to its practice in Europe. Ford buys diesels for heavy trucks from each of the three major domestic suppliers.

Cummins claimed more than half of the heavy-duty truck market for its engines for the nine years ending in 1989. Caterpillar is gaining on Cummins in the overall diesel engine business, not by large proportions, but incrementally and steadily—7 percent faster from 1984 to 1989. Cummins's greatest strength is in the heavy truck market. Each has moved to design smaller engines, but Caterpillar has only one entry in the 6 to 8-liter medium-truck size. Caterpillar is stronger in the engines larger than those used in most heavy trucks, in those employed in large stationary plants, electric generation, and marine installations. The large engine market in North America had traditionally belonged to Caterpillar; Cummins entered it in the 1970s. Half of Caterpillar's engine sales are outside the United States, almost as large as Cummins's sales volume abroad.

The competitive position of Cummins relative to Caterpillar is vulnerable, as the performance data in Table 7.3 reveal. In the last five years, Caterpillar has been able to generate more operating profits from its engine business than has Cummins. Cash flow has also been superior. Although capital spending by the two companies has been differently timed, Caterpillar is investing more in the engine business than is Cummins. Since Cummins has no major projects pending, Caterpillar appears better situated than Cummins in the foreseeable future.

Detroit Diesel's share of the market declined after the first energy crisis in 1973 and continued to worsen into the mid-1980s. Their designs were not as fuel efficient as other manufacturers' engines. Since then it has partially recovered. General Motors sold most of the division to a joint venture effective at the beginning of 1988, 60 percent controlled by the Penske Corporation, a Detroit Diesel dealer and also a large Cadillac dealer and truck-leasing firm. The losses in share by Detroit Diesel were picked up by Cummins and Caterpillar.

Mack's sales have not increased in the last five years, and it has incurred losses in three of these years. Renault had owned 44.5 percent of Mack before its recent purchase of the remaining shares. The acquisition potentially puts it in competition with its new European joint venture partner, Volvo. Mack operates only in Canada and Australia abroad.

Cummins vulnerability from vertical integration in truck manufacture lies with possible moves by foreign producers. In the immediate future that would be Daimler-Benz in a change of policy with Freightliner or Volvo in a similar move, neither of which has been indicated by actions up to the present. Daimler-Benz has brought in some smaller medium-duty truck kits for assembly in the United States, 3,000 to 4,000 annually from Germany and Brazil, but that has been the extent of its market testing.

The Japanese diesel engine manufacturers made an effort to move into the U.S. market in the early 1980s. They enjoyed a substantial price advantage and each manufacturer picked a different customer as a target. Cummins realized it needed to get its costs down and decided to meet the Japanese competition in price in anticipation of its cost reduction program, thereby denying foreign suppliers easy entry. Second, the Japanese introduced cab-over-engine models in the medium-duty range, and one tried to test-market a heavy-duty truck, with little success. Cummins has not been successful in getting as much cost out of its engines as it had hoped—22 percent instead of the 30 percent target. As a result, its profits have been squeezed. Nevertheless, the Japanese threat was forestalled.

The Cummins strategies and results can be summarized briefly. A fifty-fifty joint venture with Case in medium-duty engines was launched in 1981. Cummins provides the designs and manages the joint venture, which now supplies about half of the company's unit sales of engines. Also in the early 1980s, the Cummins licensee in Japan, Komatsu, confirmed that manufacturing costs were 30 percent lower there than in America, underscoring the urgency of its cost reduction efforts. The willingness of the company to meet Japanese prices on its 10 and 14-liter engines and the incomplete results of cost containment depressed profits. In addition, profitability comparable to the large engines has not yet been attained on the medium-range engines. Anticipated lack of growth in the North American heavy-duty truck market led to acquisitions and expansion in the markets for engine components and power systems as a way to find growth.

EUROPEAN AND JAPANESE TRUCK AND ENGINE MAKERS

The Western European market for medium and heavy-duty trucks is larger than that in the United States or Japan, which are roughly equal in numbers. Daimler-Benz is the world's leading manufacturer in these sizes, with approximately one-quarter of the Western European total and 50 to 60 percent of the German market. In 1988, it produced more than 39,000 heavy-duty trucks in Germany. Until recently when it bought some Cummins engines, Daimler-Benz had never offered any but its own engines in Mercedes-Benz trucks. Its largest foreign subsidiary is in Brazil. Recent moves have included an attempt to acquire the state-owned Spanish truck company (ENASA), actually bought by the Italian firm, Iveco; the beginning of a co-production arrangement with the state-owned East German VEB IFA Kombinat Nutzfahrzeuge; and an emerging relationship with Mitsubishi Motors. Up to now, Daimler-Benz and Volvo have sold only token quantities of trucks in Japan.

Volvo and SAAB-Scania of Sweden are in the heavy end of the European truck market. Among the European manufacturers, Volvo is thought to be the most technologically advanced in engine design. If the joint venture with Renault announced in 1990 develops as planned, together the group could be larger than Daimler-Benz. Renault leads in the truck markets in France, Spain, and Portugal, and Volvo has found its best markets among the northern European countries.

Iveco (Fiat) had been in second place through 1989, not too far behind Daimler-Benz in heavy truck production, with about one-fifth of the market. DAF of the Netherlands acquired British Leyland trucks in 1987 and is a buyer of Cummins engines. In Germany, MAN makes trucks and engines, and Klockner-Humboldt-Deutz supplies engines. These eight European manufacturers have dominated the markets in their home countries of Germany, France, Italy, and Sweden. Only the United Kingdom, among the large markets, has been relatively open to outside competition. Three of the top four also have established beachheads in the U.S. heavy truck market, as noted earlier.

The five Japanese engine and truck manufacturers—Nissan, Mitsubishi Motors, Isuzu, Hino Motors, and Komatsu—have had their own domestic market largely to themselves. After the failed attempt to assault the U.S. diesel engine business, Cummins cut the research and development access of its licensee, Komatsu, and acquired the sales company distributing Cummins's products in Japan. Komatsu appears to have been chastened by the experience and now buys engines for its U.S. joint venture from Cummins as well as a portion of its European requirements. None of the Japanese makers has scored in the U.S. heavy truck or engine business, although they remain a threat.

Probably Cummins and Caterpillar have a technical advantage on other engine manufacturers in meeting the increasingly stringent U.S. environmental controls effective in 1991, 1994, and possibly 1998. Only these companies supply their own fuel injection pumps, and the new standards will necessitate electronic fuel systems. European standards are being formulated, and their certainty has stimulated research and development efforts. Costs for developing and implementing the emerging requirements will be substantial and offer another opportunity for innovative advantage. Current cost estimates are in the 12 to 15 percent range for the addition of electronic systems that may offer a small or partial offset through improved fuel efficiency.

SMALLER ENGINES AND POWER SYSTEMS

In recognition of the increasing stability of the heavy-duty truck market and the preference for lighter, more fuel-efficient engines, Cummins decided in the late 1970s to move into midrange engines. In 1979, Case approached Cummins regarding a joint venture for medium-duty engines, which would provide for Case's needs in powering agricultural and construction machinery. The joint venture agreement establishing the Consolidated Diesel Company was signed the following year. Cummins's first 6-liter B engine was produced in 1983, and the 8-liter C engine came two years later. The engines have been well received by users.

In 1989, more than 100,000 of these engines were sold to more than 800 customers. Freightliner selected these two series to power a new line of midrange trucks. The smaller B series was selected by Chrysler to power the Dodge Ram pickup truck, and Blue Bird, the largest U.S. manufacturer of school buses, made the B series its exclusive power source. The larger C series has been engineered for use in the "Baby 8" trucks increasingly popular for highways tractors. In 1990, Ford indicated that it would soon begin using Cummins medium-duty engines. Obviously, the company has found an opportunity for sales growth.

Early in 1986, Cummins acquired 63 percent of the stock of Onan Corporation, a manufacturer of electric generator sets, small gasoline and diesel engines, and electrical control equipment. The new subsidiary assumed responsibility for combining the larger Cummins engines with generators as well. It was grouped together with McCord Heat Transfer Corporation, acquired the year before, and Cummins Electronics, also organized in 1985, and three other subsidiaries to form the rapidly growing Power Systems Group. The manufacturing capability of McCord has been improved and a minority interest traded to a German company in exchange for licenses for use of that company's technology in diesel engine cooling components.

Power systems and smaller engines are the most rapidly expanding product lines at Cummins. Since 1986 power systems has been growing more than half again as fast as engine sales and total revenues, and the medium-duty engines have increased at approximately 50 percent annually since production began. They will not continue to grow at that rate, but it demonstrates how well Cummins has done with its new engines, which have a way to go before exhausting their full potential. Cummins's challenge is to improve profit margins on them. Together, these products now account for more than one-third of Cummins sales.

COMPONENTS GROUP

Although the Components Group also was established in 1986, its four principal subsidiaries have supplied components to Cummins for many years. These are engine remanufacturing, Holset turbochargers, Fleetguard filters, and Atlas crankshafts, camshafts and gears. Four smaller component companies also have been organized, including Combustion Technologies in piston rings. An acquisition in 1985 expanded Cummins's piston ring business. Cummins's customers for components are the dealers and the other diesel engine manufacturers, including Volvo, Renault, Iveco, SAAB-Scania, Detroit Diesel, and Caterpillar to a small extent. The initial target is to generate 80 percent of component sales externally, and by 1989 the company was achieving 76 percent of sales to outside users.

Cummins claims it obtains good profit margins on its component business, which constitutes approximately one-fifth of its total volume, and expresses confidence that the group has growth potential. Since establishing it as a separate group in 1986, however, sales increases have lagged the engine and power systems business. Obviously, these are not stand-alone businesses, and depend on a close interchange between engine design, need, and component capability to maintain superiority in the marketplace. Engine remanufacturing (Diesel Recon), a service to users and dealers that generates parts business and prolongs engine life, is by far the largest of these component activities.

THE STRUGGLE TO STAY INDEPENDENT

Lackluster profits, or more accurately, the absence of profits during the last five years, has threatened Cummins with the loss of independence. During much of this time, Cummins stock has traded below book value, although on average it has been priced at a little more than book value. This has led to considerable investor scrutiny and management insecurity. Stockholding is highly concentrated with present management owning only limited amounts. Recently, five institutional investors have owned 40 to 50 percent of the outstanding stock. The resulting situation constituted a volatile ownership and control exposure for the company. Two takeover possibilities developed in late 1988 and 1989, each acquirer professing to be holding the stock for investment purposes.

In response to the question, what would one of these holders do with the company if they gained control, the answer is fairly direct. Immediate profits could be improved through reduced research and development, investment, and other expenditures. The company would be attractive for resale to a manufacturer interested in a strong North American market position, namely Ford, Komatsu, Daimler-Benz, or Volvo-GM. Other possibilities would be logical as well, such as acquisition by the Case IH division of Tenneco. (Navistar had expressed an interest in acquiring Mack if Renault had been willing to relinquish its large minority holding.)

Late in 1988, the U.S. subsidiary of Hanson PLC of London had acquired an 8.3 percent stake in Cummins. Subsequently, it added another half of one percent to its holdings. While Hanson indicated that the holding was for "investment," customers and employees of Cummins became concerned. In July 1989, three members of the Miller family, including the past chairman and founder of the company, paid $5 million more than the prevailing market price to acquire the Hanson stock. In exchange, the company gave the Millers a combination of notes and preferred stock for the Hanson stock and their own 5 percent stake, maturing in five years and yielding 10 percent, convertible to common stock at a 30 percent premium to the market value at the time. Some analysts thought the buyback was less sacrificial than it was represented as being.[1] Cummins supported the arrangement with a written opinion from its investment adviser. At any rate, the relief was short.

Within two weeks, a second investor revealed a 9.9 percent stake in Cummins. This time the acquirer was a Hong Kong subsidiary of Brierley Investments Ltd. of New Zealand, controlled by Sir Ronald Brierley. The holding was later expanded to 14.9 percent. Cummins sued and Brierley's firm counter-sued in federal court. After some initial sparring, the two firms reached a standstill agreement ten months later in which Brierley agreed not to expand its stake, to vote its shares for the election of directors in the proportion that other votes are cast, and to give Cummins the right to buy back any large blocks of stock it might wish to sell.[2]

There was still another chapter. In mid–1990, Ford and Tenneco each bought a 10.8 percent equity interest in the company, and Kubota, a Japanese maker of farm and construction machinery, acquired a 5.4 percent share. Moreover, they paid 22 percent more than the prevailing market price. Ford will purchase medium-duty truck engines from Cummins, possibly phasing out its own engine production. Tenneco is already half owner of the joint venture with Cummins for making medium-duty engines—the supplier of its Case IH division. Kubota hopes to set up a joint venture in Europe with Cummins to supply it with engines for construction equipment. Ford and Tenneco gained board seats, and Ford was given a six-year option to buy another 10 percent of stock at 20 percent over the market price and to gain another board seat. Cummins agreed not to sell voting shares to other car or truck makers unless Ford lowered its holding by more than one-third. Some of the proceeds were used to buy back the founding family's preferred shares and return them to their position prior to the Hanson deal, removing that as a possible embarrassment.[3] A coup for Henry Schacht, the CEO?

The immediate crisis of control for management passed once more, but the costs have weakened the company financially while the concentration in ownership continues. Shareholders' equity as a percentage of total liabilities and shareholders' investment declined from 40 percent at the end of 1987 to 20 percent in 1989. Because of the exchange of debt for equity and the losses of the last four years, the book value of Cummins's stock declined by 47 percent. That situation was altered again in 1990 with the injection of additional equity funds and the retirement of some debt.

Is the company's strategy adequate and will it work? It is easier to commend Cummins for maintaining its position in the engine market relative to vertically integrated truck or tractor manufacturers than to excuse its financial performance in the last decade. The two need to go hand in hand. Investor impatience is understandable. The Japanese were forestalled in gaining a position in the U.S. market by alert price action. Market position was maintained by a timely redesign of heavy truck engines. What did not follow, however, was the anticipated cost reduction, which fell short of its target.

How much of Cummins's pain was self-inflicted is hard to judge with precision, but careful attention to its chief U.S. competitor, Caterpillar, may suggest a clue. Both of the companies have taken their lumps during the 1980s and instituted cost reduction programs. Caterpillar has been more successful as its engine performance data (shown in Table 7.3) indicate. Between 1979 and 1989, Cummins sales per employee relative to that for Caterpillar declined by 10 percent.

Cummins has done much that is commendable. Its products are well engineered and accepted, and it has demonstrated sensitivity in meeting the needs of customers. Some of its independence has been surrendered to Ford and Tenneco in the sale of stock to them. It will lose more of its independence unless it can attain greater manufacturing efficiency and achieve improved profitability.

NOTES

1. Alison Leigh Cowan, "Purchase of Cummins Stake Looks Less Sacrificial Now," *The New York Times*, February 22, 1990, p. C1. The article points out that the Millers gained a higher yield and protection from loss with the sacrifice of some gain—in effect a put option.

2. Alison Leigh Cowan, "Cummins Thwarts Latest Threat," *The New York Times*, May 11, 1990, p. C1.

3. James P. Miller, "Cummins to Sell a 25% Stake to Three Firms," *The Wall Street Journal*, July 16, 1990, p. A3; Alison Leigh Cowan, "Ford and Cummins in Pact to Strengthen Relationship," *The New York Times*, July 28, 1990, p. 29.

8

CINCINNATI MILACRON: HOW THE UNITED STATES LOST MACHINE TOOL LEADERSHIP

Ten years ago, Cincinnati Milacron was still the leading machine tool company in the world, a position it held for several decades. By then, its leadership and that of the U.S. machine tool industry had eroded seriously. Milacron sales fell 40 percent from 1981 to 1983 and have not yet regained their former level. Losses occurred in three years during the 1980s and by the end of the decade there were almost a dozen machine tool builders larger than it was. In a sense, Milacron is a microcosm of the problems U.S. capital goods firms have faced in the last ten to twenty years. Like other capital goods industries, machine tools have increasingly been subjected to global competition, and for a variety of reasons, U.S. firms have lost position. Nowhere is this clearer than in machine tools, although it is more evident to the public in automobiles and consumer electronics. Machine tools, however, are at the heart of what Americans had done well since the nineteenth century.

Machine tools are used in all types of manufacturing industries that involve the cutting or forming of metals. Loss of position in the tools that perform these operations is more than symbolic of what has happened to American fortunes in a broad spectrum of manufacturing. Notwithstanding problems with currency translation, the state of various economies, and alternate material usage, the data in Table 8.1 unmistakably show the major changes that have taken place in the source of world machine tool production and exports.[1] A diffusion of the industry away from the dominant American position following World War II was to be expected. Japanese government and industry policies resulted in the production and export

Table 8.1
World Machine Tool Industry

		U.S.	JAPAN	GERM.	ITALY	SWIT.	U.K.
Production	1955	40.4	0.6	14.1	1.8	3.3	8.7
% of World	1974	16.9	13.1	17.9	6.2	3.9	4.0
	1988	6.6	23.0	17.3	7.0	4.9	4.0
Exports	1955	22.7	0.5	24.5	2.6	10.0	10.5
% of World	1974	8.4	6.4	33.2	6.5	8.2	4.5
	1988	4.4	18.9	23.6	7.6	9.4	4.0
Net Trade	1962	113	(143)	271	(46)	58	4
Balance	1974	140	133	1432	64	322	10
Millions $	1988	(1290)	2877	2803	603	1243	(45)

Source: National Machine Tool Builders' Association, *American Machinist*, February 1990.

Note: Percentages and balances calculated; deficit balances shown in parentheses.

surge in the 1970s and 1980s. West Germany led in world production in the 1960s and 1970s and continues to lead in exports, chiefly within Europe. Italy now produces more than the United States does, and exports from Italy and Switzerland in each case exceed those from America. U.S. imports now are more than 80 percent of domestic production and the largest portion comes from Japan. Japan, on the other hand, imports less than 7 percent of its machine tools.

Such drastic changes obviously exceed anything that Cincinnati Milacron or any other individual American tool maker did or failed to do. The MIT Commission on Industrial Productivity pointed to the following reasons for the competitive failure of the U.S. machine tool industry: (1) the industry did not understand what was happening to it until it was too late to fashion appropriate responses, (2) sufficient user involvement in product innovation was lacking, (3) engineering and business schools did not emphasize manufacturing technology, (4) export orientation was needed to build volume and customer responsiveness as the industry became more international in scope, (5) short-term profit orientation was harmful, and (6) several critical goofs occurred—for example, government development efforts aimed at military rather than business markets, the large makers of controls failed to move into solid state devices on a timely basis, and builders did not realize that costs come from design decisions rather than from labor.[2] These and other causes of the industry's decline, in addition to Milacron's own story, are analyzed in this chapter.

The industry is small in size and the firms had tended to be small to medium-sized enterprises, often family firms. The entire U.S. industry would rank no larger than approximately the one hundredth company in the Fortune 500.[3] Products include lathes, milling machines, drills, presses, grinding and gear cutting machines, together with the controls that automate their operation. In the past twenty-five years, users have moved from stand-alone machines to clusters of numerically controlled (NC) machines working in cells, and on to computer numerically controlled (CNC) machines within flexible manufacturing systems (FMS). Robots are found primarily in welding, painting, and material handling applications. Concentration is fairly high within the industry, despite the many small firms, because of the large numbers of specialized machines and customized systems.

CINCINNATI MILACRON AND THE U.S. INDUSTRY

Cincinnati Milacron was founded in 1884 and was led for most of its history by three generations of the Geier family until a nonfamily officer was elected CEO in 1990. The Geier family, employees, and retired employees still own a controlling interest in the company. According to a ranking by the number of wage earners in 1942, Milacron (then the Cincinnati Milling Machine Company) was already the leading U.S. machine tool company—a position it held in most subsequent years—until recent mergers increased the revenues of two firms that produce traditional metalworking machines, which are often used to define the industry.

In Milacron's case, size also was combined with progressiveness and technical leadership. Its product line spanned a wide range of typical offerings by the industry, it mounted the largest research and development program, and it had established the most extensive European manufacturing network.[4] It designed a control unit in 1955, built a manufacturing plant for controls and introduced a machining center in 1967, and developed a prototype flexible manufacturing system in 1968—all early sorties into these technologies. By 1975 half of its machines sold were numerically controlled and 10 percent computer numerically controlled. It had already moved into making machines for processing composite materials and plastics and soon moved into robotics.[5] Unfortunately, these early efforts in advanced technology were not enough to claim global leadership in the 1980s.

Markets for machine tools are found in a cross section of primarily metalworking industries, including automobiles, aircraft, electrical and electronic equipment, machinery of all types, and fabricated metal products, among others. These were the industries most seriously affected by the prolonged recession of the early 1980s and the reduced investment spending associated with slower economic growth. The rising dollar eroded export markets and invited import competition. The prominent position of the automobile industry in machine tool markets, often accounting for 40 to 50 percent of some types of tools like robots, and the declining position of the U.S. auto industry meant lower demand from that source. When foreign companies, especially the Japanese, built U.S. plants to hedge the possibility of being closed out by protectionist measures, they usually invested heavily in machine tools from the home country. The result was that U.S. machine tool output and sales plunged as the 1981–82 recession deepened, by more than half from their peak levels, and never recovered fully.

Other longer term mistakes that have affected U.S. machine tool makers adversely preceded the 1980s. The MIT investigation found weak user pull and low user sophistication in America compared to Japanese and European manufacturers.[6] Users allowed their installed base of machines to age relative to those in other countries. In particular, they were slow to adopt NC and CNC machines. For example, these machines represented only 5 percent of the installed base in the United States in 1983, in contrast to 30 percent in Japan about the same time.[7] The use of machine tools supplied by a variety of makers complicated the situation in the United States as NC and CNC machines proliferated. Rather than having one or a few suppliers of controls as the Japanese did, a dozen different systems developed in America, which led to confusion among users and resistance to adoption. In addition, "the two major domestic manufacturers of controls, GE and Allen-Bradley, were not especially responsive to either the builders or end users, and kept building very sophisticated controls."[8] Both missed the movement into solid state controls on a timely and cost-efficient basis.

MIT also found that the U.S. machine tool builders themselves had lagged in making investments in the newer technologies, not a favorable testimony to an understanding of the competitive importance of manufacturing process innovation. At the time of the study, they found that only two, Milacron and Ingersoll, had installed the latest technology—flexible machining cells and systems.[9] Engineering and business schools as well as manufacturers failed to emphasize improvements in manufacturing process as important during the last twenty-five years, turning instead to product innovation and theoretical concepts.[10]

The industry's loss of international competitive position was evident prior to the contraction of the early 1980s. Imports began to exceed exports in the late 1970s. By the mid–1980s, they were three times the level of exports, a change in the position of the industry perhaps more dramatic than any except in some consumer electronic product lines. The consequences were sobering and debilitating for U.S. tool makers.

As a result of the trauma of the 1980s, Milacron went through two restructurings during the decade, the last of which was not yet completed by 1990. Restructuring, reorganization, and termination benefits for separated employees cost more than the losses incurred during the decade. Profits exceeded losses by only a quarter for the entire decade. Dividends were maintained at the 1981 rate through the four years they were not earned, which along with the losses resulted in a one-third reduction in shareholders' equity from the end of 1981 to 1989—43 percent on a per share basis. As a consequence, the debt-to-equity ratio rose substantially, from 48 percent to 110 percent in 1987, but it was pared back to 86 percent by 1989. The first restructuring was aimed at closing unneeded plants and reducing employment by 46 percent; the second, rationalized manufacturing in "focus factories" devoted to a single product line, as opposed to multiproduct plants that had been operated earlier. This brought further employment reductions and improvements in labor productivity.

Among three efforts at diversification during the last twenty years, one has been successful. A chemical subsidiary was sold in 1980. A venture in semiconductor materials was expanded as late as the mid–1980s, but was sold to a Japanese company in 1989 after growth in silicon wafer sales failed to materialize. The successful diversification has been in plastics machinery, which has grown from 14 percent of sales in 1981 to 34 percent in 1989, and has provided a disproportionately large share of operating earnings in recent years. One other expansion into laser cutting machines in 1986 proved to be a mistake and was sold to a British machine tool company in 1990. The trial was indeed brief, although the company deemed the losses encountered as disproportionate to the technology's potential.

Milacron announced the sale in 1990 of its robotics unit to ABB Robotics, a subsidiary of Asea Brown Boveri. The company had started making robots in 1977, built a plant in South Carolina two years later, and became a major supplier of welding robots in the United States. The operation failed to generate adequate profits, however, and Milacron moved to concentrate its efforts on its core businesses—machine tools, plastics machinery, and industrial supplies. IBM, GE, and Westinghouse had left the robot business earlier.

The failure of U.S. machine tool firms to pursue foreign businesses more aggressively when they could have done so is viewed as another strategic mistake. When the dollar was depreciating in the 1970s, many firms apparently viewed foreign markets as worthy of pursuit only during U.S. business downturns and less attention was devoted to them in the good years at home. This attitude reflects the small size and provincial nature of many machine tool builders. While Milacron was better positioned abroad than other U.S. firms, it too took advantage of downward adjustments in the dollar during the 1970s to close its French and German manufacturing operations. The British facilities were consolidated in the early 1980s. After reaching a peak in sales abroad in 1980, Milacron's foreign business was flat, aside from cyclical fluctuations. The volume has been modest for a company long involved outside the United States—19 percent of sales during the 1980s. Like many other U.S. manufacturers, Milacron admitted, "We ignored the Japanese in machine tools, and now it's late; our attitude has changed, and we're trying not to let the same thing happen in plastics."[11]

Table 8.2
U.S. Machine Tool Builders' Sales (Millions of Dollars)

Company	1985	1986	1987	1988	1989
Cincinnati Milacron	732	845	824	851	851
Acme-Cleveland 9/30	214	186	177	176	191
Cross & Trecker 9/30	404	401	424	431	457
Esterline 10/31	254	236	260	284	284
Giddings & Lewis	176	135	125	169	233
Gleason	162	179	137	116	162
Litton 7/31	350	311	413	600	730
Monarch	80	66	74	91	97
Total of eight	2372	2359	2434	2718	3005

FANUC has been licensed since 1984 to jointly develop and build injection molding machines in Japan, and Daewoo was licensed to make three models in South Korea in 1986.

Roughly 500 U.S. firms are involved in machine tool building, although many of them are small, and the top dozen account for well over half of the business. The eight largest publicly owned companies are shown in Table 8.2, which omits several sizeable privately held companies, including Ingersoll, Kingsbury, and Bridgeport, and several other firms that have disappeared into larger companies, such as Ex-Cell-O, which was acquired by Textron in 1985. Mergers and rearrangements have been extensive, and a considerable number have closed. The traditional industry classification, including only new metalworking machine sales, is both arbitrary and too restrictive, since most firms perform a significant volume of rework, and the movement into plastic and composite machines, as Milacron has done, is both evolutionary and wise.

Foreign subsidiary and joint venture firms have had an increasing presence in the United States, especially since the implementation of protectionist measures in 1986. The Japanese are most extensively represented by manufacturing establishments. Some of the larger and early ones were Yamasaki Mazak (1974), Leblond Makino (1979), Hitachi Seiki (1980), and Okuma and Komatsu (both 1986). The number of Japanese machine tool firms with operations in the United States doubled from seventeen before 1987 to thirty-six by 1990 immediately following the voluntary export restraint agreement adopted by the Japanese at the end of 1986.[12] FANUC established its fifty-fifty joint ventures with GM in robotics in 1982 and with GE in controls in 1986. The Germans are represented by Trumpf and the Swiss by Oerlikon Buhrle.

JAPANESE MACHINE TOOL BUILDERS

The largest machine tool industry exists in Japan and fourteen companies account for almost two-thirds of total production approaching $9 billion, three times that in the United States.[13] Among the twelve largest firms in the world, nine are Japanese, and three American. The existence of such a large Japanese presence in this industry is the result of deliberate government policy formulated in collaboration with the industry. Japanese machine tool builders were protected by import and foreign investment restraints during the formative years from 1950 to the 1970s. The concentration of small firms into about seventy builders was fostered by MITI with the directive that they cease production of a tool if it accounted for less than 5 percent of domestic industry sales and 20 percent of its own sales. This also encouraged specialization within the firms by product. Several were affiliated with large enterprises: FANUC (Fujitsu, computers), Toyoda (Toyota, automobiles), Komatsu (construction machinery), and Toshiba Machine (Toshiba, computers and electronics). The Japanese government provided substantial research and development subsidies in the 1970s when the export drive began.[14]

Although U.S. builders had been in the forefront of early numerical control development for machine tools, the Japanese took the lead in its widespread application and use. MITI encouraged FANUC as a sole supplier of NC/CNC and the industry avoided the proliferation of different standards that impeded U.S. adoption. FANUC became the source of 80 to 90 percent of Japanese controls, it stayed with standard designs by refusing to customize, and it moved promptly into solid state technology as it became available.[15] MITI set a target for half of machine tool output to be numerically controlled by 1980, and this was achieved almost a decade earlier than in the United States. Standard computer numerically controlled lathes and machining centers became the basis for the export push into the U.S. market, and it was successful. By the 1980s, FANUC had 40 to 50 percent of the control market worldwide, and Siemens and GE joined it through joint ventures.[16] Once established, the Japanese penetration of the U.S. market continued to grow despite the 86 percent appreciation of the yen from 1985 through 1988.

Another seven-year MITI project begun in 1976 involved nine machine tool, seven electronics, and four heavy machinery firms in a $60 million research and development effort to expand the use of flexible manufacturing systems in small and medium-sized firms. One advantage of Japanese machine tool firms is the extent of their own adoption of flexible machining systems within their manufacturing operations and another is the permeation of these tools throughout Japanese manufacturing. The MIT Commission expects that the result of Japanese mastery of the high-end systems will be to challenge both the Europeans, who have specialized at that end of the product spectrum, and also the U.S. builders from Japanese-owned U.S. plants.[17]

The development of robotics is of particular interest because of the minimal role played by the Japanese government in its emergence, in marked contrast to the machine tool industry as a whole.[18] The surge in Japanese robotics manufacture in the early 1970s with labor union cooperation led to robotics usage in Japan greatly exceeding that elsewhere. In 1984, there were four and one-half times as many robots in use in Japan as in the United States, and five years later there were more than five times as many. FANUC became the largest global producer with 10 percent of its $1.1 billion sales, exclusive of its GE Fanuc Automation and GM Fanuc Robotics production outside Japan. U.S. imports of robots, largely from Japan, dwarfed domestic production in 1989. The only foreign firms that are factors in the Japanese robotics market are Asea Brown Boveri and, until 1990, Cincinnati Milacron.

THE GERMAN AND EUROPEAN INDUSTRY

West German production of machine tools recently has been more than two and one-half times that in the United States, Italian output has been slightly larger, and Swiss and British production together has been about one-third larger. The West German market for machine tools is roughly equal to that in the United States. Most of its machine tool firms are privately owned, and there are approximately 400 of them, almost as many as in America. Next to Japan, West Germany has been the second largest source of U.S. imports. The Western European market is by far the largest in the world and is likely to continue to be for the foreseeable future. East Germany in the past was the chief source of imported tools for the East Bloc countries. No attempt is made to discuss Eastern European production or markets because of the lack of data and the incomprehensibility of what is available because of quality differences and currency translation problems. However, it is reported that almost half of West German tool exports, excluding those to East Germany, were destined for East Bloc countries.[19]

The German industry gained its leadership at the upper end of machine complexity, especially in gear-cutting, grinding, and metal-forming machines.[20] In the mid–1980s, German firms were selling more than half of the world's gear-cutting machines, more than one-third of the grinders, and one-third of the metal-forming machines. Their success is partly attributed to German user interest in manufacturing processes. The MIT Commission refers to the argument of Dr. E. M. Merchant, long affiliated with Milacron as director of research, that user sophistication is one of the significant differentiating factors between the German and American industries. Another highly important factor is the extent to which training and research facilities are available within Germany. Twenty universities have research institutes for machine tools, and thirty-four Fraunhofer Institutes exist for applied research and advanced training.

The Fiat subsidiary, Comeau, is the largest machine tool maker in Europe, and more than half of its sales are to other Fiat companies. Because of its automaker tie, it engages in the production of robots. The Italian and Swiss builders are extensively involved in export business, in each case roughly twice the volume of U.S. exports.

The British industry has fared somewhat better than the U.S. industry, but it has done less well than the other three leading European countries. In 1964, the Labor government embarked on an industrial policy to encourage the consolidation of machine tool firms to make them more competitive internationally.[21] The result was almost disastrous. By the mid–1960s, Alfred Herbert became the world's largest machine tool firm as a collection of separately operated enterprises. It had to be taken over by the government in 1975 to avoid bankruptcy and was liquidated in 1982. As a result of the government's action, the industry became much more concentrated. Today it is largely self-sufficient with exports balancing imports.

FROM FIRST TO THIRD: IS A TURNAROUND POSSIBLE?

The U.S. machine tool industry is now a distant third compared to the European (or even German) or the Japanese industry. While no precise count is available, estimates indicate that at least one-quarter of the firms in the domestic industry left during the 1980s. Purchases of machine tools are now more than half dependent on imports. The MIT Commission on Industrial Productivity speaks of "the collapse of the domestic industry" and says "the industry is dissolving."[22] The following discussion describes several steps taken by the government and by the industry, collectively and individually. The chapter concludes with comments on Milacron and two other firms in response to the question posed in the section title.

The Kennedy Round tariff reductions were completed in 1967 and implemented over the next five years, bringing U.S. machine tool tariffs down to 7.5 percent. The Japanese export push of standard numerically controlled machines began soon afterward and succeeded in penetrating the U.S. market, as described earlier. This was followed by appeals from U.S. companies for fairness or protection, depending on interpretation. When Houdaille Industries, then said to be one of the top fifteen U.S. firms, charged violation of its patents and licenses, it was directed by a federal court to send an attorney to Japan to seek evidence. Japan refused to provide a visa for the attorney.[23] This led Houdaille to file a petition with the U.S. Representative for Trade Negotiations in 1982 charging the Japanese with discrimination against U.S. trade, among other accusations, and requesting that U.S. investment tax credits be rendered inapplicable to Japanese machine tools. After lengthy discussions and several studies, the administration took no action and declined an offer of a voluntary restraint agreement by the Japanese. As a result, Houdaille terminated its machine tool business.

More than three and one-half years later at the end of 1986, voluntary restraint agreements with Japan and Taiwan were announced in response to a 1983 request from the National Machine Tool Builders' Association based on national security concerns. The Japanese agreement cut computer numerically controlled machine tool imports by approximately one-fifth over a five-year period, the Taiwanese agreement provided half as large a reduction, and the government imposed restrictions on German and Swiss imports as well. Seven other countries were warned about possible action if they took advantage of the restraints. These agreements expire in 1992.

As a result of machine tool shortages during both World War II and the Korean War and the complex needs of the aircraft industry, the Department of Defense took an active interest in procurement and research during the 1950s and 1960s. These efforts were not helpful in strengthening the industry in commercial markets; they probably had a contrary effect. A problem arose because of the sophisticated nature of Air Force machining requirements and the vested interest that developed in the early numerically controlled tools to meet its needs. This detracted from the evolution of simpler NC approaches by the absorption of talent and the devotion of resources to highly complex systems for aircraft and automobile manufacturers. Things might have worked out differently if the commercial development by individual companies had not led to a cacophony of incompatible approaches and if the two larger U.S. control makers had not been wedded to their own complex systems.[24]

A further government complication and impediment for the industry was the Defense Department's interest in restricting access to a wide range of machine tools from the East Bloc countries through the Coordinating Committee for Multilateral Export Controls (COCOM). Japan and West Germany were reported to be much more lax in restrictions than the United States, and in the instance of machine tools, this probably amounted to a significant volume.[25] On occasion, it worked the other way around. When it was learned in 1988 that Toshiba Machine provided the Soviets with machines for making quiet submarine propellers, Congressional anger rose to such a pitch that the company was banned from making sales in the United States for three years.

Recently, the government has supported the industry with some funding for the industry-sponsored National Center for Manufacturing Sciences established in 1988. Initial funding came from the National Machine Tool Builders' Association, which gained 110 company sponsors among builders and users, but not Cincinnati Milacron. Research is to be backed at universities or other research organizations and at companies and shared among participants. A $19.1 million research project for the Next Generation Control was awarded in 1989 to a consortium of thirty-five companies, headed by Martin Marietta.

The arrangement of foreign alliances of various kinds has not been overlooked as a means of shoring up lagging technology, product lines, and marketing opportunities. Perhaps the broadest ones, the General Motors and General Electric joint ventures with FANUC, "were widely viewed as admissions by the American companies that they could not match FANUC's robot expertise."[26] They do, however, serve the purpose of keeping these American companies and their customers abreast of the latest in control and robot technology insofar as FANUC represents it. Cross set up an early joint venture in 1972 with Toyoda for machining centers and dissolved it a few years later to maintain its own products.[27] A Bendix agreement with Toyoda to make and market a line of machining centers in America was terminated when Bendix was acquired by Cross and Trecker in 1984.[28] Kearney and Trecker, since 1979 a part of Cross and Trecker, made an agreement with Ikegai in 1984 to replace its low-end machining center line with Ikegai machines using Kearney controls. In 1985, Cincinnati Milacron agreed to market Hitachi Seiki's computer numerically controlled lathes in the U.S. market under its own label. In the judgment of the MIT Commission staff, however, these and similar arrangements "cede the capability for designing and building low-cost, competitive products."[29]

Clearly, Milacron has done some things very well. It demonstrated technical leadership for many years, but it was not able to commercialize this leadership on a global basis. It was a leader in robotics, which have been slow to catch on in the American and European marketplaces. It diversified into plastics machinery, which required both foresight and commitment, and has been rewarded with growth and profits in that business. Recently, it is achieving some success in improving manufacturing efficiency through its focus factories. The chief mistakes have been in semiconductor materials and the brief excursion into laser machines, both of which it has exited.

In a sense, the entire U.S. machine tool industry has been the prisoner of lagging American manufacturing technology from which none escaped. Overall, Milacron looked more like a survivor in the 1980s than a leader. Others have done worse. For example, Cross and Trecker assumed too much debt in making acquisitions from 1979 to 1985 in anticipation of sales expansion that never arrived. Protracted losses and restructuring have followed. A U.S. firm showing promise recently is Giddings and Lewis. It was acquired by AMCA International in 1982 and sold again in 1989 to the public at less than half the acquisition cost, after four years of losses. It specializes in large, automated machine tools and systems having a unit value twice the industry average, and it is aggressively seeking foreign markets. Although it has installed fifty cellular systems and flexible manufacturing systems, it has yet to install one for itself.

The jury is out on the possibility of recovery in the U.S. industry. There is little likelihood that it will disappear, but there are few indications that a turnaround is imminent. If Milacron's recent curtailment of activities in laser machines and robotics is an indication of the current situation, American tool builders are returning to the basics of designing and making cost-effective machines before expanding into new product lines or challenging the Japanese where they are already strong.

NOTES

1. The table is an updated and expanded version of one presented in David J. Collis, "The Machine Tool Industry and Industrial Policy 1955–82," Case 9–387–145 (Boston: Harvard Business School, 1987), p. 2.

2. This is the author's summary of the seven causes of the U.S. industry's failure and the six factors distinguishing successful and unsuccessful countries as presented by Artemis March, "The U.S. Machine Tool Industry and Its Foreign Competitors." MIT Commission on Industrial Productivity, *Working Papers*, vol. 2 (Cambridge, Mass.: The MIT Press, 1989), pp. 33–34 and 51–53, respectively.

3. U.S. Department of Commerce, *1990 U.S. Industrial Outlook* (Washington, D.C.: U.S. Government Printing Office, 1990), p. 21–1.

4. Most of the information contained in this paragraph is based on David J. Collis, "Kingsbury Machine Tool Corporation," Case 9–388–110 (Boston: Harvard Business School, 1988), pp. 12–13.

5. Both Milacron and GM Fanuc Robotics claimed to be the largest U.S. manufacturer of robotics in 1989, and since neither publish data, it is impossible to verify either claim.

6. March, "The U.S. Machine Tool Industry," pp. 15–18.

7. Ibid., p. 16.

8. Ibid., p. 25.

9. Ibid., pp. 18–19.

10. Ibid., pp. 28–30.

11. Ibid., p. 14.

12. Jonathan P. Hicks, "Tool Plants Seek New Markets," *The New York Times*, January 30, 1990, p. C1.

13. March, "The U.S. Machine Tool Industry," p. 34 and Table 11; and 1989 Report by Joseph Jablonski and Kathleen Morgan, *American Machinist*, February 1990, pp. 59–64.

14. No data are available on the exact amount of the subsidies, although it appears to have been relatively large. The MIT Commission thought it was larger than did David Collis; see March, "The U.S. Machine Tool Industry," p. 39, and Collis, "The Machine Tool Industry," p. 26. There were also allegations by Burgmaster of patent infringement and technological theft, March, p. 36; Clyde V. Prestowitz, Jr., *Trading Places: How We Allowed Japan to Take the Lead* (New York: Basic Books, 1988), pp. 223–229.

15. March, "The U.S. Machine Tool Industry," pp. 26 and 33; Okuma Machine Works, Japan's fourth largest machine tool builder, supplies its own controls.

16. Ibid., p. 36.

17. Ibid., p. 41.

18. Much of the discussion in this paragraph follows that found in Michael E. Porter, *The Competitive Advantage of Nations* (New York: The Free Press, 1990), pp. 225–238, based on a study by Michael J. Enright.

The fact that the Japanese steel industry was one of four groups of firms making robotics contrasts with the slowness of the U.S. industry in adapting innovations. The author chided the U.S. steel industry before the Senate Finance Committee in 1967 when it first called for import quotas: "The first, second, and third largest steel companies in the United States lagged eleven, twelve, and thirteen years behind the leading foreign firm in installing the oxygen conversion process, illustrating their technological lethargy.... We simply do not believe that the American steel industry is the helpless giant that it has caricatured itself as being." Reprinted in *Steel*, April 1, 1968, pp. 43–48.

Similarly, the bankruptcy of Mesta Machine in 1983, a venerable supplier of equipment to the U.S. steel industry, which missed the conversion to continuous casting, is a later commentary on the failure to keep up with changing technology. See Robert H. Hayes, Steven C. Wheelwright, and Kim B. Clark, *Dynamic Manufacturing: Creating the Learning Organization* (New York: The Free Press, 1988), pp. 33–35.

19. Clyde H. Farnsworth, "A Debate on Controls of Exports," *The New York Times*, October 9, 1989, p. 21.

20. Information for this paragraph is chiefly drawn from March, "The U.S. Machine Tool Industry," pp. 41–51.

21. This experience is described in Collis, "The Machine Tool Industry," pp. 14–17 and 26–29; and idem, "Kingsbury Machine Tool Corporation," pp. 8–10.

22. March, "The U.S. Machine Tool Industry," p. 8, and Michael L. Dertouzos, Richard K. Lester, Robert M. Solow, and the MIT Commission on Industrial Productivity, *Made in America: Regaining the Productive Edge* (Cambridge, Mass.: The MIT Press, 1989), chap. 1, p. 20.

23. The Houdaille episode is described in Clyde V. Prestowitz, Jr., *Trading Places*, pp. 223–229; Max Holland, *When the Machine Stopped: A Cautionary Tale from Industrial America* (Boston: Harvard Business School, 1989). Holland maintains in his exhaustive study of Houdaille that Prestowitz's account is the one most sympathetic to the Houdaille petition. He argues that Houdaille had been weakened by a leveraged buyout in 1979 and was already beyond redemption as a result of its own mistakes.

24. The story is told similarly but differently by March, "The U.S. Machine Tool Industry," pp. 20–27, and Collis, "The Machine Tool Industry and Industrial Policy, 1955–82," contained in *International Competitiveness*, ed. A. Michael Spence and Heather A. Hazard (Cambridge, Mass.: Ballinger Publishing, 1988), pp. 91–94.

25. Kenneth R. Timmerman quotes State Department information that COCOM nations and Japan had shipped 6,000 embargoed machine tools to the East Bloc from 1983 to 1989. Half were from West Germany. "It's Too Early to Relax Technology Curbs for East Bloc," *The Wall Street Journal*, November 20, 1989, p. A15.

26. Michael E. Porter, *The Competitive Advantage of Nations*, p. 234.

27. Collis, "Kingsbury Machine Tool," p. 14.

28. March, "The U.S. Machine Tool Industry," p. 89, Table 5, for this and the next two sentences.

29. Ibid., p. 6.

9

CAN AMERICAN COMPETITIVE
SUPERIORITY BE REGAINED?

American superiority in capital goods is not what it used to be. In 1989, U.S. exports of capital goods were 22 percent higher than imports, up from a 3 percent advantage two years earlier when the lagged effect of the strong dollar had threatened to reverse the advantage. Recent experience is far different from the situation in the late 1960s when exports were more than four times imports, or even in the late 1970s when they were two and one-half times imports. Evidence introduced in Chapter 1 suggests that U.S. firms have made up the difference by supplying foreign markets from sources abroad and by shifting the production of goods and services offshore to overseas subsidiaries and affiliates. This is not the same as supplying markets with U.S. exports using American labor and other resources. Nor does it speak to the expansion of foreign multinational companies in the U.S. market through a combination of imports and production in foreign-owned facilities within the United States.

The ability of U.S. capital goods firms to compete in global markets at home and abroad, from sources either in America or abroad, determines superiority or inferiority. That is, if U.S. companies offer product designs and quality that interest buyers, if they are priced and financed to reflect an aggregate of costs low enough to attract customers, and if the companies are logistically able to make delivery from U.S. or foreign facilities, then we would say the balance of sales in the various global markets indicates relative competitiveness and possible superiority. We are also interested in changes in the ability of American firms to supply global markets from U.S. sources in order to show what has happened to firms employing U.S. manufacturing resources. On both of these counts, there is considerable evidence from the seven companies investigated to indicate erosion in the U.S. competitive position in capital goods during the past two decades.

This chapter commences with the findings from the analysis of the seven companies and the industries in which they participate. Recently, capital goods have constituted 36 percent of total U.S. exports of goods. The seven firms account for more than one-fifth of capital goods exports. Therefore, they represent the diversity and breadth of the capital goods industries. Collectively, the seven companies made 8 percent of the U.S. exports in the 1985–89 period, indicating their importance as beacons of leadership in American manufacturing as well as being representative of the important capital goods sector. Their experience contains elements of strength and future opportunities as well as concerns about losses in position and areas of weakness or vulnerability. The findings reach well beyond company behavior to suggest that aspects of the economic, political, and social environment are influencing the success of our firms.

This complex of macro issues, introduced in the first chapter and referred to in several specific instances as influencing the experience of the companies, is addressed in the second section of this chapter. These issues include the cost of capital and related macroeconomic questions, and encompass economic growth and foreign exchange rate fluctuations, labor costs and quality, educational preparation and training, some aspects of product and manufacturing technology, market size and firm concentration, and government antitrust and trade policy. Most of these issues were raised earlier as background influences. Here they are dealt with as they impact individual companies in the capital goods field.

In the third section, the peculiarities of competing with Japanese companies in Japan are presented. Charges of anticompetitive conditions and discriminatory behavior relative to imports and foreign investors are reviewed. Alarms have been sounded from a number of quarters regarding dependence on or dominance of Japanese suppliers of semiconductors and machine tools. An effort is made to consider and respond to these concerns. This is approached with recognition of the political and economic ties and realities between the United States and Japan and the time that any such adjustment may require.

In the fourth section, the position of U.S. capital goods firms and their European competitors is explored as the European industrial situation evolves. Of particular interest are the European Community changes to be completed by the end of 1992, the reunification of Germany, and the freeing of the other Eastern European economies. American capital goods manufacturers are well established in Europe—six of the seven companies in this study have more than one European facility. European capital goods firms are also increasingly well established for global competition—seven of thirteen large European competitors of the companies in this study have plants in the United States.

Finally, the last section of this chapter attempts to deal with the question of what the focus of U.S. attention should be to improve our competitive position. A response is framed by filtering from the complex of issues those that are most important. These are (1) improving U.S. investment, including spending on research and development, (2) remedying our most egregious educational deficiencies, and (3) better corporate decision making to develop and capture comparative advantages in the context of global competition. A broad approach attending to many deficiencies is necessary, but success is not likely to follow unless there is a concentrated effort on these crucial determinants.

A SUMMARY OF FINDINGS

Five of the seven leading U.S. capital goods companies have lost share in world markets during the last twenty years, and the other two are more vulnerable to loss than they were twenty or even ten years ago. World leadership has been lost by two firms—General Electric in electrical equipment and Cincinnati Milacron in machine tools. The other five are still on top, although arguably less secure in most cases than in earlier years. The losses in global market share range from radical in the case of machine tools to moderate or slight in the instances of Kodak or GE. As might be expected, the reasons are complex and varied. In some cases, there were product problems; in others, costs and prices were permitted to get out of line. There are more than a few instances where the firms were unresponsive to competitive thrusts. Kodak's nemesis is Fuji Photo Film; Caterpillar's, Komatsu. Most situations are less clear. Other factors include primary markets that declined more than those of competitors, lagging U.S. manufacturing technology, and market inaccessibility. Rather than throwing up our hands at this tangle of causes, the purpose of this section is to sort out, insofar as possible, those that really mattered among the plethora of factors.

Six of the American leaders were affected by product technology innovations of competitors or by competitive quality improvements reducing preexisting market preferences. IBM's product leadership in mainframes has been a phenomenon. However, its midrange line was poorly defended for more than twenty years, and some products like workstations were missed entirely for extended periods. For the first time in almost three decades, Boeing is about to face across-the-board competition from a family of Airbus transport airliners. However, it never really enjoyed the monopoly some critics claim to recall—it was lucky or wise enough to develop the right concepts early. GE's customized approach to nuclear power plants lived less well for users than the standardized designs of CGE–Framatome in France, and now it is adapting, hoping for a renewed U.S. market. Kodak and Caterpillar sat by while Fuji Film and Komatsu closed much of the quality gap and broadened their lines and marketing. Caterpillar also lagged in introducing hydraulic excavators, while its competitors enjoyed an expanding product line. The Japanese onslaught in standardized numerically controlled and computer numerically controlled machine tools caught the U.S. industry and Cincinnati Milacron with a babel of incompatible machines, despite their earlier introduction of these products. Only Cummins has maintained continued product leadership, but this has been a profitless success for other reasons.

These setbacks should not be misinterpreted as a loss of product leadership by U.S. capital goods firms. IBM, Boeing, Kodak, Caterpillar, and Cummins appear to have a definite hold on product leadership in their industries, if not as commanding as they were in 1970. In addition, GE has no peer in steam and gas turbines. GE's $750 million order to supply power systems along with Toshiba and Hitachi to a nuclear project for Tokyo Electric Power in 1989 demonstrates that it is a leading player. Its reactor and transmission and distribution equipment, however, have yielded global position. Similarly, if U.S. machine tool firms are no longer ahead, Milacron appears to be the world leader in plastics molding machinery, a contention supported by FANUC's licensing of its technology.

At least four of the companies suffered cost problems of a serious nature—serious enough in three instances to involve the firms in multiyear losses and to require major restructuring in all four. Both Kodak and Caterpillar fell seriously behind their leading Japanese competitors in manufacturing costs. Each was sluggish in recognizing and adjusting to the problem, and this delay required radical surgery, extensive product redesign, and process revamping. Cummins recognized the necessity for product redesign and cost reduction somewhat earlier from signals indicated by its Japanese licensee. It became a "benchmark" example for factory rearrangement utilizing CNC machines and flexible systems.[1] To date, these actions have not helped Cummins's profits because of softness in the truck engine market and failure to meet its cost targets, although they may have forestalled more fundamental competitive inroads. In the case of machine tools, the problem appears to rest with the failure of U.S. manufacturers generally to be interested early in process improvement. Machine tool builders also failed to invest in upgraded manufacturing technologies themselves. Although not slow to enter new product technologies, Milacron's first FMS installation in its own facilities did not become operational until 1986.[2]

In contrast, both IBM and Boeing won special comments from the MIT Commission on Industrial Productivity for their attention to manufacturing processes and costs.[3] IBM also has taken steps recently to assist other U.S. semiconductor manufacturers and semiconductor equipment makers.

Labor costs are a declining element of total product costs, particularly in the case of sophisticated capital goods. Only at Caterpillar did differing labor costs appear to play a key role in disadvantaging the U.S. company. It is locked into an industry compensation pattern set by the protected auto industry, which has little relevance to the competitive situation in construction machinery. In the last ten years, three of the four principal American companies in the industry have unsuccessfully sought to alter the pattern. The result may force more of the industry offshore. Caterpillar gained some concessions from the UAW through collective bargaining in the 1980s and reduced the number of job classifications that make shifting assignments difficult. Caterpillar representatives point out, however, that they still have sixty manufacturing job classifications in Peoria compared to three at the new Mitsubishi Motors-Chrysler (Diamond Star) automobile assembly plant forty miles away. Job classifications at Caterpillar's Belgian and French plants were eliminated several years ago.[4]

Caterpillar also has concerns about the educational backgrounds of U.S. employees. Manufacturing vice president Bernard Sorel states, "In Japan people running even small manufacturing systems are professional engineers. In Europe they would be technicians. Here in the U.S. we sometimes start with people with very little education." Relative to education, Don Fites, the CEO commented, "I do not think it's a matter of literacy.... But numeracy is important. We have to reeducate people in the short term." In 1989, Caterpillar spent $125 million on training.[5] Contrasting the difference in cultural approaches to manufacturing costs, a Japanese engineer at the Shin Caterpillar Mitsubishi facility in Japan, where American and Japanese engineers work together in designing hydraulic excavators, said, "The Japanese engineer tends to consider the impact of his design on cost or manufacturability.... The Americans ... want to know whether it can be done from an engineering point of view."[6]

Marketing facilities and efforts of U.S. capital goods companies are generally superior to their global competition. Nevertheless, important changes are apparent in this realm as well as others. Fujitsu and Hitachi have made progress in expanding U.S. marketing efforts, largely at the expense of IBM's American competition. Boeing competes with governmental financing and subtle marketing pressures on behalf of its primary rival. Public ownership of utilities and closed bids have blocked GE's access to many foreign markets, while foreign inroads have been possible in the United States. This may be changing with the company's joint ventures in Europe and the possible opening of bid practices. Kodak's marketing presence is better than that of any competitor in most areas except the Japanese market, but the establishment of an aggressive presence by Fuji Film both in America and Europe will be a factor for it to contend with in the future. Similarly, Caterpillar's distribution network of independent dealers is superb, but Komatsu has measurably improved its coverage through joint ventures and acquisitions in the United States and Europe and it has broadened apace its distribution facili-

Table 9.1
Company Leadership by Region

Measure	U.S.	Europe	Japan
Manufacturing Cost	1	0	5
Product Acceptance	5	1	1
Market Share Gain	0	2	4
Entrepreneurship	2	2	3
Totals	8	5	13

ties. In diesel engines, Cummins aims its marketing efforts at users and also at vehicle manufacturers. Its success in blocking Japanese and European competitors has not been as effective against Caterpillar, which appears more formidable than other domestic competitors who are disappearing from the American scene. Neither Milacron nor any other American tool maker ever effectively established a global presence, and now the Japanese are here in force along with some German, Swiss, and other tool makers.

An attempt to capture what is happening in the capital goods industries globally is presented in Table 9.1. The leading companies in the three principal industrial regions are tallied, based on who is lowest in manufacturing cost, which companies lead in product design and quality, who has gained market share, and who has displayed the best entrepreneurial decision making in the last decade. Two of these measures are almost wholly objective, while two involve opinion or subjective judgment. Only twenty-six first-place rankings are indicated because data are lacking to determine which region is the lowest cost manufacturer in electrical equipment, and no significant change has occurred in the diesel engine share by region. Japan leads in lower manufacturing costs as expected, and Boeing is America's only claim in this category. U.S. products are still the best in five industries, European electrical equipment has been better accepted, and Japan and Germany are close competitors for superiority in machine tools. The United States has lost market share in six industries, while Japan has gained in four of these. Entrepreneurship claims are more diffuse. The U.S. firms have demonstrated initiative in computers and diesel engines; the Japanese, in photographic equipment and supplies, machine tools, and construction machinery; and the Europeans, in aircraft (with considerable public assistance) and electrical equipment.

The seven companies discussed in these pages are the leaders in U.S. capital goods because their performance exceeded many if not most of those in their industries. As global competition increased, there was convergence in industrial technology among the economies of North America, Europe, and Japan. There was also more than convergence occurring. During the decade of the 1980s, employment was lost overall in U.S. capital goods industries. Modest employment gains took place in computers and aircraft, serious reductions occurred in electrical equipment and photographic equipment and supplies, and catastrophic losses were suffered in construction machinery and machine tools. Cummins maintained relatively stable employment overall, but redistribution took place away from its home plant in Columbus, Indiana. Within the electrical equipment, construction machinery, and machine tool industries, economic and competitive forces led to the closing of many plants and the merger or liquidation of more than a few companies. These realignments are not likely to be reversed, and in a changing world, these industries are not going to stay the same for long either.

THE COMPLEX OF ISSUES

A great deal of discussion and writing has been devoted to the subject of American competitiveness in recent years. In 1987, the *Harvard Business Review* published the results of a survey of its readers on the question and received almost 4,000 responses. Overwhelmingly, more than nine out of ten respondents believed that competitiveness was deteriorating, and they offered more than enough causes. The problem was overidentified, and that may be part of the difficulty. The written views of twenty-three leaders were published, including seventeen business executives, two labor leaders, and four government officials. Ten of them named the budgetary deficit and the inadequacy of investment in their statements. Five criticized protection abroad as fundamental to the problem, including both labor leaders. One took the trouble to say that trade policies were not the problem. Only two stressed improvements in education as necessary, although among the 4,000 general respondents, more than one-third wrote out their views, and of these 43 percent thought that education needed to be emphasized.[7]

Two years earlier, the President's Commission on Industrial Competitiveness had published its views on the problem.[8] In 1988, the National Academy of Engineering issued the report of its Committee on Technology Issues That Impact International Competitiveness, and the Cuomo Commission on Trade and Competitiveness also made its report.[9] The following year the sixteen-member faculty Commission on Industrial Productivity from MIT, which used a staff of thirty-two people who worked for the better part of two years, plus an additional thirty faculty serving on study groups, filed its report: *Made in America: Regaining the Productive Edge* and two volumes of *Working Papers*, which included the results of hundreds of field interviews.[10] Finally, in 1990, Harvard Business School Professor Michael E. Porter's massive study, *The Competitive Advantage of Nations*, was published, assisted by groups of researchers from ten nations.[11] The purpose here is not to attempt a summary of this extensive literature, but to emphasize several contributing economic and social causes, common to many of the studies, that played a role in the experience of the seven companies discussed earlier.

Table 9.2
Net Saving and Capital Formation, 1989 (Percentages of GDP)

Country	Gross Fixed Capital Formation	Net National Saving
U.S.	17.1	2.9
Japan	30.6	19.0
France	20.1	8.0
Germany	19.9	12.3
Italy	19.9	9.8
U.K.	19.2	4.6

Source: OECD *in Figures*, 1990 edition.

Each of the seven leading U.S. capital goods companies was found to be making substantial capital expenditures to restructure plants and reduce manufacturing costs in order to become more competitive. To the extent that they were deterred from pursuing these programs or handicapped by higher capital costs, these companies operated at a significant disadvantage relative to their principal competitors in Japan and Europe. Chapter 1 notes that capital costs were in fact much higher in the United States than in Japan or Germany, the domiciles of the chief competitors. In explaining the differences, the Federal Reserve Bank of New York pointed to lower U.S. household saving, "stable growth in Japan . . . , stable prices in Germany," and the greater reliance on debt financing in these two countries.[12] Evidence of the extent of the actual differences in net saving and capital formation in 1989 is shown in Table 9.2, where the inferior position of the United States in both measures is convincingly clear. Persistent and large-scale federal deficits throughout the 1980s contributed significantly to the U.S. savings deficiency and intensified the problem by utilizing domestic saving to finance the deficits. The direct effect of lowered capital formation on capital goods sales is underscored by the composition of capital formation—almost half for producers' durable equipment, half for structures, and a small fraction for additions to inventory.

Reliance on foreign sources of capital investment, which was encouraged by the low rate of U.S. savings, ballooned upward in the 1980s and probably contributed to exchange rate instability. The appreciation of the dollar from 1980 to early 1985, shown in Figure 1.2, partially in response to the inflow of investment funds, made U.S. exports less attractive in foreign markets insofar as the appreciation was reflected in higher prices. Subsequently, after 1986 the buildup of foreign investment in the United States subsided and the flow of investment funds even declined a little. This roughly coincided with the rapid decline of the dollar from early 1985 to the end of 1987 (see Figure 1.2). As pointed out earlier, not all the harm done to U.S. exporters by the rapid rise in the dollar early in the 1980s was offset by its equally rapid fall. An argument was made by Robert L. Bartley, editor of *The Wall Street Journal*, that the end of the fixed exchange rate regime in 1973 and the subsequent instability of exchange rates has not been good for the growth of the international economy.[13] When flexible exchange rates are combined with an unfettered federal budgetary policy, as happened during the 1980s, international businesses and U.S. employment dependent upon exports become pawns that may be sacrificed in the exchange rate swings inspired by erratic capital movements.[14]

Investment spending influences the technological level of a nation by creating the opportunity for introducing technical changes. Research and development spending is another form of investment in new technology, most of which is charged to current operations by businesses. A third form of spending, not often thought of as embodying some investment, is that involved to establish distribution outlets, service, finance, and other support facilities offering opportunities for change and improvement in the delivery of products and services. The extent to which companies are willing to buy their way into foreign markets by acquiring local firms is evidence of the worth of these investments, especially in gaining access to overseas markets.

Having expressed concern about the relative level of U.S. fixed capital formation, we now turn to the level and content of research and development spending. Few question the U.S. position in basic research—Americans have won almost twice as many Nobel awards in science since 1946 as have Europeans, and the Japanese have received a mere handful. The record is less favorable for America when the focus is on applied research and development or the use of external technology. Unfortunately, observers frequently place too much emphasis on the level of research and development spending, rather than its effectiveness. Actually, while Japanese research and development spending has been rising faster than in the United States, as a proportion of manufacturing sales or GNP, it is currently not much different than here.

A recent study by Edwin Mansfield on research and development by 200 Japanese and American firms is very instructive. He found "that the Japanese tend to have significant cost and time advantages over U.S. firms."[15] The Japanese required only three-quarters of the time and only half the cost that the introduction of similar innovations did in the United States from 1975 to 1985. They relied more heavily on suggestions from users and production people for guiding research and development efforts, while the U.S. leaned more on ideas from within the research and development group itself. As a result, the Japanese spent about twice as large a portion of their funds for "tooling and manufacturing equipment and facilities" and only half as much for initial marketing efforts.[16] A further difference revealed that, between fifty matched pairs of companies in the chemical, electrical equipment, machinery, instrument, rubber, and metals industries, which accounted for one-quarter of research and development spending in each country in these industries, U.S. firms directed two-thirds of their funds toward better product technology and only one-third toward process technology, whereas in Japan the proportions were reversed.[17] These results are very useful in explaining why the Japanese seem to do so well in lowering manufacturing costs, in choosing appropriate products to develop, and in getting them introduced quickly.

With the engrained tradition of Yankee ingenuity and the practical accomplishments of American business in our minds, we may be shocked to learn that some other group or nation can apply the fruits of scientific advance better than we can. But it is also positive and encouraging to remember that industrial development occurs in the thousands of small steps and incremental innovations required to bring a new technology into widespread use, and that successful research and development is not a series of bold breakthroughs, but rather painstaking small steps and improvements. Downstream activities in the development process and the careful "coordination of product design and manufacturing functions" are perhaps more important in determining competitive success than industrial targeting or superhuman dedication to workplace ethics.[18]

Innovation and technology lead directly to the question of manufacturing productivity. As noted in Chapter 1, there are measurement problems, and the MIT Commission on Industrial Productivity has suggested a broader concept of "productive performance" to include quality, timeliness, and other aspects of products and services not included in traditional economic measurements. Nevertheless, there is concern about the superior productivity performance of Japan and Germany, although U.S. manufacturing gains in the 1990s were better than those in Germany. After an exhaustive investigation of comparative productivity for more than a century, three economists—William J. Baumol, Sue Anne Baty Blackman, and Edward N. Wolff—argue that the high catch-up rates of productivity growth abroad following World War II will gradually converge toward U.S. levels. They hold that the imitative behavior of businesses is more important to productivity growth than where invention originates. This is reassuring but not necessarily sanguine for the United States. The economists point out that, if the total productivity gains of the most progressive economies fell in the future to half of their advantage over the American rate of progress, the United States would need to increase its rate of overall productivity increase by one-third from that of the 1950 to 1979 period in order not to find itself behind Germany, Japan, and perhaps several other countries soon after the year 2000.[19] This may not be an easy increase for the United States to achieve. The authors indicate, as this study also emphasizes, that the chief determinants of productivity growth are investment, research and development, educational achievement, and business management (entrepreneurship).

The ties between productivity and educational attainment are close, although not completely understood. Increasingly, concern is being expressed about U.S. shortcomings in education, chiefly at the primary and secondary

Table 9.3
Science Achievement Test Rankings

```
Grade Level US Japan England Italy No. of
----------- -- ----- ------- ----- Countries

   4-5       8    1     12      7      15
   8-9      14    2     11     11      17
 12-13
   Biology  13   10      2     12      13
   Chemistry 11   4      2     10      13
   Physics    9   4      2     13      13
```

Source: International Association for the Evaluation of Educational Achievement, *Science Achievement in Seventeen Countries: A Preliminary Report* (New York: Pergamon Press, 1988). Published in *Science*, March 11, 1988, p. 1237.

levels. At the college and graduate levels, U.S. education is still viewed with admiration, but deficiencies in earlier mathematics and science schooling are contributing to increasing dependence on foreign graduate students in technology and the sciences. For the large numbers of working people who do not go beyond high school (and less than three-quarters reach that level), the story is different. Until well after World War II, the heterogeneous educational system had served America well, reaching a broader proportion of our population than in other industrial countries. However, in the last twenty-five years problems have emerged. Most other advanced societies have moved beyond the educational attainment levels of new workers in the United States. Deficiencies are being recognized in basic skills, in the ability to read and understand written instructions, to perform rudimentary mathematical manipulations, and to solve problems of a scientific nature. The difficulties are revealed in such ways as the adoption of flexible manufacturing systems, the subject of a recent investigation comparing American and Japanese experiences.[20] The reasons are readily apparent—twelfth grade American students fall below the median levels in all categories of mathematics, and the average Japanese student "scores as well as the top 5 percent of American high school seniors in math and science."[21] Comparisons of achievement test rankings in science at various levels are shown in Table 9.3 (German data are not available for comparison).

Repeated calls have been made for improvement, including the following statement from the president of the American Association for the Advancement of Science: "Our education system needs drastic improvement if we are to maintain a competitive edge in a world that increasingly uses and depends on science and technology."[22] The U.S. president emphasized the urgency of reform by calling state governors to an educational summit and including educational goals in his State of the Union address to Congress in 1990. School problems will not be easy to resolve, however, because they are rooted in ethnic and urban questions, in poverty and broken families.

Moreover, the control of American schools is highly decentralized among the fifty states and local districts. Also, while parents, politicians, and business leaders are stirring, the call for improvement has not reached the level of a national crusade, or even intensified to the post-Sputnik period of excitement.

Another set of issues arises from the diverging growth rates of markets in the three major industrial regions and the differing public policy agendas of governments and their constituents. The commanding position of the North American market relative to others is likely to erode significantly during the 1990s. The twelve European Community and the six European Free Trade Area countries together make up an aggregate market roughly paralleling the United States and Canada in size, although they include approximately one-third more people. If the 1992 Single European Act incentives and a portion or all of the six Eastern European countries become economically associated with Western Europe and lead to more rapid growth, then the total European market will become significantly larger than the North American market by the end of the decade, given a reasonable range of economic increases for each region.

Similarly, the economies of the Far East have been growing faster in the last ten years than any other region of the world. They, too, are becoming more interdependent and integrated economically. A combination of nine countries, with Japan as the center and including Australia and New Zealand, the four tigers (South Korea, Taiwan, Hong Kong, and Singapore), plus Malaysia and Thailand, have an output about two-thirds that of the United States and a population that is almost 15 percent larger. If they grow half again as fast as the U.S. economy—less than their expansion rate in the last decade—their combined output would be three-fourths that of the United States by the year 2000. This would occur without any contribution from increased market opportunities that might arise from the six large-population, low-income countries that are located nearby—China, India, Pakistan, Bangladesh, Indonesia, and the Philippines. With this potential rate of increase, Far Eastern markets for capital goods will in many cases become larger than those projected in North America.

Although the U.S. companies in this study are large—five are among the first 102 firms in *Fortune*'s Global 500 in 1989—a cursory review suggests their European and Japanese competitors are more conglomerated in capital goods markets than they are. This is in accord with the higher business concentration ratios in Japan and the former cartel preferences among many European countries. For example, within the seven industries examined, there are only two instances of multiple industry participation (excluding IBM's limited venture into factory automation)—GE in electrical equipment, aircraft engines, and factory automation, and Caterpillar in construction machinery and diesel engines—ten entries for seven companies. For eleven of their chief competitors abroad (six European and five Japanese), there are twenty-seven entries within the seven industries. Nevertheless, competition is intensifying with the globalization of capital goods markets, and American firms as well as U.S. consumers have nothing to gain and much to lose by any relaxation of competitive forces. Enforcement of statutes against anticompetitive behavior by U.S., Japanese, or European authorities is a long-run guarantee that each competitor has a fair chance to succeed based on its merits.

Arguments against protectionism are equally compelling. At the present time voluntary restraint agreements are in force against imports of semiconductors and machine tools into the United States. Not so subtle pricing restraints are being exercised by the European Community in semiconductors. The opening of competitive bids to government-controlled corporations in aircraft, electrical equipment, and telecommunications is problematic. Japan has removed formal trade restraints, but the distortion of trade in manufactured goods clearly implies the existence of limits. These subjects will be taken up in the next two sections. The Uruguay Round GATT negotiations were resumed in 1991, and an early conclusion will be required to avoid further backsliding from open markets in the immediate future. Protectionism is not the basis for building global competitive firms. When governments err in their macroeconomic policy decisions, the correction ought to be in their decisions, not in a new round of protectionism.[23]

COMPETING WITH THE JAPANESE

Within the past fifteen years, Japanese firms have established themselves as competitive forces to be reckoned with in global markets for capital goods. NEC now ranks third worldwide in computers, Fujitsu is fourth (second after the ICL merger), and Hitachi sixth. If the merchant semiconductor business is broken out separately, Japan has five of the leading seven sellers, adding Toshiba and Mitsubishi Electric to those listed above. In electrical equipment, Hitachi is third globally, Toshiba ranks sixth, and Mitsubishi Electric seventh. Fuji Film has fought its way to second place worldwide and also in the United States. Komatsu is clearly Caterpillar's leading contender in practically all markets. And in the critical field of machine tools, Japanese firms constitute nine of the top dozen on a global basis, including Komatsu and the leader in controls, FANUC, founded and 39 percent owned by Fujitsu. When added to the well-known penetration in the U.S. automobile and consumer electronic industries, many Americans view the Japanese economic success as threatening to the United States. Business investment in Japan is already exceeding U.S. capital spending, and their research and development effort is on a par with U.S. business outlays as a percentage of sales. Furthermore, their expenditures appear to be more effective than U.S. spending in the cost of achieving similar innovations or in the time required for their accomplishment. Warnings have gone out from the Department of Commerce, *The New York Times*, and business analysts indicating further erosion in the U.S. competitive position if current trends continue.[24]

Actually, popular impressions sometimes outrun the realities of the situation, and an antidote needs to be injected. U.S. productivity and per capita income level are still the highest in the world based on purchasing power comparisons. In the latest data available, Japan ranks sixth among the twenty-four OECD countries in per capita gross domestic product, approximately three-quarters of the U.S. level.[25] Nevertheless, this could change in little more than a decade should recent trends persist. The warnings and the basis for them need to be carefully evaluated in considering the U.S. competitive position.

During the first two to three decades after World War II, Japan utilized protectionist measures to promote its domestic industrial development, as the United States had in the period from 1862 until 1934. They went further, however, in tightly controlling foreign investment in Japan, which largely excluded foreign control of industrial concerns. MITI targeted sectors for promotion, controlled licensing, and subsidized research and development. A different approach to patents and other intellectual property rights makes it difficult for foreign corporations to obtain protection similar to that which they enjoy in other industrial areas. The trade and investment restraints were mostly lifted by the end of the 1970s, but institutional and strong behavioral patterns still persist, favoring an export surplus and shunning imports particularly of manufactured goods. Some of these pernicious practices continue, while Japan appears to be making progress in dismantling many of its aversions to imports.

One of the stronger and best articulated concerns was expressed recently by Charles H. Ferguson, a former IBM analyst now associated with the MIT Center for Technology, Policy, and Industrial Development, in a lead article in the *Harvard Business Review*. His contention is that Japan's success in semiconductors is being followed in personal computers, and that a convergence of digital technologies in several key industries, ranging from computers to consumer electronics, will expose large segments of the American and European economies to Japanese dominance. He believes they have used and will continue to employ predatory pricing and collusion in forcing licensing, blocking patent applications, and other means of withholding access to technology and markets. Americans are insufficiently aware of what is happening and have adopted inadequate responses of either partnership or individualism. His proposal is to form a "Euro-American keiretsu" grouped around IBM, DEC, Xerox, Motorola, Siemens, and Philips.[26] This would not be an appropriate course.

Others have chronicled the Japanese excesses, American mistakes, the academic analyses of what transpired, and a possible course of future action that might be acceptable to both the Japanese and Americans in the search for solutions to the economic antagonisms. Edward J. Lincoln of the Brookings Institution describes Japan's distorted trade pattern in *Japan's Unequal Trade*.[27] Manufactured imports are less than 3 percent of the gross domestic product in Japan compared to more than 7 percent in the United States and from 10 to 17 percent for the four large European economies. Japan's exports are more concentrated in a few industries than are those of other industrial countries, and Japan engages in far less importing and exporting of similar products than is the case elsewhere.[28] Lincoln goes on to offer reasons why the Japanese trade as they do, focusing on their aversion to the importation of manufactured goods. He concludes that "the general bias against imports and the lack of intra-industry trade" (imports and exports of similar products) "in Japan are the results of factors that run far deeper and are more complex than traditional, identifiable import barriers."[29]

All of these barriers may be changing. Imports of manufactured goods have been rising rapidly in dollars since 1985 and in yen beginning a year later. The large appreciation of the yen was a major factor in the change, but other things are changing, too, including the attitude of MITI, other agencies, and business organizations. The Structural Impediments Initiative discussions between U.S. and Japanese negotiators were concluded favorably in 1990 with both sides pledging action. The Japanese will increase imports, remove distribution practices that deter foreign firms, and enforce anticompetitive legislation more vigorously. Critics will argue that the Japanese have made empty promises before, yet to assume that they will want to continue the large export surpluses of recent years indefinitely is to imply that they will not ultimately act in their own interest. Businesses and consumers may wish to take advantage of lower prices from abroad, and the Japanese may wish to spend more on themselves, both as consumers and to remedy major deficiencies in housing and public works.

Americans also may react in their own interest and stop the heavy dependence on external capital encouraged by federal deficits and excessive consumption. The outrage at real and perceived injustices by the Japanese may give way to a realization that Americans cannot withdraw from the fray, as business and economic relationships are already too extensive. Since the Japanese are destined to play a major role in the Asia and Pacific region, engagement, pressure, and negotiation are more rewarding courses of action.

Exposure and censure of one-yen bids by Fujitsu and NEC in the fall of 1989 prove the extent to which leading Japanese firms were (and are) willing to go and the fact that enforcement and tolerance of such practices may be changing. Fujitsu made a one-yen bid to supply a $78,000 computer system for mapping and controlling Hiroshima's waterworks believing that the experience gained would bring it a sizeable volume of similar business in the future. When the Hiroshima waterworks publicized the practice, it was revealed that both Fujitsu and NEC had made similar bids on other recent projects. MITI denounced the practice and the Japan Fair Trade Commission investigated; the bid was withdrawn and Fujitsu and NEC apologized. Foreign companies have frequently complained about unfair bidding practices on public projects by Japanese firms.[30]

Japan's response to foreign firms in technology matters poses questions of fair play or discriminatory treatment. For example, Texas Instruments, one of the developers of integrated circuits along with Intel, applied for Japanese patent protection in early 1960. After wending its tortuous way through Japan's system for thirty years, it was finally granted a patent in October 1989, effective for twelve years. This patent is expected to provide Texas Instruments with hundreds of millions of dollars in license fees annually. Under a new ten-year cross-licensing agreement with Toshiba alone signed in 1990, Texas Instruments is expected to receive several hundred million dollars in 1991 royalties. However, it will not be permitted to recover revenues lost prior to 1989 because of the delay. Three years earlier, TI had won suits against the major Japanese semiconductor manufacturers for chip sales in the United States. Patent applications in Japan require five to seven years for processing. Bell Laboratories has had applications pending on optical fiber technology for more than ten years.[31] Delaying tactics and pernicious administration of patents are among the unresolved problems on the 1989 agenda of the U.S. Trade Representative for Japan.[32]

Another illustration of the extent to which a leading Japanese computer firm would go to obtain proprietary information on a competitor occurred in 1982. Hitachi, a maker of IBM-compatible machines, was caught buying trade secrets on the new System 3081 by the FBI. The sting involved multiple contacts with Hitachi people, including the general manager of its mainframe computer plant in Japan. Hitachi pleaded guilty. The disappointing aspect of the case was that Hitachi was assumed to be the victim in Japan after news media there portrayed it as a "dirty Yankee trick, aimed at bashing the Japanese."[33] Fujitsu later paid IBM $833 million to settle a software copyright dispute involving the mainframe operating system.[34]

These examples—one-yen bids, apparent patent discrimination, and criminal violations—ought not be taken as a basis for generalizing that all Japanese firms or governmental agencies act in this fashion. They are indicative, nonetheless, along with other evidence cited earlier, such as the distorted trade pattern, that Japan has some problems to remedy if it wishes to continue to enjoy the benefits of an open trading system. Correction of such problems should not be expected to remove the bilateral trade deficit with the United States. Nevertheless, it would help to clear the atmosphere clouding trade relations between the two nations.

Probably the greatest competitive threat from the Japanese at the present time lies in manufacturing efficiency. It appears that, in five of the seven capital goods industries, they possess at least some significant manufacturing process advantages. In computers, the advantage currently lies in semiconductors. In film and standardized CNC machine tools, the cost differentials are substantial. In construction machinery and diesel engines the differences are more marginal, although they have been large enough to cause major problems in the 1980s. The ability of the Japanese to design and tool-up quickly for new models or products, to employ flexible manufacturing systems and robotics, to handle just-in-time inventory systems efficiently, and to deliver quality products was acquired by conscientious effort. Americans must master these techniques and improve upon them if we are to remain competitive.[35]

The presumed advantage that Japanese firms possess in terms of labor costs may not be immutable, as recent changes suggest. Convergence is not likely. Employee relations are vastly different in the two societies. In a review of the autobiographies of three of Japan's great postwar business leaders— Koji Kobayashi of NEC, Konosuke Matsushita of Matsushita, and Akio Morita of Sony—*The Economist* states that: "all preach the gospels of training, good employee relations, the importance of trust rather than contracts and of quality rather than price."[36]

There are American business leaders who emphasize good employee relations, but a sampling of achievers in the last forty-five years would be unlikely to reveal similar unanimity of stress on the importance of working relationships. Lifetime employment in Japan may be yielding to gradual modification. American manufacturing management will very likely have to learn how to reduce its dependence on frequent worker redundancy in order to be competitive, as the present practice is too costly in wasted talent. Training is more extensive in Japan than in the United States, and job rotation is much more common. American management already is learning from the Japanese the value of flatter organizations with less hierarchy. American unions appear to have limited tolerance for Japanese-style working relationships. Nevertheless, the Japanese are convinced enough of the superiority of their own system to attempt implementation in their U.S. subsidiaries. More than one in ten of the initial work force of the Mitsubishi-Chrysler joint venture were sent to Nagoya for training, and this is a fairly common practice among Japanese-operated auto plants in the United States.

Educational differences are even more fundamental. Japanese children spend considerably more time in school than do those in other industrialized countries, and a much higher percentage (90 percent) complete the twelve years through high school at a higher average level of achievement than in the United States. Homework starts earlier, evening or weekend cram courses are common in order to compete in a meritocratic system of admission to higher education, and mothers who generally do not work play a significant role as the driving force for achievement. These facts are fairly well known. More university graduates are prepared in engineering than in America, although the content of the curriculum is less practically oriented than here. Even at the universities, the first two years are devoted to general studies. Most research is carried out in corporations rather than universities, and most vocational training occurs within the companies as well, although there are some vocational high schools and technical colleges. Retraining is also a responsibility assumed by large companies as a necessary part of the lifelong employment commitment. The results are manifestly evident in a relatively homogeneous society. Whether they enjoy the pressure or not, the Japanese work force is very competent in comparison to American workers, something that could not have been said twenty to thirty years ago.[37]

The drive for economic achievement has been the principal thrust and motivating force in Japanese society since the Meiji restoration in 1868, interrupted by their aggressive excursion into militarism in the 1930s and 1940s. The Japanese have become able competitors and need to be taken seriously and respected as such. Their society is also evolving and changing. The large export surplus is a phenomenon of the last decade, as their high savings proclivity was utilized earlier by the government to finance its own deficits. With incomes rising and sizeable business investments in North America, Europe, Asia, and the Pacific, Japanese behavior is likely to change in keeping with these new roles.[38]

A REINVIGORATED EUROPE

The Europeans are ahead of the Japanese in three of the seven capital goods industries examined—aircraft, electrical equipment, and heavy trucks and diesel engines. They lag behind the Japanese and the United States in computers and chips, photographic equipment and supplies, and construction machinery. More machine tools are produced in Europe, but their firms are generally smaller than the Japanese with a few exceptions for affiliates of large engineering concerns. Asea Brown Boveri has emerged as the world's largest maker of electrical equipment, and the second company in the industry also is European. Airbus has become the second largest builder of commercial aircraft, and Rolls-Royce occupies third position in aircraft engines. Daimler-Benz is first as a global manufacturer of heavy trucks, closely followed by Volvo and Renault with their fast-growing alliances. None appears to have displaced Cummins to any significant extent from its leading position in diesel engines. The Europeans' poorest showing is in computers, where their leading firms rank eighth, ninth, and tenth globally. Agfa ranks third in film, and the two European construction machinery companies rank about fifth and sixth. More than a spate of merger activity has been spurred by the preparation for economic union after 1992, and developments in Eastern Europe have added a new flurry of alliances in that direction.

Since the collapse of Communist regimes in Eastern Europe, attention has focused on Western business interests there, with German reunification occupying center stage. The early conversion of East German marks into deutsche marks and massive aid from West Germany will accelerate the reform and recovery there. Still, it will take years to privatize 8,000 firms that were state owned, and the rush by Western firms to acquire desirable investments will not bring immediate prosperity. Since most Eastern European manufacturing enterprises are expected to be less than competitive with Western firms, a transition period of high unemployment is anticipated before new investment, new products, and new manufacturing processes are introduced. Each country will adapt in its own fashion. Hungary and Poland are moving more quickly to sell some state-owned enterprises than are East Germany and Czechoslovakia.[39] As investment funds roll in, however, larger markets for Western capital goods will exist and should prove to be a stimulus to the European economy, particularly Germany. The rise in economic activity in Germany should spillover in the form of increased imports, including capital goods, from its trading partners in Europe and the United States, which furnished 67 percent and 8 percent of its imports, respectively, in 1989.[40]

Internal discussions to deepen the economic relationships among the twelve countries (the 1992 objectives) before widening the European Community have had to accommodate the realities of German reunification and the needs of the other Eastern European nations. The momentum of 1992 was well established before the historic Eastern European opening occurred in 1989. The Single European Act became effective in mid–1987, and some of its practical effects have already been seen in the combination of Asea and Brown Boveri (firms headquartered outside the European Community), GEC-Alsthom, and the alliance of Volvo and Renault, among others. The movement within the Community toward legislating the 279 stipulated measures proposed, the European Monetary Union, a special arrangement for the six European Free Trade Area countries, and possible political union—all have gone beyond the point of no return and will result in a real economic fillip to Europe during the 1990s. Measures of the increment to be added differ substantially. The most popular estimates range from the official 4.3 to a 6.4 percent addition to GDP after six years, although a number of economists have suggested that these may be too limited.[41]

A number of European Community practices are worrisome for future U.S. relationships. The extensive resort to subsidies is troubling as emphasized in conjunction with commercial aircraft manufacture. The twelve member nations plus the Community itself spend almost 3 percent of GDP on subsidies, contributing potent amounts when concentrated in particular industries.[42] Other issues of concern to capital goods makers include technical standards, rules of origin combined with local content requirements, and governmental procurement procedures. Semiconductors bear a rather high tariff of 14 percent coming into the Community. In addition, integrated circuits have been subjected to a local content requirement since 1989 which necessitates that the diffusion process in chip making be performed in Europe.[43] As a result, Intel is having to build a plant in Ireland. Government procurement is big business in the Community, representing 15 percent of GDP, and is of importance to the aircraft, computer, electrical machinery, telecommunications equipment, and construction machinery industries. At this time, it is not apparent that the opening of bid practices within the Community will include sources outside the Community.

European investment levels are uniformly higher than in the United States, as the data in Table 9.2 reveal. In 1989 gross-fixed capital formation ranged from 12 percent higher in the United Kingdom as a proportion of GDP to 32 percent more in Spain. This completes a decade of moderately higher investment rates. The cause, of course, is found in a much lower net national saving rate in the United States and in the macroeconomic policies that brought that result. Already, direct investment by European Community firms in the United States is larger than by U.S. firms in Europe (at book value) and is expected to grow more rapidly.[44] As yet, this is probably not true for the capital goods industries, although the trend is in that direction. Of the seven industries investigated, U.S. direct investment in Europe appears to outweigh European investments in the United States in computers, photographic equipment and supplies, and construction machinery. The reverse is true in electrical equipment, heavy trucks, and machine tools, but the aggregate is smaller in these three industries than in the former ones. Aircraft industry investments are quite small in either direction.

Research and development efforts by the member countries' firms will receive new stimulus through implementation of the Single European Act.[45] Joint projects already initiated include, among others, Airbus, Esprit (dozens of microelectronic projects), Eureka (297 commercial technology projects), Joint European Submicron Silicon (JESSI, semiconductors), Joint European Torus (JET, nuclear fusion reactor), and Race (telecommunications). These are included in the government subsidies mentioned earlier and are an indication of the interventionist commitments by Europeans. Admission of foreign firms, both Japanese and American, to these research consortia, based on their ownership of European subsidiaries, is bound to be a lively topic of discussion and negotiation in the immediate future. Recently, IBM was admitted to JESSI following a reciprocal invitation for European firms to join its research in X-ray lithography—a technique for making future generations of semiconductors.

The same American worries exist regarding education and training in Europe. Many people are concerned that the Europeans will gain competitive advantages over the United States, as in the case of Japan. Similarly, they are chiefly concerned about training programs and primary and secondary education rather than higher education. Obviously, with more than thirty distinct educational systems, few generalizations are possible with respect to Europe. Questions have also been raised about the inadequacies of U.S. training, and even research, specifically concerning German apprenticeship training and research institutes for manufacturing technology. More generalized inadequacies linked to the scientific preparation of U.S. students are apparent in the testing information from which Table 9.3 is drawn. Scores available for eight European nations provided thirty-five different comparisons with the United States in which the European children ranked higher in twenty-nine instances. Insofar as these kinds of inferiority are accumulating in U.S. work force entrants and get translated into productivity differences, a legacy of deficiency is being left to the next generation.

European integration has come a long way since the Treaty of Rome was signed in 1957, creating the European Community. The 1992 initiative and the opening of Eastern Europe will add impetus to European growth and unity throughout the next decade. This will probably mean that European-based firms will grow more rapidly than those based in the United States and become more competitive globally. Gary Hufbauer expects the number of European companies in the top 100 industrial firms to grow, and he is probably right. From 1970 to 1989, the share of U.S.-based company sales in the top 100 declined from 69 percent to 40 percent as the number of U.S. firms included has been reduced.[46] International competition in capital goods is also likely to intensify and include more industries where previously national champions or regional competition have prevailed—especially in the markets for diesel engines, electrical equipment, and telecommunications equipment.

THE CRUCIAL DETERMINANTS

Near the outset of this chapter in "The Complex of Issues," a half dozen studies of U.S. competitive problems are cited from among a larger group addressing the subject. The reports give rise to a still larger number of recommendations—five imperatives and thirty strategies from the MIT Commission and from *The Wall Street Journal* seven broad themes to deal with the "strained alliance" between the United States and Japan.[47] This empirical study of seven industries has uncovered no small number of problems. There are, nonetheless, several recurrent themes that emerge from the public discussion now underway and the stories of the capital goods companies that are the center of the examination. These are three in number and are restated again for emphasis in this concluding section. This does not imply that a larger series of recommendations are irrelevant once the need for change is understood and the implementation of required remedies is begun. The challenge is to gain the attention of articulate members of this nation regarding the fundamental problems that exist and to provide guidance on the key questions that must be addressed if constructive change is to occur.

The conclusions of this study are compatible with and contained in most other reports, including the MIT Commission and the Baumol study of productivity.[48] They are stated here as three crucial determinants to focus attention on the essence of our difficulties and to emphasize their impact on America's important capital goods manufacturers.

Investment

Information presented in this investigation has emphasized the high U.S. capital costs relative to our principal international competitors, Japan and Germany. These costs discourage business investment in new facilities that afford an opportunity for the introduction of new technology. Heightened present value relative to future value, an accompaniment of higher capital costs, encourages short-range as opposed to long-range thinking on the part of management.[49] Research and development spending, which requires foregoing present returns for later benefits in the longer run, also is deterred by high capital costs. Insofar as the capital goods industries are both capital and research intensive, they suffer in particular from these costs.

The problem must be laid at the feet of government policy makers who have resorted to excessive deficit financing and permitted greater inflation relative to other competitive societies. Inflation was reined in during the 1980s after considerable competitive damage had been done, but it continued through the balance of the decade at a rate higher than in either Japan or Germany. Federal deficits were reduced somewhat following the Gramm-Rudman restraint, yet the government continued to absorb the scanty personal savings, leaving the economy dependent on attracting investment funds from abroad. The many calls for greater fiscal responsibility on the part of the administration and Congress must receive a more positive response if the U.S. competitive disadvantage in capital costs is to be removed. The Federal Reserve Bank of New York absolves income tax structures of blame for differences in capital costs and concludes regarding fiscal measures that "eliminating the double taxation of dividends in the United States could only work in the direction of improvement. But a lower level of government dissaving is also important."[50]

Similarly, George Hatsopoulos, Paul Krugman, and Lawrence Summers argue that "if the rate of growth of U.S. consumption could be kept even 1 percent below the rate of growth of U.S. output from now until the year 2000—and the reduced consumption to be replaced by increased exports and investment—the U.S. would be strongly placed to regain the position of international economic leadership that its natural advantages should entitle it to."[51]

The low rate of personal saving in the United States is very real, but not well understood. The disincentives for saving can be adjusted if we wish to increase the savings rate. Tax policies can be shifted to encourage saving and discourage certain forms of consumption. Current tax policy favors expenditure for housing through tax-deductible interest, and interest on savings accounts is fully taxed, in contrast to tax-free saving in Japan. Furthermore, one of the largest disincentives is the taxing of total returns on investment, as opposed to taxing only the after inflation or real returns.

In this investigation several examples have emerged regarding the disadvantageous effects of high capital costs on investment. Small start-up firms in various branches of the computer industry were hobbled from time to time in search of capital, and occasionally resorted to foreign financing and sale of assets or equity. Cummins was involved in a several-year search for secure equity financing to avoid takeover by British, New Zealand, and possibly Japanese interests. Cincinnati Milacron wished to remain a publicly held company subject to family control and resorted to debt financing to accomplish that objective. In each of these situations, the outcome at the margin would have been more favorable to the U.S. firms if capital costs had not been higher here than abroad.

Edwin Mansfield's work on U.S. research and development relative to that in Japan suggests that American manufacturers should carefully consider how their projects are chosen, with the possibility of greater payoffs in the area of adaptive or applied (downstream) research on the one hand, and shifting toward more process-oriented as opposed to product-oriented research on the other. Obviously, we should not lose the ability to lead in basic research; the objective is to regain the art of quick adaptation and imitation, which once served America well.

Another question, on which there is no consensus, relates to the need for more cooperative and government-sponsored industrial research. There are many calls for this effort, especially in areas such as semiconductors or machine tools, where targeting by the Japanese was successful. Interestingly, much less is heard about the failures of the Japanese in building aircraft or the British in the manufacture of machine tools. Undoubtedly, there are appropriate areas for some forms of collaborative research; attempts to duplicate foreign successes under much different circumstances appear delusive. The problem is to determine when private gains are likely to be inadequate to obtain the benefits of new technology and to allocate the costs of social benefits fairly.

Education and Training

The shortcomings of U.S. education have been accumulating for twenty-five years and are diverse in nature and cause. They range from the functional illiteracy of up to one-quarter of the work force to the engineering and business schools ignoring manufacturing technology. A large part of the deficiency lies in the primary and secondary schools, although there are shortfalls relative to other nations in science and engineering as well. To a considerable extent, homogeneous industrial societies abroad have eliminated their preexisting educational deficits.

Because of easier agreement on goals and methods of achievement, they have moved beyond what was America's preeminent position in breadth of attainment. In the meantime, our schools have been caught in state and local fiscal constraints, debates over control, collective bargaining disputes, desegregation litigation, and deteriorating discipline. Efforts at serious reform are just beginning. Before they are fully developed, we shall have accumulated a sizeable addition of poorly educated people who will require extensive remedial training if Americans hope to be competitive with their counterparts abroad.

Training is a company responsibility to a much greater extent in Japan than in the United States. In Germany an apprentice system prepares factory workers, while what apprentice training exists in the United States is in rapid decline. In fact, the transition from inadequate high school preparation to jobs in America is very haphazard. An educational burden awaits U.S. firms if these poorly trained workers are to be molded into a fully competitive work force in the years ahead. A few companies are beginning to recognize this problem and are accepting the burden as one they must carry. Others will learn to do so as the numbers of young work force entrants shrink in the early 1990s and they are left with those who have been passed over. Motorola, the largest U.S. merchant chip maker, increased its training budget from $7 to $60 million annually in the 1980s. According to the vice-president for training and education, "We discovered . . . that much of our work force was illiterate. They couldn't read. They couldn't do simple arithmetic like percentages and fractions. . . . About half of our . . . manufacturing and support people in the United States failed to meet the seventh grade yardstick in English and math."[52]

Evidence of education and training problems has been found among the seven capital goods firms examined. When the management at IBM's Austin plant learned that they could save $60 million by buying rather than making circuit boards, they reorganized the operation and launched an education and training program costing 5 percent of its payroll in order to close the gap.[53] Across the board, from technical manpower to dependence on European and Asian scientists, IBM leadership expresses concern about the availability of competent people.[54] Observers question Boeing's ability to maintain a competent labor force with the U.S. practice of hiring and layoff. Kodak is involved with other business firms to upgrade Rochester's public schools. Caterpillar management finds unfavorable U.S. comparisons in worker qualifications with those in its European and Japanese facilities. That was not the case twenty-five years ago. Along with others in the machine tool industry, Cincinnati Milacron faces companies with better trained work forces in Germany and Japan and manufacturing customers who may be unable to claim the superior capabilities of CNC and FMS machines because of the background of their employees.

Decision Making: Entrepreneurship

Perhaps the most striking result of the *Harvard Business Review* survey of readers regarding U.S. competitiveness was the almost unanimous response (97 percent) that the solution was to be found in "more effective management" and that almost nine out of ten placed responsibility for the problem with managers.[55] Without these findings, it might appear that a call for improved decision making is too easy a prescription. Entrepreneurship is admittedly an elusive concept, and too readily credited when luck is flowing and the enterprise is "running with the wind," and too routinely missing when adversity strikes for enigmatic reasons. Nevertheless, one does not need to search long to find examples of U.S. management problems. The most obvious is hubris, the cardinal sin of pride and arrogance, found in reward systems built on size of organization rather than performance, golden parachutes for protected sinecures, and immobility in the face of failed strategies. Others are not hard to find.

Americans were once good at technology transfer when they sought to obtain the benefits of industrial processes from the British. Perhaps we are learning again, now that it is clear that the Japanese and Europeans have something to teach us. Why did this recognition take so long? The answer lies partly in arrogance and partly in lack of global perspective. Why else would Kodak and Caterpillar allow their Japanese competitors free boarding rights to markets they had dominated for so long? After establishing the framework for a global logistical system in the twenty years after 1948, Caterpillar failed to expand it more than proportionately during the next fifteen years, until forced to do so by the rising dollar. That was human error, given the depreciation of the dollar from 1971 to 1980. Flexible exchange rates are free to move in either direction, and the company paid a price to learn this. Most machine tool makers failed to anticipate the consequences of opening international markets. Now, it is late and re-engagement, more difficult.

Military-style managerial hierarchies are poorly adapted for late twentieth century business. This realization has come slowly to many U.S. managers, and the fact that Japanese management demonstrated many useful innovations in manufacturing organization took some time to sink in. Few cross-cultural transfers run smoothly without some adaptation; direct transplantation seldom works in employee relations. Flatter organizations are becoming more popular. Adversarial labor-management relations and resorting to layoffs to adjust to changing demand conditions are aspects of U.S. business that are poorly adapted to world competition. Cooperation and retraining skills need to be learned if the United States is to become more competitive. How the costs should be shared between business and government are questions that should be addressed with political skill rather than vindictiveness. Investments in people are not reflected in financial statements, but are nonetheless real.

If U.S. manufacturing companies are to become more competitive, they will need to reestablish interest and prestige in the manufacturing process and recapture the intrigue of how to do it better. Business and engineering schools are as remiss in this area as business organizations, but they are beginning to change. Guidance will be needed to shape an appropriate preparation, just as manufacturers need help to allocate research and development funds more profitably. Product design and manufacturability testing can and should move forward together. Again, we are beginning to learn. The watchword of the past several years has been for companies to concentrate on one or a few technologies that they understand and do well, in terms of product design, marketing, and manufacturing efficiency, and to avoid excessive diversification as was the practice in the first post–World War II generation. This seems to have been taken seriously in the late 1980s, as firms shed product lines not central to their missions.

One of the contributions of the microelectronic revolution of the last twenty years was to prove that the font of U.S. entrepreneurial activity had not run dry. The innovative creativity in semiconductors, personal computers, software, components and various niches in the field has demonstrated again the availability and response of Americans to new engineering and business challenges. Weaknesses appeared quickly in many cases; hitting the market first and hard with one good product did not often establish a sustaining enterprise. Even a number of the larger, bureaucratic companies in the industry managed to discard old habits and run with the bulls (if not the gazelles). Business opportunities exist in global competition for the quick and the fleet, the competent and the wise.

SUMMARY

A number of accumulated mistakes have contributed to the declining competitive superiority of U.S. capital goods companies. Beginning with the educational malaise in the 1960s, the mistakes continued on into the inflation of the 1970s and the budgetary deficits of the 1980s. In several cases, companies intensified their own problems by inattention to international competition and by insensitivity to manufacturing costs and product preferences of customers. These difficulties will not be overcome quickly, but they can be reversed if priority is given to their solution.

The seven companies focused on in this study have demonstrated their inherent and continuing strengths as well as their vulnerabilities. Most are still in a leading position. Unfortunately, there is evidence of deterioration in most cases. Public mismanagement of the economy must bear a large share of the responsibility for the troubles of U.S. capital goods manufacturers relative to their principal competitors in Japan and Europe. Despite these mistakes, if the government and the people take steps to correct the shortfalls in U.S. investment and are serious about the improvement of education, then the experience of the next ten to twenty years may be different. Competitive superiority can be maintained and enhanced. The opportunity exists, but it will require dedication, patience, and persistence.

NOTES

1. Associated Press release on Xerox benchmarking companies, April 23, 1990. Also see Ravi Venkatesan, "Cummins Engine Flexes Its Factory," *Harvard Business Review* (March-April 1990): pp. 120–127.

2. Artemis March, "The U.S. Machine Tool Industry and Its Foreign Competitors," MIT Commission on Industrial Productivity, *Working Papers*, vol. 2 (Cambridge, Mass.: The MIT Press, 1989), p. 19.

3. Prepared by Commission Working Group, "The U.S. Semiconductor, Computer, and Copier Industries," MIT Commission on Industrial Productivity, *Working Papers*, vol. 2 (Cambridge, Mass.: The MIT Press, 1989), p. 28, and Artemis March, "The U.S. Commercial Aircraft Industry and Its Foreign Competitors," MIT Commission on Industrial Productivity, *Working Papers*, vol. 1 (Cambridge, Mass.: The MIT Press, 1989), p. 50.

4. Nick Garnett, "Caterpillar Gets Dug in to $2 billion Factory Modernization," *Financial Times*, June 6, 1990, p. 14.

5. Ibid.

6. Alan Murray and Urban C. Lehner, "Strained Alliance: What U.S. Scientists Discover, the Japanese Convert—Into Profit," *The Wall Street Journal*, June 25, 1989, p. 1.

7. "Competitiveness: 23 Leaders Speak Out," *Harvard Business Review* (July-August 1987): pp. 106–123; "Competitiveness Survey: HBR Readers Respond," *Harvard Business Review* (September-October 1987): pp. 8–12. The survey form was published in the May-June 1987 issue.

8. *Global Competition: The New Reality* (Washington, D.C.: U.S. Government Printing Office, 1985).

9. *The Technical Dimensions of International Competitiveness* (Washington, D.C.: National Academy of Engineering, 1988); *The Cuomo Commission Report: A New American Formula for a Strong Economy* (New York: Simon & Schuster, 1988).

10. Michael L. Dertouzos, Richard K. Lester, and Robert M. Solow, *Made in America: Regaining the Productive Edge*, MIT Commission on Industrial Productivity (Cambridge, Mass.: The MIT Press, 1989).

11. Michael E. Porter, *The Competitive Advantage of Nations* (New York: The Free Press, 1990).

12. Robert N. McCauley and Steven A. Zimmer, "Explaining International Differences in the Cost of Capital," Federal Reserve Bank of New York, *Quarterly Review* (Summer 1989): p. 7.

13. Robert L. Bartley, "The Great International Growth Slowdown," *The Wall Street Journal*, July 10, 1990, p. A18.

14. A recent survey by the central banks indicated that in April 1989 total daily

transactions in foreign exchange markets were approaching $500 billion daily. This compares to world trade in goods of only six times as much annually. Jonathan Fuerbringer, "Foreign Exchange Trading Rising, Central Banks Say," *The New York Times*, September 14, 1989, p. 29.

15. Edwin Mansfield, "Industrial Innovation in Japan and the United States," *Science*, September 30, 1988, p. 1770. His research, the source of the paragraph in the text, is also presented in the following articles, with some repetition: "Industrial R and D in Japan and the United States: A Comparative Study," *The American Economic Review* (May 1988): pp. 223–228; "The Speed and Cost of Industrial Innovation in Japan and the United States: External vs. Internal Technology," *Management Science* (October 1988), pp. 1157–68; and "Technological Creativity: Japan and the United States," *Business Horizons* (March-April 1989): pp. 48–53.

16. Mansfield, "Industrial Innovation in Japan and the United States," table 2, p. 1770.

17. Ibid., p. 1772.

18. Nathan Rosenberg and W. Edward Steinmueller, "Why Are Americans Such Poor Imitators," *The American Economic Review* (May 1988): pp. 229–234. This source provides a brief discussion of Japanese success in research and development.

19. William J. Baumol, Sue Anne Baty Blackman, and Edward N. Wolff, *Productivity and American Leadership: The Long View* (Cambridge, Mass.: The MIT Press, 1989).

20. Ramchandran Jaikumar, "Post-Industrial Manufacturing," *Harvard Business Review* (November-December 1986): pp. 69–76; "In the Japanese companies I studied, more than 40 percent of the work force was made up of college-educated engineers, and all had been trained in the use of CNC machines. In the U.S. companies studied, only 8 percent of the workers were engineers, and less than 25 percent had been trained on CNC machines." p. 70.

21. Walter E. Massey, "Science Education in the United States: What the Scientific Community Can Do," *Science*, September 1, 1989, pp. 915–921; and Urban C. Lehner and Alan Murray, "Strained Alliance: Will the U.S. Find the Resolve to Meet Japanese Challenge," *The Wall Street Journal*, July 2, 1990, p. A1, quoting James Powell, president of Reed College.

22. Massey, "Science Education in the United States," pp. 915–921.

23. A contemporary discussion of trade policy alternatives for the United States is contained in Robert Z. Lawrence and Charles L. Schultze, eds., *An American Trade Strategy: Options for the 1990s* (Washington, D.C.: The Brookings Institution, 1990).

24. Eduardo Lachica, "Japan Could Surpass the U.S. in Output of Electronics Soon, New Report Says," *The Wall Street Journal*, June 11, 1990, p. B4; "Computers and Other Targets," editorials, *The New York Times*, May 10 and 11, 1990, pp. A18 and A14; Charles H. Ferguson, "Computers and the Coming of the U.S. Keiretsu," *Harvard Business Review* (July-August 1990): pp. 55–70.

25. Organization for Economic Cooperation and Development, *OECD in Figures: Statistics on the Member Countries*, supplement to the *OECD Observer* (June/July 1990): pp. 26–27.

26. Ferguson, "Computers and the Coming of the U.S. Keiretsu," pp. 55–70.

27. Edward J. Lincoln, *Japan's Unequal Trade* (Washington, D.C.: The Brookings Institution, 1990).

28. Ibid. pp. 19, 29–37, and 39–60.

29. Ibid. pp. 92–93.

30. Jacob M. Schlesinger, "Fujitsu Ltd. Shows Money Is No Object in Winning Contract," and "Fujitsu, NEC Offer Apologies for 1 Yen Bids," *The Wall Street Journal*, October 31, 1989, p. A17, and November 2, 1989, p. A15; David E. Sanger, "One-Yen Bid Withdrawn by Fujitsu after Protests," *The New York Times*, November 1, 1989, p. D5.

31. Thomas C. Hayes, "U.S. Chip Gets Patent in Japan," and "Japan Grip Still Seen on Patents," *The New York Times*, November 22, p. C1, and November 24, 1989, p. C1; Andy Zipser, Stephen Krieder Yoder, and Jacob M. Schlesinger, "U.S. Chip Firms Expect Little Fallout from Texas Instruments Patent Award," *The Wall Street Journal*, November 24, 1989, p. C8; and Andrew Pollack, "Toshiba Royalty Pact for Texas Instruments," *The New York Times*, December 12, 1990, p. C3.

32. Lincoln, *Japan's Unequal Trade*, p. 154.

33. David B. Tinnin, "How IBM Stung Hitachi," *Fortune*, March 7, 1983, pp. 50–56.

34. Michael W. Miller, "Fujitsu Can Legally Clone IBM Software; The Question Now: Will It Be Able To?" *The Wall Street Journal*, December 1, 1988, p. B1.

35. These techniques are best described in the MIT study of the worldwide automobile industry: James P. Womack, Daniel T. Jones, and Daniel Roos, *The Machine That Changed the World* (New York: Rawson Associates, 1990).

36. *The Economist*, August 19, 1989, p. 71.

37. For a current survey of Japanese education and training see Ronald P. Dore and Mari Sako, *How the Japanese Learn to Work* (London: Routledge, 1989).

38. The polar positions on Japan's future role are expressed by Ezra F. Vogel, "Pax Nipponica?" *Foreign Affairs* (Spring 1986): pp. 752–767, and Bill Emmott, *The Sun Also Sets: the Limits to Japan's Economic Power* (New York: Times Books, 1989). Obviously, the author of this book takes an intermediate position based on his work in the capital goods industries.

39. Steven Greenhouse, "East Europe's Sale of the Century," *The New York Times*, May 22, 1990, p. C1. A change in the leadership of the agency that is handling East German privatization could lead to a speedup in that case. See "Turmoil at the Treuhandanstalt," *The Economist*, August 25, 1990, p. 58.

40. Unpublished paper by Edward M. Bernstein, "Some Aspects of the Unification of Germany" (July 6, 1990).

41. See "Symposium on Europe 1992," *Brookings Papers on Economic Activity*, 1989–2 (Washington, D.C.: The Brookings Institution), pp. 277–381; "The Lure of 1992," *The Economist*, November 18, 1989, p. 77. Both sources discuss the official European Community document, the Cecchini report, and the work of Richard Baldwin. The first source includes an extensive bibliography.

42. Gary A. Hufbauer, ed., *Europe 1992: An American Perspective* (Washington, D.C.: The Brookings Institution, 1990), p. 31.

43. Ibid., pp. 40–41.

44. Ibid., p. 45.

45. Linda F. Powers, "The Single European Act and '1992,' " *1992—New Opportunities for U.S. Banks and Business in Europe* (New York: American Bar Association, 1989), pp. 15–16, quoted in Hufbauer, *Europe 1992*, p. 58.

46. Hufbauer, *Europe 1992*, p. 45.

47. Dertouzos, Lester, and Solow, *Made in America*, pp. 129–167; Alan Murray and Urban C. Lehner, last article in a series of five, "Will the U.S. Find the Resolve to Meet Japanese Challenge?" *The Wall Street Journal*, July 2, 1990, p. A1.

48. The four "kinds of investment" advocated in "Providing for the Future" in the MIT report are (1) "invest in basic education and technical literacy, (2) develop long-term business strategies, (3) establish policies that stimulate productive investment, and (4) invest in infrastructure for productive performance"; Dertouzos, Lester, and Solow, *Made in America*, pp. 143–145.

49. This point is made by George N. Hatsopoulos, Paul R. Krugman, and Lawrence H. Summers, "U.S. Competitiveness: Beyond the Trade Deficit," *Science*, July 15, 1988, p. 303.

50. McCauley and Zimmer, "Explaining International Differences in the Cost of Capital," p. 26.

51. Hatsopoulos, Krugman, and Summers, "U.S. Competitiveness," p. 299.

52. William Wiggenhorn, "Motorola U: When Training Becomes an Education," *Harvard Business Review* (July-August 1990): pp. 71 and 78.

53. Albert R. Karr, "Workplace Panel is Urging Changes in Schools, on Job," *The Wall Street Journal*, June 19, 1990, p. A10, from a report of the Commission on the Skills of the American Workplace.

54. John A. Armstrong, vice president for Science and Technology, interview by John Markoff, "IBM's Top Scientist," *The New York Times*, July 9, 1989, p. F5.

55. "Competitiveness Survey," *Harvard Business Review* (September-October 1987): p. 9.

BIBLIOGRAPHY

BOOKS AND ARTICLES

Abegglen, James C., and George Stalk, Jr. *Kaisha: The Japanese Corporation*. New York: Basic Books, 1985.

Aerospace Facts and Figures, 1988–89. Washington, D.C.: Aerospace Industries Association of America, October 1988.

Anchordoguy, Marie. *Computers, Inc.: Japan's Challenge to IBM*. Cambridge, Mass.: Harvard University Press, 1989.

Baily, Martin Neil, and Alok K. Chakrabarti. *Innovation and the Productivity Crisis*. Washington, D.C.: The Brookings Institution, 1988.

Baldwin, Robert E., and Anne O. Krueger, eds. *The Structure and Evolution of Recent U.S. Trade Policy*. A National Bureau of Economic Research Conference Report. Chicago: The University of Chicago Press, 1984.

Bartlett, Christopher A., and Susan Ehrlich. *Caterpillar Inc.: George Shaefer Takes Charge*. Case 9–390–036. Boston: Harvard Business School, 1989.

Bartlett, Christopher A., and U. Srinivasa Rangan. *Komatsu Limited*. Case 9–385–277. Boston: Harvard Business School, 1985.

Baumol, William J., Sue Anne Baty Blackman, and Edward N. Wolff. *Productivity and American Leadership: The Long View*. Cambridge, Mass.: The MIT Press, 1989.

Chposky, James, and Ted Leonsis. *Blue Magic: The People, Power and Politics Behind the IBM Personal Computer*. New York: Facts on File Publications, 1988.

Christopher, Robert C. *Second to None: American Companies in Japan*. New York: Crown Publishers, 1986.

Coleman, Wendy. *Airbus Versus Boeing B: The Storm Intensifies*. Case 9–388–145. Boston: Harvard Business School, 1988.

Collis, David J. *The Machine Tool Industry and Industrial Policy 1955–82.* Case 9–387–145. Boston: Harvard Business School, 1987.

———. *Kingsbury Machine Tool Corporation.* Case 9–388–110. Boston: Harvard Business School, 1988.

"Competitiveness: 23 Leaders Speak Out." *Harvard Business Review,* July-August 1987.

"Competitiveness Survey: HBR Readers Respond." *Harvard Business Review,* September-October 1987.

"Competitiveness Survey Form." *Harvard Business Review,* May-June 1987.

Crandall, Robert W., and Kenneth Flamm, eds. *Changing the Rules: Technological Change, International Competition, and Regulation in Communications.* Washington, D.C.: The Brookings Institution, 1989.

Davidson, William H. *The Amazing Race: Winning the Technorivalry with Japan.* New York: Wiley, 1984.

Dertouzos, Michael L., Richard K. Lester, Robert M. Solow, and the MIT Commission on Industrial Productivity. *Made in America: Regaining the Productive Edge.* Cambridge, Mass.: The MIT Press, 1989.

Dore, Ronald P., and Mari Sako. *How the Japanese Learn to Work.* London: Routledge, 1989.

Eckley, Robert S. "Caterpillar's Ordeal: Foreign Competition in Capital Goods." *Business Horizons* (March/April 1989): pp. 80–86.

Fisher, Franklin M., James W. McKie, and Richard B. Mancke. *IBM and the U.S. Data Processing Industry: An Economic History.* New York: Praeger, 1983.

Fisher, Stanley, Zvi Griliches, Dale W. Jorgenson, Mancur Olson, and Michael J. Boskin. "Symposium on the Slowdown in Productivity Growth." *The Journal of Economic Perspectives* (Fall 1988): pp. 3–97.

Fishman, Katherine Davis. *The Computer Establishment.* New York: McGraw-Hill, 1981.

Flamm, Kenneth. *Targeting the Computer: Government Support and International Competition.* Washington, D.C.: The Brookings Institution, 1987.

———. *Creating the Computer: Government, Industry, and High Technology.* Washington, D.C.: The Brookings Institution, 1988.

Gilder, George. *Microcosm: the Quantum Revolution in Economics and Technology.* New York: Simon & Schuster, 1989.

Hatsopoulos, George N., Paul R. Krugman, and Lawrence H. Summers. "U.S. Competitiveness: Beyond the Trade Deficit." *Science,* July 15, 1988, pp. 299–307.

Hayes, Robert H., Steven C. Wheelwright, and Kim B. Clark. *Dynamic Manufacturing: Creating the Learning Organization.* New York: The Free Press, 1988.

Holland, Max. *When the Machine Stopped: A Cautionary Tale from Industrial America.* Boston: Harvard Business School, 1989.

Horn, Julia L. *Caterpillar and the Construction Equipment Industry in 1988.* Case 9–389–097. Boston: Harvard Business School, 1989.

Hufbauer, Gary A., ed. *Europe 1992: An American Perspective.* Washington, D.C.: The Brookings Institution, 1990.

Jenkins, Reese V. *Images and Enterprise: Technology and the American Photographic Industry 1839 to 1925.* Baltimore, Md.: The Johns Hopkins University Press, 1975.

Joskow, Paul L. "The International Nuclear Industry Today: The End of the American Monopoly." *Foreign Affairs* (July 1976): pp. 788–803.

Kipnis, Stuart, and Clyde Huffstutler. "Productivity Trends in the Photographic Equipment and Supplies Industry." *Monthly Labor Review* (June 1990): pp. 39–49.

Klein, Norman, and Stephen A. Greyser. *Navistar International Corporation: Charting a New Course*. Case 9–589–068. Boston: Harvard Business School, 1988.

LaMond, Annette. *The Loss of U.S. Dominance in DRAMs: A Case History (1976–1984)*. Case 9–689–067. Boston: Harvard Business School, 1989.

Lawrence, Robert Z., and Charles L. Schultze, eds. *An American Trade Strategy: Options for the 1990s*. Washington, D.C.: The Brookings Institution, 1990.

Lincoln, Edward J. *Japan's Unequal Trade*. Washington, D.C.: The Brookings Institution, 1990.

Lipsey, Robert E., and Irving Kravis. "The Competitiveness and Competitive Advantage of U.S. Multinationals, 1957–83." National Bureau of Economic Research Working Paper No. 2051. Cambridge, Mass., October 1986.

Mansfield, Edwin. "Industrial Innovation in Japan and the United States." *Science*, September 30, 1988, pp. 1769–1774.

Marcom, John, Jr. "Behind the Monolith: A Look at IBM." *The Wall Street Journal*, April 7, 1986, pp. 25–28.

Marston, Richard C. "Price Behavior in Japanese and U.S. Manufacturing." National Bureau of Economic Research Working Paper No. 3364. Cambridge, Mass., May 1990.

Massey, Walter E. "Science Education in the United States: What the Scientific Community Can Do." *Science*, September 1, 1989, pp. 915–921.

McCauley, Robert N., and Steven A. Zimmer. "Explaining International Differences in the Cost of Capital." Federal Reserve Bank of New York. *Quarterly Review* (Summer 1989): pp. 7–28.

McKenna, Regis. *Who's Afraid of Big Blue: How Companies Are Challenging IBM—and Winning*. Reading, Mass.: Addison-Wesley, 1989.

Merry, Glenn W. *Polaroid-Kodak*. Case 376–266. Boston: Harvard Business School, 1976.

MIT Commission on Industrial Productivity. *Working Papers*. 2 vols. Cambridge, Mass.: The MIT Press, 1989.

Moore, Taylor. "The Rise of International Suppliers." *EPRI Journal* (December 1988): pp. 4–15.

Moran, Ursala H. *The Airframe Industry in 1987*. Case 9–588–014. Boston: Harvard Business School, 1987.

Newhouse, John. *The Sporty Game*. New York: Knopf, 1982.

Ohmae, Kenichi. *Triad Power: The Coming Shape of Global Competition*. New York: The Free Press, 1985.

———. *The Borderless World: Power and Strategy in the Interlinked Economy*. New York: Harper Business, 1990.

Orr, James. "The Performance of the U.S. Capital Goods Industry: Implications for Trade Adjustment." Federal Reserve Bank of New York. *Quarterly Review* (Winter-Spring 1989): pp. 69–82.

Pedigree of Champions: Boeing Since 1916. 6th ed. Seattle: The Boeing Company, May 1985.

Porter, Michael E., ed. *Competition in Global Industries.* Boston: Harvard Business School, 1986.

———. "From Competitive Advantage to Corporate Strategy." *Harvard Business Review* (May-June 1987): pp. 43–59.

———. *The Competitive Advantage of Nations.* New York: The Free Press, 1990.

Porter, Michael E., and Mark B. Fuller. *Polaroid-Kodak* (B–1, 2, 3, 4, 5, 6, 7, 8, 9, 10, and 11). Cases 378–173, 174, 175, 176, 177, 178, 179, 180, 181, 182, and 379–149. Boston: Harvard Business School, 1978–1979.

Prestowitz, Clyde V. *Trading Places: How We Allowed Japan to Take the Lead.* New York: Basic Books, 1988.

Rangan, U. Srinivasa. *Caterpillar Tractor Co.* Case 9–385–276. Boston: Harvard Business School, 1985.

Sculley, John, with John A. Byrne. *Odyssey, Pepsi to Apple...A Journey of Adventure, Ideas, and the Future.* New York: Harper & Row, 1987.

Sieling, Mark Scott. "Semiconductor Productivity Gains Linked to Multiple Innovations." *Monthly Labor Review* (April 1988): pp. 27–33.

Sinrich, Irene L. *Airbus Versus Boeing (A): Turbulent Skies.* Case 9–386–193. Boston: Harvard Business School, 1986.

Spence, A. Michael, and Heather A. Hazard, eds. *International Competitiveness.* Cambridge, Mass.: Ballinger, 1988.

Statistical Yearbook of the Electric Utility Industry/1985. Washington, D.C.: Edison Electric Institute, 1986.

"Symposium on Europe 1992." *Brookings Papers on Economic Activity,* 1989–2. Washington, D.C.: The Brookings Institution. pp. 277–381.

Taylor, John W. R., ed. *Jane's All the World's Aircraft, 1987–88.* London: Jane's, 1987.

United Nations Industrial Development Organization. *World Non-Electrical Machinery: An Empirical Study of the Machine-Tool Industry.* New York: United Nations, 1984.

U.S. Congress. Office of Technology Assessment. *Paying the Bill: Manufacturing and America's Trade Deficit.* Washington, D.C.: U.S. Government Printing Office, 1988.

U.S. Department of Energy. Energy Information Administration. *Annual Energy Review 1988.* Washington, D.C.: U.S. Government Printing Office, 1989.

Valery, Nicholas. "High Technology: Clash of the Titans." *The Economist,* August 23, 1986.

Venkatesan, Ravi. "Cummins Engine Flexes Its Factory." *Harvard Business Review* (March-April 1990): pp. 120–127.

Warshofsky, Fred. *The Chip War: The Battle for the World of Tomorrow.* New York: Charles Scribner's Sons, 1989.

Watson, Thomas J., Jr., and Peter Petrie. *Father Son & Co.: My Life at IBM and Beyond.* New York: Bantam Books, 1990.

Wiggenhorn, William. "Motorola U: When Training Becomes an Education." *Harvard Business Review* (July-August 1990): pp. 71–83.

1989–1990 Wolfman Report on the Photographic and Imaging Industry in the United States. New York: Diamandis Communications, 1990.

Womack, James P., Daniel T. Jones, and Daniel Roos. *The Machine That Changed the World.* New York: Rawson Associates, 1990.

Yoffie, David B. *Cummins Engine Company in 1979.* Case 9–387–066. Boston: Harvard Business School, 1986.

————. *The Global Semiconductor Industry, 1987.* rev. ed. Case 9–388–052. Boston: Harvard Business School, 1990.

TRADE PUBLICATIONS

American Machinist. Penton Publishing, 122 E. 42nd Street, New York, NY, monthly.

Datamation. Cahners-Zift Publishing Associates L. P., 275 Washington Street, Newton, MA, twice monthly.

Electric Light & Power. Pennwell Publishing Company, 1250 S. Grove Avenue, Barrington, IL, monthly.

Electrical World. McGraw-Hill, Inc. 1221 Avenue of the Americas, New York, NY, monthly.

EPRI Journal. Electric Power Research Institute, Inc., Palo Alto, CA, eight times per year.

Power Engineering. Pennwell Publishing Company, 1250 S. Grove Avenue, Barrington, IL, monthly.

Transmission & Distribution. Andrews Communications, Inc., 5123 West Chester Pike, Edgemont, PA, monthly.

GENERAL AND BUSINESS PERIODICALS

The Economist, London.
The Financial Times, London.
Fortune.
The New York Times.
The Wall Street Journal.

INDEX

ABB Asea Brown Boveri Ltd., 7, 67, 70–73, 75; acquisition of Westinghouse transmission and distribution equipment, 73, 76; Barnevik, Percy, 73, 75; Cincinnati Milacron, sale of robotics to, 121; Combustion Engineering and, 5, 75; Japanese robotics market and, 124; joint venture with Siemens, 72; rank, global, 148

Abegglen, James, 101

Acer, Inc., 35

Achievement, science, grade level by country, 141

Acme-Cleveland Corp., 122

Advanced Micro Devices, Inc., 34

AEG, division of Daimler-Benz, 73–74; gas turbine sale to European Gas Turbine, 74; steam turbine sale to ABB, 74

Aeritalia, subsidiary of Instituto por la Ricostruzione Industriele (IRI), 51, 59

Aerospatiale, 53, 61

Agfa-Gevaert AG, 79, 84–85; Bayer and, 84; Gevaert and, 84; market, European, 84; market, Japanese, 85; market, U.S., 81, 84; market, world, 84; rank, global, 148; sales growth, 79–80

Airbus Industrie, 4, 47, 50–53
—aircraft: A300, 51–52; A310, 52; A320, 52–53; A321, 61; A330, 53; A340, 53
—design requirements, 48
—engines for, 56
—organizational problems, 61
—rank, global, 148
—subsidy of, 53, 57, 60–61
—success achieved, 52, 60
—summary, 133
—supersonic aircraft, 58

Aircraft, commercial transport, 6–7, 47–63; demand for, 47; shipments, 50; subsidies, 53, 57–58, 60–61; subsidies, Japanese, 58–59; supersonic, 57–58. *See also* Concorde

Aircraft engines, 55–57; joint ventures, 56

Akers, John F., 40, 43, 45 n.15

Alcatel N.V., subsidiary of CGE, 5. *See also* Compagnie Générale d'Électricité

Alfred Herbert, British machine tool firm, 125

Allen, William, 49

Allis Chalmers (AC): construction machinery sale to Fiat, 100; electrical equipment sale to Siemens, 71

About the Author

ROBERT S. ECKLEY is President Emeritus of Illinois Wesleyan University in Bloomington, Illinois, and was manager of the Business Economics Department of Caterpillar Tractor Co. He has published articles in *Business Horizons*, *The Brookings Review*, *Harvard Business Review*, and *The American Economic Review*, among others.